THE SOCIAL ECONOMY
AND THE DEMOCRATIC STATE

The Social Economy and the Democratic State

A new policy agenda

edited by
Pete Alcock
Andrew Gamble
Ian Gough
Phil Lee
Alan Walker

The Sheffield Group

foreword by
David Blunkett MP

LAWRENCE AND WISHART
LONDON

Lawrence & Wishart Limited
144a Old South Lambeth Road
London SW8 1XX

First published 1989

Photoset in North Wales by
Derek Doyle & Associates, Mold, Clwyd
Printed and bound in Great Britain by
Billings & Sons Ltd, Worcester.

Contents

Preface

The Sheffield Group first came together after the Labour Party's third consecutive election defeat in 1987. It appeared to us that the case for a popular form of socialism was compelling, could be electorally appealing and was not even being put. This was not only due to political faint-heartedness, but also to an absence of feasible socialist policy options and *realistic* strategies for their implementation. The 'new' Conservatism was making all the electoral and intellectual running and our first major concern was how to reverse this.

Debate in the Labour Party at a national level seemed locked into a series of frozen dualisms – policies were either short term and electorally feasible or long term, 'socialist' and unthinkable. Economic goals were constantly count-erposed to, and elevated above, so-called social aims. Similar dichotomies seemed to pervade the Left's thinking generally with debates conducted through anachronistic concepts that always led to questions about whether you believed power could either be seized or managed.

Much intellectual energy was spent, but it was either devoted to the immediate management of the economic *status quo* and/or indefensible social institutions, or to the drawing up of principles for some distant future utopia. The twain never seemed quite to meet.

Meanwhile, the combination of world economic develop-ments and Thatcherism was significantly altering not only the social contours of British society but also the rules governing electoral politics. Many in the Labour Party still seemed mesmerised by the success of 'third' forces rudely coming between them and their exclusive battles with the Tory enemy. Times were changing rapidly but the Left's thinking and strategies were not changing with them.

Some developments seemed to contain the seeds of new

thinking, and promised optimism. Those local authorities that had made explicitly political appointments and established limited institutionalised resistance to the Thatcherite onslaught had begun to pose some of the right questions. The 'new social movements' – feminist, anti-nuclear, anti-racist and ecological groups – posed many more, and proffered, in some cases, realistically attainable solutions.

Just coming to intellectual grips with Thatcherism has meant that many other long overdue issues have had to be engaged with: questions about the appropriate scope for market intervention; the sexist and racist nature of much social democratic welfare provision; constitutional reform and the protection of civil rights; and about how initiatives by the state can be planned in a truly democratic manner not involving top-down imposition.

The Sheffield Group wants to act as a focus for an intellectual renaissance both in the way the British Left thinks about the relation between economic and social policy, and political strategy in, and around, the Labour Party. We want to encourage the development of a *credible* case for socialism.

This volume is a contribution to a process, in which we invite others to participate, of developing *popular* policies that can benefit and empower people. It is envisaged that this publication is the first of many to be published annually to coincide with the Labour Party Conference. Alan Walker took major responsibility in writing the introduction, agreed by the group. Editorial tasks were shared, with Phil Lee acting as general editor. We do not, nor do our contributors, agree on everything, but we all do share the central aims of breaking down the barriers between economic and social policy, and inserting the state and democratically collectivist principles into civil society. At root, ours is a realist concern with practical socialist politics and their realisation within Britain in the near future.

The Sheffield Group, February 1989

David Blunkett MP
Foreword

What is needed on the Left of British politics is confidence –
confidence not simply in a set of policy proposals but, more
fundamentally, in the values and principles which underpin
them. In short, we must have a conviction which shines
through everythig we say and do, so that mistakes or
diversionary activity can be seen in their rightful context.

That is why *The Social Economy and the Democratic State*
is a timely publication; it draws together progressive and
forward-looking proposals developed from an analysis which
rises to the ideological challenge of the 1990s. The time has
come to stop apologising for our commitment to democratic
socialism and to speak out in language which strikes a chord
with millions of people who are currently confused as to
what the Labour Party stands for, and how our alternative to
a decade of right-wing assertiveness might work in practice.
Our task is to appeal to the inherent good in people and give
them the confidence that decency, fairness and justice are
not only right but practical, effective and forward-looking.
Self-doubt has arisen not because of the intellectual or moral
supremacy of our opponents – far from it – but because of
our own timid approach in putting forward ideas which
reflect our values in a modern technological era where
international influences have changed the nature of
economic and political activity.

Never before have we needed to embrace the socialist
values of mutuality, interdependence and co-operation as
we do today. Technology offers us great opportunities if we
can embrace and shape it for the well-being of all. The
productivity that could be ours needs to be used in a way
which shares its fruits and directs its potential to meet the
needs of humanity. Without our intervention in the

9

processes of the international market economy, individual men, women and whole communities will simply become the flotsam and jetsam of a tide which carries all before it. Market economic forces challenge the supremacy of participative and representative democracy, and deny the political process which offers power to those without the wealth, property or privilege which enables others to maintain and extend inequality and injustice.

Only socialism can offer sustainable and renewable growth and can seek to build a world where what we do today enhances the lives of those who come tomorrow. In the current climate, future generations will be denied the natural resources to sustain life or maintain material standards of living, unless we conserve the resources we use in a responsible way. A 'free for all' can never renew what is taken from the earth around us or protect us from the very exploitation which short-term self interest has as its *raison d'etre*. Protecting and enhancing the quality of life means working with the natural environment and developing a sense of community. Our dependence on combining our talents is therefore reinforced – we must accept our obligations to each other and seek to develop our rights as citizens, consumers or employees.

This view leads to a reassertion that meeting need and developing aspirations must be a primary task of government and not merely left to market forces. This means that welfare is at the heart of socialism. However, the term welfare is not intended to suggest narrow welfarism or the welfare state, but rather a commitment to enhancing the well-being and quality of life of everyone. Despite the ten year sustained attack on the institutions and processes which embody a sense of community and interdependence, the political Right have failed to destroy people's basic belief in a world where working together is preferable to individual self-interest. Ideas for putting into practice the principles of liberty, equality, fraternity and community are as important today as when they were first annunciated. This means a rejection of bureaucracy and over-professionalism, which separate the user or consumer from the provider or supplier. It entails an emphasis on decentralising decision making and developing the concept of an enabling and responsive government which uses the state as a tool for people's well-being. This means a bottom-up approach where government is the servant of people and not their oppressor. It entails an acceptance that dependence, either on the state or the charity of others, does not enhance the self-respect which comes from taking responsibility for ourselves.

What is true for the individual is equally true for society as a whole. It is therefore valuable to see that the provision of essential services – thus meeting individual and collective need – is a major contributor to economic prosperity rather than detracting from it. An understanding of the inter-relationship between wealth-creating manufacturing industry and spending on services is important in rejecting the myth that we do what is right, decent and morally just, only when we have created a world where economics is superior to political decision making and making money is superior to meeting need. The truth is that economic well-being and an acceptable quality of life for all are inseparable. What we spend on ensuring good health, on developing transport and communications, on educating and training our people, on housing families and caring for the elderly all contribute towards a prosperous and competitive economy.

Democracy is the tool which makes all of this possible and shakes off the patronage of private dominance or public oppression. Extending and developing democracy has to be our task in the decades ahead. Our aim is to empower people – protected from, as well as by, their government – since we must recognise that for many, living their lives in peace is all that they desire. Democracy should not and must not depend on the income or position of the individual. It has to be based on citizenship and a willingness to be involved and that involvement will depend on circumstances and will vary from time to time, as well as between one individual and another. The test of our success in making democracy work has to be the experience of men and women in their everyday lives. Freedom without the power to exercise or enforce it, is no freedom at all. It is travelling and not merely arriving that distinguishes democratic socialism from the oppression of international financial interests or well-meaning but bureaucratic oligarchies. How we set about reaching our goals is as important as attaining them. It is unacceptable to achieve the right objective by the wrong means.

Transnational corporations and international financial institutions respect no boundaries and are not accountable to elected representatives. This is why the development of countervailing power both in the community and through national government is so important in re-establishing confidence in democratic processes. The development of genuine social ownership in services and industries has to be felt (as well as proclaimed) to be in the interests of those who consume as well as those who produce. Community facilities or the provision of services must be responsive and accountable. As we approach the 21st century, new thinking is needed to be able to put into practice what the cynics assign to theory alone.

As we approach the Single European Market in 1992, developing social policies to protect and promote the interests of the majority of people will be vital if communities and individuals are to benefit from this new economic freedom. Democracy can help people not merely to defend themselves but to make a positive contribution towards progress, without some being the victors and others the victims of change. Shaping change and providing the means for self-determination will enable us to bring our ideas to fruition, and empower the powerless.

This book seeks to stimulate debate and to contribute to the reassertion of democratic socialism, not merely as morally and intellectually superior to the harsh and divisive doctrines of the Right, but as simple common sense which has universal appeal. If the review and updating of policies is to be successful, it must be seen as an on-going process within which imaginative ideas are welcomed. It requires a new morale on the Left in British politics to achieve that determination and conviction which will inspire the committed and win over the doubters. We need the vision and self-confidence of those early pioneers who faced the same ideological opponents across the same philosophical divide. The world has moved on and we must move with it; but while circumstances and solutions are different, the underlying values remain the same. In the late 20th century, as much as in the 19th, to win people over to what we stand for is to convince them that we stand for them.

The Sheffield Group
Introduction: Bringing Socialism Back In

How can democratic socialism be transformed from an important and influential set of social and political ideals into a potent electoral force? This question has been confronting the labour movement with ever increasing urgency over the last ten years. However, after a decade of some of the worst electoral and other political reverses suffered by the Left in the post-war period, a coherent answer does not appear to be any nearer than it was following the shock defeat of the Labour Party in 1979.

This is not to suggest that the Left has been idle, far from it. The Thatcher years have generated a host of new political initiatives, from the Socialist Society to the Labour Party's Policy Review, from the Socialist Conferences in Chesterfield to *Marxism Today*'s 'New Times'. This activity has already produced an unprecedented amount of policy debate and even more column inches. But none of this has made much headway in the struggle for ruling ideas, big or small, with the New Right. Indeed for various reasons which we explore below, the struggle has been rather one-sided.

It is partly in recognition of the ascendancy of new right ideas, especially in the economic sphere, that a series of broad-based 'non-Right' initiatives, such as Charter 88 and *Samizdat*, have been launched. These initiatives raise fundamental issues of principle, particularly the inherent weaknesses of the British electoral system, the increasing centralisation of power and the purposeful erosion of civil liberties; however they are not concerned directly with the current plight of democratic socialism in Britain. It is not simply a matter of getting elected but doing so with a coherent set of policies designed to introduce socialism in a steady and sustained way. In other words, it is to the renewal

13

of the whole socialist project that the energies of democratic socialists must be addressed if the Labour Party is to represent a genuinely democratic socialist position, if it is to get elected and if, therefore, a coherent socialist programme is to be introduced.

At the heart of this process of renewal is the re-fusion of economic and social policy. Indeed the failure to recognise the inter-relationship between economic and social policy is one of the main reasons why democratic socialism has been in the doldrums for a decade. Yet paradoxically this is one of the chief lessons from the last ten years: the Thatcherites were sure from the outset about the need for an integrated economic and social policy and, in power, they have used monetarist and neo-monetarist economic management very successfully to promote the social objective of an increasingly unequal and individualised society, dominated by a narrow utilitarian financial calculus.

Despite the striking success of Thatcherism, the labour movement has not yet produced a socialist strategy that matches its vision and coherence. It is not just that proposals from the Left must necessarily fight for legitimacy in a capitalist system. Some of the packages produced over the last decade have lacked both credibility and conviction. However the process of policy renewal is underway, especially within the Labour Party, and this book is intended as a contribution to this process of evolving a feasible democratic socialist programme. It centres on what we regard as the main missing link in the Left's search for an alternative agenda: the re-fusion of economic and social policy in the context of constitutional reform. In the place of the free economy and the strong state of the New Right we want to see the social economy and the democratic state.

We invited a group of distinguished policy specialists associated with the labour movement to couple a critique of Tory policies with an outline of what a realistic socialist policy alternative would look like, and these chapters form the bulk of the book. Some key policy issues are missing. But our aim was never to be comprehensive: the project was originally planned as an annual one and, of course, no single volume can hope to cover the full range of relevant policy issues. We have included many of the key policy concerns for the early 1990s and they are intended as examples of the policy agenda that a feasible democratic socialist framework might produce. In the conclusion we outline in some detail our strategy for socialism, democracy and welfare and the mechanisms for achieving it.

There are some clear differences in approach and emphasis between contributors but these have been left intact as we regard them as 'creative tensions'. For instance, Dave Purdy argues for a guaranteed minimum income while Ruth Lister puts the case for radical improvements in the present benefit structure. The latter concentrates on the short to medium term within current employment-income relationships whereas the former looks to the longer term where this relationship will be dissolved. Within a democratic socialist programme they can be seen to be wholly complementary. A more significant political problem for socialists today, and one shared by all the contributors, is how to draw the fine line between those market principles that should be endorsed and those that should be subordinated to social rights. Mike Rustin argues there are limits to an individualism of the Left, and that would-be defenders of public provision can make too many concessions to consumerism. He may feel that one or two other contributors are insufficiently precise in their placement of this line.

The purpose of this introductory chapter is to set the scene: how can socialism be brought back in? What are the conditions for its renewal and the development of a socialist strategy based on the re-fusion of social and economic policy? We do so first by discussing the changed context which socialist policies must reflect in the 1990s. Secondly the approach of the New Right is discussed. This is followed by an examination of the Labour Party's Policy Review and, finally, we outline the main elements of a democratic socialist strategy.

The Changing Context of Political Debate

During the last twenty years the context and the issues of political debate have altered substantially, and with them the prospects of socialism. At first in the years after 1968 socialism seemed to be renewing itself intellectually and politically, but more recently there has been much questioning of its continuing relevance and validity. Socialism has been criticised by the Right both as an outworn political creed, incapable of adjusting to the changes that are taking place in the world around it, and also as a doctrine that is based on a series of intellectual fallacies.

These two challenges have been particularly evident in Britain. The Labour Party suffered a major drop in its support after 1979, and has faced a Conservative government which has seized both the political and ideological initiative and has grown in confidence in its ability to dictate the political agenda.

The dominance of the Right in the 1980s has elicited a range of responses from socialists, both fundamentalist and revisionist. The Labour Party and its future has been a central feature of this debate. The Labour Party policy review is an attempt to modernise the party and rethink the essentials of socialism. Modernisation has been interpreted by some in the party as an attempt to dilute the party's principles and its socialist commitments, while others doubt that the kind of modernisation contemplated in the policy review is adequate to the kind of challenge the Left now faces.

To think clearly about these questions requires an understanding first of all of the changing context in which socialists are obliged to operate and the nature of the intellectual and political challenge which they face.

Changes Within Capitalism

The major changes that have been identified include the increasing pace of internationalisation, changes in the labour process and the organisation of production, and changes in the working class. In many accounts these amount to a major change in the regime of accumulation, a transition from Fordism to post-Fordism, or from organised to disorganised capitalism. The scope and permanence of some of the changes has been questioned, but there is general agreement that the 1970s is a watershed in the history of capitalism, a decade which saw the ending of the long boom and the opening of a period of greater conflict, experimentation, and uncertainty.

The search for the conditions that will restore stability to the global and domestic accumulation of capital has dominated the politics of the 1970s and 1980s. Parallels have been drawn with the last great cataclysm of the world economy, the slump and depression of the 1930s. But there have been major differences this time.

One of the most important is that far from the recessions of 1974-5 and 1980-1 leading to a fragmentation of the world economy into hostile and competing trade blocs, the pace of internationalisation of the economy has increased. The flows of capital and trade have accelerated. National economic controls have been weakened not strengthened as a result of the downturn.

The most dramatic example of this has been the internationalisation of the world's financial markets which followed the breakdown of the attempt to maintain fixed exchange rates. The recognition of the interdependence of economies in the world economy has led many states, including Britain in 1977-9, to abandon all exchange controls.

Such a move has serious implications for the viability of national economic management. With the further enhancement of the power and reach of transnational companies, and the increased incentive for all companies to become at least multinational in their operation, the idea of national economies as a significant economic space, over which national governments might hope to exercise some control, has faded.

The increasing internationalisation of the economy has weakened the scope for governments to exercise discretion in managing the economy. The transition from a Keynesian to a monetarist perspective in the course of the 1970s was powerfully assisted by this fact. National Keynesianism made most sense when economies were relatively closed. As economies became more open during the long boom, the difficulties of discretionary economic management by national governments increased. In the circumstances of the 1970s national governments found that there were heavy costs to be paid for departing too far from the policies being pursued by the leading economies and favoured by the financial markets. Attempts to insulate a national economy from the pressures of the world market were sometimes still made but had to be quickly abandoned.

A second major change has been the transformation of the labour process. The exhaustion of the boom was simultaneously the exhaustion of the regime of accumulation that had sustained it – Fordism. Fordism was based on mass production and mass consumption. The creation of assembly lines, the de-skilling of the workers who worked on the lines, the design, production, and marketing of standardised products gave capitalism enormous momentum from the 1920s onwards, reaching its zenith in the successful Fordist economies of the United States, Europe and Japan in the 1950s and 1960s.

When Fordism began to weaken, much else began to weaken with it. National economic management to maintain high levels of employment and a steady rate of economic growth had been an important stabiliser of demand in many Fordist economies. Similarly strong trade unions, and free collective bargaining where they became established, had helped maintain high levels of demand and mass consumption. Government spending programmes on transport, communications, education, health, and the great urban centres which Fordism required all flourished under a Fordist regime of accumulation.

As a principle of industrial organisation Fordism is still very much alive and still being applied to new areas. But in many new and some established sectors it is being replaced by different patterns of organisation in response to new technologies and new marketing strategies. These involve batch production in smaller plants, diversification and decentralisation, and a different pattern of industrial relations. A group of core workers become more separated than before from those who are more peripheral to the firm's operations. The latter are casual workers or limited contract staff and have much inferior conditions of employment and pay in comparison with the core workers (Leadbeater and Lloyd 1987).

This new pattern of industrial relations has major consequences for the third change – the change in the working class. The working class occupied a central role in a Fordist economy through their contribution to both production and consumption. Organised in strong trade unions and voting for social democratic parties, the working class was often able to secure not merely legal protection of its bargaining position in the factories, but also state intervention in the economy to promote full employment and state spending programmes to provide collective social security, health and education.

The decline of organised labour has been the decisive change for many on the Left in the 1970s. Whereas Fordism helped to unify the class and provide a set of common work and consumption experiences, the new patterns of work organisation, consumption, and leisure are tending to fragment it. The working class has become more sectional, and also more diverse, as new occupational categories have arisen. The manual working class, the backbone of the Fordist workforce, has been shrinking steadily. The new occupations tend to be white collar jobs in the service class. The old common culture of the working class has been fragmented by new kinds of consumption and new ways of spending free time.

This has produced a crisis of identity for socialists. The privileged agent of the transition to socialism, the organised working class, is no longer the force it was. The structures within which it used to operate – the large-scale industrial plant, the nation-state, and the city – have all less importance now than in Fordism's heyday (Lash and Urry 1987).

The strategy for a transition to socialism through the agency of social democracy was always problematic, but at least the fundamentals of the project were clear. A majority for socialism was to be built by rallying the organised working class around a programme which promised the extension of citizenship rights and national control of the economy. Some argued that the organised working class on its own was too small, and that it needed alliances with other parts of the working class and crucially with elements of the progressive middle class, but there was no doubting the central role which the organised working class was intended to play.

It is this strategy which has become unhinged in the post-Fordist era. One response in Britain has been to argue that the key problem has been the narrow strategy of the Labour leadership which needs changing in order to avoid the isolation of the old labour movement. A more radical response has been to question whether the starting point for strategic thinking on the Left should any longer be the organised Fordist working class, because this is to give priority to a political formation which is predominantly male and white (Wood 1986; Laclau and Mouffe 1985).

The question that the era of post-Fordism raises for the Left is what kind of political formation is socialism to be? What are to be the priorities and assumptions that are to guide the building of a coalition of interests and groups into a force that can challenge the political and ideological dominance of the Right? The old kind of Labourist coalition was barely sufficient even in the period of its greatest success. It is plainly inadequate today.

The choice, however, is not simply between reverting to a traditional Labourism and building a new broad coalition. There is no choice if Labour is ever to form another government. But there is still great scope for argument as to the kind of coalition Labour should attempt to build, and what importance class should have within it. Here there is a basic divide: on the one hand there are those who believe that since class exploitation remains the foundation of a capitalist economy and society, a socialist politics has to be a class politics, and the wider coalition has to be assembled around a class conscious vanguard; on the other, there are those who argue that class is only one form of domination and oppression, alongside gender and race, that it should have no special priority within the socialist project. On this second view a socialist politics has to be a democratic politics, and the coalition for socialism has to be built around demands for extending individual choice, autonomy and control.

The real or alleged changes within capitalism have tended to dominate the debates on the future of socialism in the 1980s. But the changes in world politics are also extremely important. Three are singled out for comment here: the change in relations between the superpowers; the renewed momentum of the European community towards integration; and the north/south divide.

The first has two major aspects: the decline of United States hegemony, and the programme of perestroika in the Soviet Union. The decline of US hegemony is due to the global over-extension of the United States which has helped erode the technological lead of its industries, destroy its financial dominance, and create the trade and budget deficits. But although the United States has lost ground to Japan and to the European Community it remains overwhelmingly dominant within the military and political alliances of the western world.

The managing of US decline has become a central concern for its allies. The possible withdrawal of US military and nuclear guarantees, or the introduction of protectionist measures, have been sufficient to persuade other leading states to continue funding the American deficits. It would not be feasible to do this indefinitely however if the deficits were to continue to grow. The paralysis of decision making within the United States makes an internal cure to the deficits difficult.

This situation is likely to persist and casts a cloud over prospects for the world economy. So far, however, the pressures for maintaining interdependence and co-operation have outweighed the pressures towards a major slump and breakdown.

The other major change in this area has been the programme of perestroika launched by the Gorbachev leadership in the Soviet Union. After the new cold war of the late 1970s and 1980s which was used by the United States to bolster its flagging authority over its allies, a new period of detente and arms reduction has opened. If the momentum is maintained, then there may be far-reaching consequences for the solidity of the two blocs which have faced each other in trench warfare for the last forty years.

Defence and security policy may be transformed by such developments. Still more important is the changed perception of socialism and the Soviet Union that may follow in the wake of perestroika. If the cold war were finally to end and the mobilisation of western societies against the ideological and military threat posed by the Soviet Union were to be relaxed, one of the greatest obstacles to the development of socialism in the capitalist world would have been removed.

Perestroika is, however, double-edged, since it is unclear whether its outcome will be the creation of a viable socialist economy, a more market-oriented socialism, or even the re-emergence of capitalism. The current lack of any society which the Left regards as a model for socialism, in the way that Milton Friedman regards Hong Kong as a model for capitalism, is a serious disability. The USSR once provided such a model. Despite recent events it is unlikely to become so again, although the negative image for socialism which it has increasingly projected is likely to disappear.

Partly as a result of the way the roles of the two superpowers are changing, the moves to integrate the European Community both politically and economically have been gathering pace. Labour's divisions over British membership of the European Community in the 1970s was partly due to the widespread fear on the Left and among the unions that membership meant losing the ability to manage the economy according to national objectives.

The reality of increasing internationalisation and interdependence has made the economic nationalism of the Alternative Economic Strategy of the 1970s unattractive as well as impractical. In the 1980s Labour has come to terms with Europe and now perceives it as necessary ground on which any struggle for socialism will have to be fought. It is becoming accepted that Europe is potentially not just a set of rules about markets but a set of rules about social citizenship, with all that that implies for common policies and common laws and the need for democratic accountability.

The third major change is the relationship between north and south, between the rich and the poor nations. Two key aspects are worth highlighting here – the Third World debt problem and the global environmental crisis. Third World debt is the large bomb under the world economy but no-one knows what, if anything, will detonate it. The persistence of this colossal imbalance is one of the chief obstacles to a return to the growth of the long boom.

Finding ways to remove the burden of the debt and create

the conditions for a more balanced development of the world economy are priorities for any socialist politics. So intractable have these problems become that only international co-operation to solve them offers any chance of success. A more integrated Economic Community and a reformed Soviet Union would be important steps to achieving that kind of action.

The final change that has altered the context of domestic politics in the last twenty years is the recognition that the world is facing a global environmental crisis of uncertain but possibly catastrophic proportions. This is directly linked to the operation of transnational economies in a global economy and to the pressure for development in poor countries in the Third World. The destruction of rain forests, the release of carbon monoxide and harmful chemicals into the atmosphere, the threatened extinction of many species of plant and animal life, and the build-up of toxic wastes, all pose severe challenges to the traditional politics of both Left and Right which have assumed that continuing economic growth is unproblematic. The integration of green perspectives into the politics of production, distribution and exchange, which have always lain at the heart of the socialist approach to politics, has hardly begun.

The Challenge of The New Right

The spaces which have been opened up by the changes of the 1970s and 1980s have been colonised most purposively by the New Right. The new politics has so far been a conservative politics in Britain and the United States. In some other countries the initiative has been seized by political forces of the Left, as in New Zealand, but their programmes and new ideas have often been taken from the New Right. The old intellectual confidence of the Left has weakened. Most of the confidence these days about diagnosing problems and prescribing solutions comes from the Right. Even more important, the moral certainty of the Left that it knew how to create a better society seems to have passed for the moment to the New Right.

Any renewal of the socialist project has to take the New Right very seriously, and understand the power of its arguments and the appeal of its programmes. It challenges both the moral integrity and the intellectual coherence of socialism. For many of the adherents of the New Right, socialism is an exhausted and discredited creed, with more prospects currently of withering away than the state ever had (Graham and Clarke 1986).

A common response on the Left has been to treat the New Right as though it was not new at all, but a simple rehashing of old *laissez-faire* ideas. This is to misunderstand the New Right. Although it draws on long and well-established intellectual traditions, its greatest strength is the originality with which it has analysed the problems of contemporary capitalism and linked them to the rise of democracy and the growth of the state.

The New Right is not a unified movement or doctrine. It has many different strands within it. Some commentators have used the term to refer exclusively to the market liberal right; others have used it to refer to the new intellectual movements of the conservative right, such as the neo-conservative in the US, the Salisbury Group in the UK, the *nouvelle droite* in France, and the *nuova destra* in Italy. But although the different currents of the New Right do need identifying and analysing, it is important to recognise that they are united by their hostility to socialism as an ideology and to the extended state created and legitimated by social democracy.

The vehicle for uniting the various strands of New Right opinion has often been a political party or political leader. Politicians like Reagan and Thatcher have provided a focus for opposition to social democracy and extended government, and have helped create a new right-wing agenda, behind which very disparate elements of a right-wing coalition could rally. Often the hopes and expectations such politicians aroused far exceeded what they intended or proved able to deliver, but at the very least what they have done is to shift the terms of the debate on policy.

The liberal and conservative strands of the New Right are marked by distinct discourses, although there is much overlapping between them. The market liberal strand focuses on the requirements for a free economy, while the neo-conservative strand is more concerned with the conditions for maintaining and restoring authority throughout the key institutions of society. Both accept the need for the economy to be free and the state to be strong, but the relative emphasis is reversed. For the market liberal the state has to be strong primarily to uphold the rules and conditions for the market order, while for the conservatives the economy has to be free because private property is an essential bulwark of state authority (Gamble 1988).

Economic and Social Strategy

The New Right in Britain is most closely identified with the macro-economic prescriptions of monetarism and, since 1985, neo-monetarism. At a technical level monetarism is concerned with the control of the money supply to generate non-inflationary economic growth. It is the duty of a responsible government to ensure that the rate of growth of the money supply does not exceed the growth of output, otherwise inflationary pressures will occur. This was the macro-economic strategy adopted, albeit in a weak form, by the last Labour government in 1976/77 and taken on in a more committed and thorough-going way by the first Thatcher administration. Moreover this supply-side approach has increasingly dominated the macro-economic policies of other Western (and some Eastern) societies and is the established orthodoxy in the international monetary agencies.

But as well as being a doctrine of economic management, monetarism is the macro-economic element of a much broader economic and social philosophy. The policies of the Thatcher governments over the last decade cannot be understood properly unless the other key elements of this philosophy are taken into account.

At the heart of the New Right's economic and social strategy is the commitment to individualism. In the economic sphere there is the conviction that if the economy is free it has an inherent capacity to expand and prosper. In other spheres a similarly negative concept of freedom – freedom from coercion – also reflects the sanctity of the individual. Economic and social order spring from the unplanned and unintended consequences of co-operation between self-interested individuals. In these conditions free enterprise will operate to full effect, spearheaded by a minority of entrepreneurs and risk-takers, and will promote economic growth (Friedman and Friedman 1980). Thus economic growth forms a primary integrative force in society through the commitment it commands from individual economic 'men' operating in a free market to maximise their welfare. The market is idealised to the point that it is regarded as the most efficient mechanism for distributing virtually all goods and services.

The strategy of the New Right is not based solely on a eulogy of the effectiveness of the free market, there is also a strong underlying belief in the damaging effects of state intervention in the market. The New Right does not oppose all forms of state intervention, indeed such measures may be necessary to promote the free market system, but rather any attempt to plan or 'politicise' the market itself (Bosanquet 1982, p7). Thus the Thatcher governments have concentrated on the removal of direct state intervention in the market, including the labour market, by de-regulation, but have increased the regulations governing trade unions. There are also severe dangers said to be associated with the growth of public expenditure in both crowding out private investment and in the deleterious impact of high tax levels on entrepreneurship and financial incentives. Hence the numerous measures taken to limit the growth of public spending over the last ten years.

As the embodiment of the interventionist sentiments of the post-war settlement, the welfare state has attracted much of the New Right's philosophical and practical attention. In the first place it offends their belief in the primacy of the market in responding to demand, ensuring choice and containing costs. Secondly, it entails high rates of taxation which damage incentives and restrict the freedom of individuals to spend their own money. Thirdly, the welfare state is said to create dependency by making people reliant on welfare. Fourthly, like all bureaucracies it has a tendency to expand and serve its own interests. Fifthly, welfare measures aimed at the redistribution of income are misplaced because, once absolute poverty has been abolished, inequalities are held to occur naturally since they result from social freedom and individual initiative.

Although the various elements of Tory social and economic policies can be analysed separately, the strategy underlying them consists of a coherent fusion of the economic and the social. This much was clear from the very early days of the first Thatcher administration. For example Sir Geoffrey Howe's first Budget speech stressed four 'principles' going far beyond conventionally defined economic management:

> First, the strengthening of incentives, particularly through tax cuts, allowing people to keep more of their earnings in their own hands, so that hard work, ability and success are rewarded; second, greater freedom of choice by reducing the state's role and enlarging that of the individual; third, the reduction of the borrowing requirement of the public sector which leaves room for the rest of the economy to prosper; and fourth, through firm monetary and fiscal discipline bringing inflation under control and ensuring that those taking part in collective bargaining are obliged to live with the consequences of their actions.
>
> (House of Commons, 1979, col 240)

Thus 'monetarism' was the leading edge of the New Right's economic and social strategy aimed at promoting inequality, reducing the role of the state in a wide range of long accepted areas, encouraging free enterprise and individual initiative and breaking the power of trade unions. Moreover this was obviously conceived of as a strategy to transform economic and social relations permanently and not one for the lifetime of a single Parliament that might be overturned by the whim of the electorate. The establishment of a free economy and low tax regime would reduce the scope for future government intervention to alter the distribution of income in favour of greater equality. A smaller and tightly controlled public sector coupled with strong and poorly regulated financial markets would ensure that any politicians tempted to argue for increased public expenditure would be kept in check. With a small state, closed to corporatist influences, and in the face of a dual labour market, it was expected that trade unions would also be exposed to the discipline of the market.

Impact of the New Right Strategy

In other words the government had a very clear idea about the sort of society it wanted to create. For example, the over-riding priority given to inflation in the government's macro-economic policy, at the expense of mass unemployment and the accompanying degradation and misery for those it affects, represented an unequivocal choice about which groups in society would prosper and which would be left behind. Similarly with the policy of tax cuts. Out of a total of £12,000 million that has been cut from income tax since 1979 over two-fifths went to those on incomes of £20,000 per annum or more (one in ten taxpayers) compared with just under one-fifth for those with incomes of £10,000 or less (one-half of taxpayers). (Moreover there is a substantial regional imbalance in the distribution of tax cuts with, for example, 60 per cent of the tax cuts in the 1980 Budget going to the South East of England and only 6 per cent to Scotland.) At the same time an equal sum, £12,000 million, has been cut from the social security budget. Tax cuts for the better-off and benefit cuts for the poor may be justified officially in economic terms but this policy is a clear expression of social values. In 1925, when monetarism was also the economic orthodoxy of the British government Keynes (1972, p207) described the policy as 'simply a campaign against the standard of life of the working classes [operating through] the deliberate intensification of unemployment ... by using the weapon of economic necessity against individuals and particular industries'.

A combination of economic and social policies has been employed, very effectively, over the last ten years to restrict the role of the welfare state, reduce the rights of workers in relation to employers and encourage low wages. This strategy has already had a devastating impact on many of those reliant on state welfare, which has been documented in detail in a series of reports (Walker, Ormerod and Whitty 1979; Bull and Wilding 1983; Lee *et al* 1983; Walker and Walker 1987). If the government is re-elected for a fourth term we are likely to see state welfare becoming more and more residualised, harder controls on those claiming welfare benefits and a continuation in the social and economic polarisation between rich and poor and between private affluence and public squalor.

Key aspects of government policy over the last decade, including their detrimental impact, are analysed in subsequent chapters. To what extent, though, has the New Right established itself as part of the changed economic and social circumstances that socialists must now address? There are both negative and positive lessons for socialists to draw from the 1980s Thatcher administrations. On the negative side there is a tendency in some parts of the labour movement to argue that, because the New Right's strategy is so demonstrably shallow, once elected it will be a relatively simple matter of overturning the policies of the last decade. This is to grossly underestimate the importance of the New Right.

First, there is no doubt that the conventional wisdom concerning economic and social policy has been changed significantly. The importance of tight monetary policy and cost-efficiency in the delivery of public services are obvious examples. Second, as we have seen, the government has shaken the foundations of the welfare state and has begun to make substantial inroads through (subsidised) private welfare. It will be no easy matter to reverse these major institutional changes in the structure of welfare provision. The restructuring of public housing, education, pensions and social services now represent major obstacles to the introduction of a socialist welfare strategy. For example, by the early 1990s the number of private beds in residential and nursing homes for the elderly will significantly exceed those in the public sector. A traditional cornerstone of Labour Party support, the welfare state, is being transformed. Third, one of the most important aspects of the New Right policies of the 1980s may have been to profoundly reduce popular expectations about what is economically feasible. The slogan 'there is no alternative' has proved very effective in both silencing critics and stifling debate about credible alternatives. Fourth, the caricatures of the market as the basis of free choice and the state as the source of dependency have been entrenched very persuasively and represent attitudinal challenges to any socialist welfare strategy.

On the positive side, the relative simplicity and, in its own terms, effectiveness of the New Right strategy must, surely, convince socialists that we must also have a clear idea about the sort of society we want to create and that economic and social policies have to be integrated in order to produce the desired result. Second, like it or not, the New Right has taught socialists and social democrats some important home truths about the state, and the welfare state in particular. State provided welfare arising out of the post-war settlement, and closely associated with the Labour Party, is heavily professionalised and bureaucratic, relatively unresponsive to need and lacking in democratic accountability to users. Third, the New Right has been quite successful in appearing to be in tune with changing social and economic circumstances, such as the increasing flexibility of the labour market. Indeed the government has actively encouraged several of the developments that have been regarded subsequently as the inevitable result of economic change, including the rapid decline of the British steel producing industry. Nevertheless the Left must also ensure that its policies are adjusted to fit the changing (if not entirely 'new') times.

Fourth, while the success of Thatcherism can be demonstrated clearly in material terms, there is little evidence of any major success in altering the fundamental values on which British society is based. This is particularly true for those social values that have given sustenance to social democratic and socialist aspirations: a belief in 'fair shares' in income, wealth and taxation, support for the principle of free universal access to certain (if not all) welfare services and endorsement of the principle of class solidarity within trade unions (though not necessarily endorsement of all traditional forms of trade union action). For example, a recent MORI opinion poll revealed that 84 per cent of respondents thought that the gap between the rich and the poor is too wide (*Sunday Times*, 12 June 1988). Opinion polls and survey evidence regularly report support for higher levels of personal taxation in order to finance improved state welfare for the poor. In fact it is the positive attitudes of the British people towards welfare that distinguish them significantly from their counterparts in the USA. This helps to explain why social policy appeared at the top of the government's agenda following its re-election for a third term. The New Right regard continuing popular support for important aspects of state provided welfare as a major challenge to their strategy. However this means that the Left has a powerful value and attitudinal base on which to build a socialist strategy.

Remaking Labour Party Policy

It has been noted previously that the Left has not been quiescent during the Thatcher years in office. For its part, following three successive defeats the Labour Party has embarked on a comprehensive review of its policies. The first stage of this review, *Social Justice and Economic Efficiency*, was published in mid 1988 and, although, at the time of writing it is much too soon to judge the final outcome, the review has advanced sufficiently to allow a preliminary assessment.

The Labour policy review is potentially of enormous sigificance. The very fact that it is taking place appears to signify that the party has recognised the need to rethink its policies in the light of the changing economic, political and social context, including the influence of the New Right-inspired Thatcher administrations, discussed above. The review also suggests that the Labour Party is serious about getting elected. This is an important development away from the incredible introspection of many earlier policy discussions within the upper echelons of the party, responsible for producing documents such as *Labour's Programme* (1982), and the 1983 manifesto, cruelly dubbed the longest suicide note in history. Instead the party has grasped the fact that some compromise is necessary on some issues if, against all the odds, the tide of Tory electoral success is to be turned and a Labour government elected. It is now attempting to derive a policy package that is acceptable to the electorate. As if to emphasise this aim the Labour Party also conducted a parallel 'Labour Listening' campaign in 1988: a series of open meetings around the country at which senior Labour politicians publicly listened to the views of voters.

The review process inevitably poses difficult questions concerning the extent of any policy compromises. There are still those in the Labour Party who hold that a fundamental review of policy is not necessary and who are suspicious that the intention of the leadership is to sell out socialism. However, in early 1989, following the acceptance of *Social Justice and Economic Efficiency* by a substantial majority at the last conference and well into the second stage of the review process, these purist critics have, for the time being, been isolated. Of far greater importance are the differences between key participants *within* the review process itself. An early focus for these was provided by the Joint National Executive Committee (NEC) and Shadow Cabinet discussion of values and principles, on 4 and 5 February 1988.

This discussion was based on a 'Statement of Democratic Socialist Aims and Values' prepared by Neil Kinnock and Roy Hattersley. However, at the same time an 'unofficial' statement of the Labour Party's aims and values, by David Blunkett, a prominent member of the review, and Bernard Crick, was also circulated widely (Blunkett and Crick 1988). These two documents reveal some of the inherent tensions in the review process, between those seeking a stronger and more popular expression of democratic socialism and those who appear to doubt the electoral viability of such a programme and, therefore, want to take the accommodation to social democracy (for a discussion on the nature of social democracy see Hindess 1983, and Murray 1984) and the market somewhat further.

One or two examples serve to illustrate these differences in emphasis that underlie the whole review process. The main thrust of the Kinnock/Hattersley statement is the creation of a genuinely free society: 'the true purpose of socialism'. Thus the principle economic aim of socialism is to create 'the material ability to make the choices that a free society provides'. Whereas the Blunkett/Crick statement is concerned primarily with the core socialist values of equality, liberty, democracy and 'fraternity'. Moreover they highlight the centrality of the attack on class stratification to the democratic socialist project, which Kinnock and Hattersley do not discuss directly. There is also a stark contrast between the individualism of the Kinnock/Hattersley statement 'socialism is the gospel of individual rights' and the emphasis given to community and fraternity by Blunkett and Crick.

The 'official' statement of aims and values, by Neil Kinnock and Roy Hattersley, comes dangerously close to 'essentialising the market' (Hindess 1987) and, thereby, seeming to promote the system that the Labour Party has least public credibility to manage. According to the Kinnock/Hattersley statement, the first role of government is to 'help to stimulate the enterprise and innovation that creates the wealth upon which future generations will depend'. Furthermore their statement caricatures the distinction between the market and a centrally planned economy, and so damages the credible alternatives to *both* the market and a command economy. On the positive side, however, the Kinnock/Hattersley statement does give prominence to a number of important democratic socialist goals: the need for greater equality, the importance of environmental issues, guaranteeing the rights of citizenship, and the crucial role of the state in relation to 'basic provision' such as health care, education, social security, housing and transport.

Ideological differences such as these have existed within the Labour Party since its formation and it will be a severe test of the review process to see whether a new settlement between the social democratic and democratic socialist strands of the party can be achieved. As we have noted the fact that the review is taking place at all is of major significance. Final judgement must await the end result, but, at the mid-point, what can be said so far about the review?

Social Justice and Economic Efficiency

First the review process itself. It was established by the NEC following the decision by the 1987 annual conference to undertake a comprehensive review of party policy. It consists of seven review groups with joint membership and Chairpersons drawn from the NEC and Shadow Cabinet, with some external advisers. There is no doubt that the policy review is a serious and substantial undertaking, reflecting a genuine desire to find ways of translating socialist values into credible policies for the 1990s. Each review group was set the clear tasks of establishing the context for policy development over the next decade, outlining the impact of political, social and economic change, setting out Labour's values and priorities in relation to the groups' specific policy areas, outlining the main themes of Labour's new approach and indicating where major new policy work was required. In other words the first stage was concerned with identifying the key issues and a framework for the more detailed policy development in the second stage to be completed in time for the 1989 party conference. The groups were requested to pay special attention to the perspectives of women and racial minorities (a separate *ad hoc* group was set up to review draft reports from a women's perspective).

The main problem with the review process is the obvious difficulty of co-ordinating seven separate groups. Links are rarely made between overlapping areas being considered by different groups and, inevitably, there are resulting gaps in the first report. In a laudable attempt to work across traditional Whitehall boundaries broad areas of investigation were established, including 'Consumers and the Community', but this means that some specific aspects of policy, such as the future of local government and housing, have not received sufficient attention. These difficulties of co-ordination might have been eased procedurally by, for example, periodic conferences for all review group members, by the advance issue of a general survey of the key social and economic factors likely to confront a Labour government in the 1990s to accompany the statement of aims and values and by establishing an overarching theme, such as democratic citizenship, to be pursued by each review group. As Plant (1988, p 7) has observed there is not a clear link between them which could hold together the main issues pursued separately in the different review groups, including individual choice, the role of the market, social insurance, increasing democracy and consumers' rights.

Another problem is that, despite the 'Labour Listening' events, there is little evidence of direct grassroots input into the policy review process. Attempts are being made to rectify this during the second stage by holding seminars to discuss important policy issues, by seeking the views of constituency parties and by holding regional conferences. Inevitably, however, the public events tend to be dominated by special interests, such as the trade unions, and it is more unusual for the voices of the users of services to be heard.

Turning to *Social Justice and Economic Efficiency*, how can we assess this report on the first stage of the review? There is not space to examine each proposal in detail; and in any case it is more important for our purposes to ask three specific questions: has Labour got the message about the need for an integrated social and economic policy? Is the emergent programme a democratic socialist one? Is the programme beginning to look like a positive and salient package that might form the basis of the next election manifesto?

On the first question, there are some signs that there is a growing commitment to planning social and economic policy consecutively, particularly in the section on Economic Equality. Similarly, in A Productive and Competitive Economy, the goal of reversing the economic policy bias in favour of asset holders and against the creators of wealth is established. But it is still the case that economic and industrial policy figure much more prominently than social policy. For example, the central role accorded to economic growth in the creation of a fairer and more equal society is a sure sign that orthodox economic hegemony still exerts its powerful influence throughout the labour movement (Walker 1983). This means that human needs and social development continue to be subordinated to the narrow concerns of financial investment and management.

Second, the report suggests that democratic socialist forces are at least holding their own against the social democratic ones. The report expresses the key democratic socialist goals of greater equality and the abolition of poverty, social insurance, democracy, full employment, community involvement and social ownership. (This suggests that the thematic, rather than departmental, approach has paid dividends.) However these important themes are scattered throughout the report rather than being carefully linked together. Moreover despite these optimistic signs, there still remain strategic social democratic policies such as means testing and national insurance contributions which, if they remain, will limit the coherence and potential effectiveness of the final package. In addition there is the complete failure of both wings of the party to grasp the constitutional nettle and support a Bill of Rights and proportional representation.

Third, although the sections of the report are patchy, there are good indications that Labour's programme is being adjusted convincingly both to the nature of the 1990s and the need to win an election. For example the section A Productive and Competitive Economy takes on board the changing economic context and attempts to synthesise macro-economic expansion with supply-side control. In addition this review group is in the process of developing new forms of social regulation and social ownership as alternatives to nationalisation. Similarly the Economic Equality section recognises the profound changes in British society that will have taken place by the early 1990s, especially the polarisation between rich and poor. It could be argued, however, that several of the review groups, including Economic Equality and Consumers and the Community, have underestimated the extent of the changes that will have been made in the pattern of social security benefits and social services, as well as the balance between public and private welfare, by the time of the next election. Furthermore, there is danger in some of the sections that the need for modernisation and accommodation to Thatcherite domination of the policy agenda might have gone too far. For instance the Consumers and Community section walks a narrow line between a consumerist strategy and a participative one.

Overall, a mid-term report on the Labour Party review might conclude that there are strong indications of the emergence of more attractive and salient policies. This includes important elements of a democratic socialist strategy for the 1990s. But the review is crying out for a dominant and persuasive theme.

Conclusion: A Social Economy and a Democratic State

The ensuing chapters provide, we believe, the main elements for the theme that might give purpose and direction to the democratic socialist project: a social economy and a democratic state. This would entail on the one hand a re-fusion of social and economic policy geared to meeting human needs and, on the other, a more open, participatory and democratic state reflecting both the rights and duties of citizenship. Thus the main tasks facing democratic socialists, within the Labour Party and outside it, are threefold.

First, it is necessary to argue for a new conception of welfare based on common human needs. This implies the transformation of social welfare from a residual economic category depending on surplus growth into the rationale for economic management. The New Right's narrow and divided conception of welfare – conditional welfare benefits and services for the poor and generous fiscal and private welfare for the rich – would be replaced by universal provision based on common needs and common citizenship.

Second, it is essential for democratic socialists to renew their confidence in collective provision both by recognising the strengths and weaknesses of collectivism and by challenging market provided welfare. While it is only the state that can guarantee universal rights to welfare and democratic accountability for the management of welfare services, in practice the post-war welfare state fell far short of these ideals.

Throughout the 1960s and 1970s left-wing critics of the welfare state, both within and outside of the Labour Party, rightly attacked welfare services for their statism, their paternalism, their sexism and their racism. Many people were in fact excluded from the supposed advantages of state welfare for all, most notably women and black people in Britain. Even those who did gain access to services were excluded from any involvement in their management or delivery. Too much of welfare was provided *by* the state on terms dictated by the state, and by the professionals employed within it; and thus it became divorced more and more from the people *for* whom it was being provided. Thus any attempt simply to repackage the welfare state is not likely to succeed; it must be replaced by a genuinely collective and participatory welfare society.

It is essential too for democratic socialists to challenge the simplistic assertions that the market is the source of choice and a democratic voice for consumers, while the state is the source of dependency. This is as misleading as the dichotomy between market and plan. There is no single market form and while markets may be appropriate allocators of some resources they will be entirely inappropriate in the allocation of others. Similarly with state planning. Moreover users may be dependent under *both* market and state, for example the status of an elderly person in residential care may differ little between public and private sectors. Furthermore the 'voice' of consumers is often illusory, for example in a market dominated by a transnational corporation. Thus it is not to the abolition of markets that our attention should be addressed but, where necessary, to their regulation.

Third, there is the renewal of the concepts of citizenship and democracy. Both of these concepts have been central to debates, both within and outside of the Labour Party, in the late 1980s. Citizenship was discussed by the Labour Policy Review, but mainly in relation to civil liberties; yet it could have provided the linking theme between consumers' rights, regulated markets, social insurance, greater equality and democracy on the one hand and the commitment to full employment on the other. Citizenship and democracy are also central to the contributions to this volume – most notably in the recognition that new social and economic policies must be linked to demands for constitutional reform (see Mike Rustin's contribution and our concluding chapter). If the Left is to mount a successful electoral challenge to Thatcherism, these concepts must also be at the centre of planning for the welfare state. Only in this way can the moral support for welfare (which so manifestly was not enough to bring electoral success for Labour in the 1980s) be harnessed to the real concerns of people for a welfare service that works for them.

As we discuss in our final chapter, this will involve both top-down and bottom-up planning. The central state is not, as Thatcherism claims, incurably bad. But it is also not, as post-war Labour governments appeared to believe, unquestionably good. The relative roles of the state and civil society need to be measured against differing social needs and forms of provision in different welfare services.

Here the renewal of the concept of citizenship is of fundamental importance. Not the 'active', individualistic citizen with responsibility only for individual philanthropy recently championed by the Prime Minister; but a collectivist concept of citizenship as guaranteeing social and economic rights and entailing social and economic duties. In this way the free economy and the strong state might be replaced by the social economy and the democratic state.

References

D. Blunkett and B. Crick 'The Labour Party's Aims and Values', the *Guardian*, 1 February 1988, p 24.

N. Bosanquet, *After the New Right*, Heinemann, 1982.

D. Bull, and P. Wilding, (eds), *Thatcherism and the Poor*, CPAG 1983.

M. Friedman, and R. Friedman, *Free to Choose*, Pelican 1980.

A.M. Gamble, *The Free Economy and the Strong State*, Macmillan 1988.

D. Graham and P. Clarke, *The New Enlightenment*, Macmillan 1986.

B. Hindess, *Parliamentary Democracy and Socialist Politics*, RKP 1983.

B. Hindess, *Freedom, Equality and the Market*, Tavistock 1987.

Hansard, vol 968, 12 June 1979.

J.M. Keynes, *The Economic Consequences of Mr Churchill*, Hogarth Press, 1925, republished in the *Collected Writings of John Maynard Keynes*, Macmillan 1972, vol 9, pp 207-30.

Labour's Programme, Labour Party 1982.

Social Justice and Economic Efficiency, Labour Party, 1988.

E. Laclau, C. Mouffe, *Hegemony and Socialist Strategy*, Verso 1985.

S. Lash, and J. Urry, *The End of Organised Capitalism*, Polity 1987.

P. Lee *et al*, 'Banishing Dark Divisive Clouds: Welfare and the Conservative Government 1979-83', *Critical Social Policy*, Issue 8, 1983, pp 6-44.

R. Murray, 'New Directions in Municipal Socialism', in B. Pimlott (ed), *Fabian Essays in Socialist Thought*, Heinemann 1984.

R. Plant, 'Citizenship and Society', *New Socialist*, December 1988 pp 7-9.

A. Walker, 'Labour's Social Plans: the Limits of Welfare Statism', *Critical Social Policy*, Issue 8, 1983, pp 45-65.

A. Walker, P. Ormerod, L. Whitty, *Abandoning Social Priorities*, CPAG 1979.

A. Walker and C. Walker (eds), *The Growing Divide: A Social Audit (1979-87*, CPAG 1987.

E.M. Wood, *The Retreat From Class*, Verso 1986.

Michael Rustin

A Constitution for a Pluralist Democracy?

A singular failure of the Labour Party's Policy Review has been the refusal to engage with the urgent issues of constitutional reform. This has clearly not happened through inadvertent neglect. At the 1987 Party Conference a resolution calling for a review of the electoral system was brutally put down by Roy Hattersley on behalf of the National Executive Committee. At the 1988 Conference, a broader composite resolution, asking for a review of constitutional issues including the call for a Bill of Rights, was again defeated at the behest of the NEC. There have been some later moves on less contentious constitutional matters, probably in pre-emptive response to Charter 88 and the large support ir received. But Labour's conception of what is wrong with Britain today still does not for the most part include its system of gevernment.

Britain is famous of course for its 'unwritten constitution'. This alleged triumph of consensus over mere rules is supposed to have made possible the gradual adaptation of Britain's form of government to new historical circumstances, without the eruption of the revolutions and bloody conflicts which marked the history of so many continental nations. The enfranchisement first of the middle class, then of the working class; the eventual admission of women to political citizenship; the diminution of the powers of the monarchy and the House of Lords; the vast 20th century growth in the powers of government and the social rights of citizenship which some of these powers were designed to further: it was held to be a virtue of our unwritten constitution that such profound changes could be effected and civil peace still be maintained.

This system relied on 'understandings' where other systems of government depended on entrenched constitutional laws. Since the function of government in society is in large part to reconcile and resolve conflicts of interests, the British system of government has long depended on a stable, tacit division of powers between contending elements in the body politic. For centuries, the critical balance was struck between Crown and Parliament, with the aid of a civil war in the 1640s and a coup d'etat in 1688. But there was also a balance between Crown and central government, on the one hand, and the landed interest throughout the country on the other, whose judicial powers and role in local administration impeded the development of a modernising absolutism in Britain. And later, as mass political parties grew, understandings between them concerning the *de facto* limits to the powers of governments holding a parliamentary majority became a crucial self-denying ordinance of the British system. The fact that the state as a system of government pre-existed modern parties, and was, so to speak, put at their disposal when the monarch appointed a Prime Minister, no doubt made it easier for elected governments to accept as legitimate such constraints on the power of mere parties.

Regulated Conflict

Britain (excluding Ireland) seemed uniquely to organise itself around a series of binary oppositions regulated by custom and practice, and rarely breaking into all-out struggle. (For an interesting argument on this theme see Boyle 1988.) These dualisms were of very different kinds, but had in common the idea of 'regulated conflict' or competition, and the notion that, given restraint by all parties, these central axes of division could be reconciled with the survival and well-being of the larger society of which they formed part. The idea of 'loyal opposition' and the 'good loser' also formed part of the national psyche as a result of this recurring situation of regulated and bounded conflict. The dualisms of King and Parliament, Lords and Commons, Church and Chapel, Oxford and Cambridge, gentlemen and players, and the various mutations of party conflict – Tory-Whig, Tory-Liberal, Tory-Labour (the greater historical persistence of the first of these two terms should not be overlooked) characterised British society.

For a period after the Second World War, even the

relations between trade unions and their employers, and between the TUC and CBI, were constructed on this model. However, this proved an unstable relation. It was over-dependent on governmental tinkering and support, and led to catastrophic breakdown in the 1970s, with the defeat of three successive governments, in effect, at the hands of the trade unions. One reason for the peculiar anomaly of Northern Ireland within the so-called United Kingdom is that in Northern Ireland the relations between the major contending forces, though dualistic in character, have not been amenable to regulation by convention and mutual restraint between the contending parties. The ruling axiom there has always been, 'winner takes all', and all the armed and persuasive powers of mainland governments have failed to achieve a local consensus in favour of some more self-restrained form of 'power-sharing' – the explicit term used in one phase of constitutional experiment in the 1970s – in preference to all-out conflict. In mainland Britain, these constitutional oppositions were always serious, but the importance of most of them could be over-estimated if the subordination of these antagonisms to the idea of nation was not fully recognised, especially as common loyalties seemed rarely to need explicit declaration. Ireland, as always, was the exception, the intractability of its conflicts being under-estimated rather than the reverse, even after more than twenty years of armed conflict.

An equally decisive aspect of British constitutional arrangements has been the insulation of many powerful institutions and instruments of government from party or partisan intervention. Most importantly, of course, in maintaining a long tradition of civil government, is the 'non-political' status of the armed forces, however much, and with whatever good reason, this might be doubted as a dependable condition by the Left. But the convention of the political neutrality of the civil service is also important; it is required to serve different political masters even-handedly, and accrues considerable powers for itself from the convention which distinguishes matters of government from matters of party politics. At the level of local government a similar convention obtains, professional officers being entrusted with the implementation of policies determined by elected councillors. The relative power of local government officers may be even greater, since local politicians are often even less well-equipped than their national counterparts to challenge the expertise and judgements of their officials.

This convention of non-partisanship included the judiciary (however conservative its members and ethos might in practice be), and extended to many other quasi-governmental institutions, as the powers of the state have grown. These have included numerous public authorities such as those responsible for utilities like electricity and water; other nationalised industries; national cultural institutions such as the BBC, the Arts Council, the University Grants Committee, and the Research Councils; and the Health Authorities. Sometimes, as with the older universities, an original institutional autonomy has been partially respected even as dependence on public funds has grown. In other instances, new government-funded institutions have been deliberately set up on a principle of semi-autonomy or arms-length independence, as an established British convention. The working ethos of the administration of these bodies has tended to be one of public service, and recruitment to top posts, at least until recent years, was liable to take the form of a circulation of elites between senior military, academic, civil service, and political positions, rather than drawing mainly from the world of business.

This is a convention that the Thatcher government has rejected, adopting the business ethic and cost-effective management as the preferred alternative to the public service ideology of intrinsic ends and bureaucratic means. The relative freedom of many significant public institutions from direct central, and especially party political control was previously seen as a strength and a virtue. The other side of the coin, however, has been the weakness and technical incompetence of interventions by British governments; in particular in relation to the productive economy, when it has attempted what David Marquand (1988) has called a 'hands-on' approach to economic management. (See also Barnett 1986).

The ultra-constitutionalist Labour Party has usually accepted these conventions of the British system of government, and indeed in certain important areas (for example the construction of the nationalised industries) has helped to invent them. Only when Labour governments have failed has a more critical view been taken of these arrangements, and blame been assigned to administrators and 'the establishment' for the ultimate failure of Labour's programmes of reform. Since one of the dominant conventions (if in practice misleading considering the rarity and brevity of periods of Labour majority government) of the British system has been the idea of the alternation of the two major parties in power (the natural-seeming 'swing of the pendulum'), acceptance of the rules of the game seemed to guarantee Labour a fair chance to effect its reforming programmes when in office.

Harold Wilson for a brief period in the 1960s made a long-term shift in political balance seem an attainable objective, within these conventions, when he envisaged Labour as 'the natural party of government'. Many critics of 'Labourism' have blamed these constitutional delusions for Labour's repeated failures in office (See Anderson 1987; Nairn 1981 and 1988), but more contingent explanations of these cannot be ruled out. After all Labour governments, whether of the 1940s or the 1960s, did not explore very fully the limits posed to reformism by the constitutional system. The weakness and ill-preparation for office of the institutions of the party, and the inadequacies of its strategies and means in the field of economic development and conflict-resolution, seem to have been more decisive in undermining it in government. Nor can the element of sheer blundering by political leaders be overlooked. It does, after all, seem that Labour governments have unnecessarily surrendered office, through tactical misjudgements, in 1951, in 1969-70, and in 1978-79. Who can say what might have been the fortunes of the party if better judgements regarding the timing and conduct of elections had been made by party leaders on these successive occasions?

A 'New' Bourgeois Revolution

However, if the constitution cannot be entirely blamed for past failures (except perhaps in the unambitious and complacent habits of thought it has nurtured), the severe problems it has posed for Labour and social democracy in the last decade are a different matter. The Thatcher governments have shown that it is possible for a government of the Right to hi-jack this constitutional system, to tear up many of its informal understandings and self-denying ordinances, and to use constitutional rules unashamedly as an instrument of class power. Whether a government of the Left could have achieved its own equivalent of this 'irreversible shift of power', given the different balance of extra-parliamentary and extra-national forces that usually confront radical governments of the Left and Right is another matter; as also is the political and ethical question of whether Labour governments *should* make such an attempt.

The Thatcher governments have set out to use the unlimited powers given to the 'Crown in Parliament' to a formidable degree, against their political and class opponents, and against the insulation from ideological definition and pressure of many hitherto important and relatively independent institutions. One example is the removal of trade unions from their previously central role in the institutions and practices of 'corporatism' which developed during the 1960s and 1970s. Another instance is the subordination of local government to limits on spending imposed by ministers, thus gravely restricting the powers of this subordinate level of government to make public policy or redistribute resources.

A significant degree of politicisation seems to have taken place in the appointments to key positions in the higher civil service, and to other public bodies such as Health Authorities, on the 'is he one of us?' principle. Pressure has been brought to bear on the broadcasting authorities with regard to the range of political dissent given access to television, and a narrower and more government-decided definition of the public interest has been imposed. These are important examples of the flexing of the government's muscles in the cause of political control, which has led to numerous cases of pressure and interference with broadcasters' decisions (the Zircon affair, Thames Television's broadcast before the Gibraltar inquest, etc). The field of education, where the government has sought more direct control over curricula, teaching, and subject-balance at all levels of the education system, is another example of adoption of a more politicised approach to hitherto relatively self-governing institutions.

Mrs Thatcher has a well-known aversion to the idea of 'society' as an entity distinct from its individual members. This is consistent with her governments' many-headed attacks on institutions of civil society, which stand mid-way between individuals and the state. Many of the institutions deliberately attacked, constrained, or 'de-recognised' by the Thatcher government see themselves as corporate entities, embodying not merely interests, but also distinctive social or moral identities. This is the case, for example, with trade unions (by some self-definitions anyway), with the entities of local government and the would-be institutions of peripheral national government in Scotland and Wales, with universities, and with the professional institutions of broadcasting. Antipathy to the churches' pronouncements on questions of social values signify a similar distaste for the idea of civil institutions whose moral and social claims transcend those of individual interest.

One of the few trans-individual entities that has been affirmed and celebrated by the Thatcher government is that of the British national state, which is upheld to make claims on citizens' obedience that overrule all other conflicting loyalties and considerations. This view of overriding national sovereignty has justified the priority given to security and state interest, whether over the rights of trade union membership in the GCHQ affair, or over public rights to access to information in the various legal battles over official secrets. The continuing British interest in spy-cases of the past reveals an obsessional distrust of claims on individual loyalty other than by the nation itself. This distrust goes beyond its ostensible objects and extends to the whole upper class social network in which such dissidence, disloyalty, and ultimately treason could find support. It is interesting to note however that the 'treachery' for which Peter Wright is condemned by the Thatcher government seems to consist only of his breach of obligations to the secret service not to disclose official secrets, not his self-confessed criminal misdeeds against the elected Labour government.

Since 1979 a certain kind of bourgeois revolution has been taking place in Britain (at long last, some might say). Corporatist and tacitly consociative relations between class and other interests, and all the consensual custom and practice which have supported them, are being rejected in favour of an alternative definition of a single nation composed solely of individuals. (Or rather of individuals-in-families, since family is the second institutional exception, with the nation, to the proscription of all trans-individual identities and claims.) This late bourgeois revolution, motivated by the unviability of the old order, as revealed by the crises of government of the 1970s, has taken the form of a virtual elective dictatorship (a term initially coined by Viscount Hailsham to describe the dangers of left-wing majority government) of the bourgeoisie, or a large fragment of it, in the form of Mrs Thatcher's governments. The institutions of labour and the class alliances of social democracy have been most heavily subject to attack in this process, while the more paternalist and corporatist survivals of aristocratic influence in British politics have also incidentally been brushed aside.

It is the natural tendency of the representatives of aristocracy to regard other social classes as corporate entities with whom power in the nation is to be shared (albeit on unequal terms). This view is unwelcome to the Thatcherites, whose hegemonic vision of the world denies the corporate existence of classes. Aristocracy has sought, (in both 19th and 20th century Britain) an accommodation with rival classes which allows its representatives to hold on to many of the strings of power and office, while acknowledging the subordinate existence and claims of other classes. Matthew Arnold, an early advocate of the rational state, saw the class question as the central one; he saw the conflict of the three great classes (barbarian aristocrats, philistine bourgeois, and the 'sleeping giant' of the proletariat) as needing to be resolved through the mediating and leading role of state functionaries and the 'culture' which was their distinctive gift, and he anticipated the later growth of the state bureaucracy and the ethos of public service as a means of class reconciliation. The most militant advocates of bourgeois interest, on the other hand (and both Mrs

Thatcher and David Owen fall into this category) seek to deny the existence of classes and to conceal the separate interest of the bourgeoisie in the universal concept of the individual, linked by contracts (regulating exchanges of land, capital, and labour in markets) and by the common subordination of all to the sovereignty of the nation alone.

This has represented a volcanic change in a national political tradition which has hitherto had a mainly sedimentary character. Through most of British history, the separate corporate interests of new historical classes – aristocracy, bourgeoisie, proletariat – have simply been piled on top of one another under the leadership of aristocracy. The fact that feudal and aristocratic conceptions of the social order always assumed the existence and relationship (in a hierarchical structure) of different estates, classes, and levels of society made this framework very capable of adapting to new social claims, so long as they could be kept within the limits of ultimate subordination.

The acceptance by the 'aristocracy of labour' (significant term) of a status of respectability within a social hierarchy, after the democratic insurgency of the Chartist 1840s, was an important reinforcement of this structure. Though the larger mass of the urban and industrial working class in the latter part of the 19th and most of the 20th century was less hierarchical in its attitudes, the Labour Party's high-minded middle class leadership and extreme constitutionalism had the effect of containing this new social force. The national mansion could be shared, so long as the residents were prepared to stay on their own separate floors and keep upward movement and joint arrangements for good government to a necessary minimum. The idea of common nationality and its insular and imperial reinforcement helped this cohesion, especially during the two world wars. Internal class tensions could often be deflected into common hostility to the foreigner, and the miracle of British social harmony and constitutional government celebrated in contrast to the absolutist tyrannies being fought elsewhere. The Falklands War won support in Britain as a struggle on behalf of democracy as well as nationality, and the collapse of military dictatorship in Argentina *was* one of its consequences, intended or otherwise.

Getting Labour Elected Again

The lack of historical imagination shown by the dominant factions of the Labour Party in choosing not to think about constitutional questions is remarkable, considering the near-revolution that is being accomplished by the Thatcher governments' repudiation of past conventions which called for bi-partisanship and self-restraint to be practised by the government in power. Hardly anyone believes that the working class 'estate' which the Labour Party was created to represent any longer exists in sufficient number or strength to generate a majority of votes. Harold Wilson's brilliance, in the early 1960s, in constructing a class alliance for modernisation to prop up the already-declining strength of the working class now looks like an unrepeatable *tour de force*, not, as many thought, the initial crystallisation of an emerging hegemonic force. It owed its success to the still great strength of the working class movement (after two decades of peacetime full employment); to Wilson's skilful polarisation of elements of the new middle class against the vulnerable upper class and exclusionary forces of old Toryism, no longer now the forces for good or ill that they were; and also to the existence of the institutions and governmental practices of the post-war class truce, whose general logic and direction (economic interventionism, state-guided modernisation, the development of the welfare state), Labour was in any case seeking only to mildly inflect to the left when it came to power in 1964 and 1974.

Previously, Labour in office could count on a substantial and powerful supporting constituency outside (which brought its own problems), and on some consensual framework for policy-making and implementation inside the government system. Neither of these conditions – of a massive class base or interventionist consensus – any longer exist, and this suggests that the future difficulties for Labour in implementing a reforming programme are likely to be even greater than they were in the past. The greater exposure of the economy to international pressures, in part deliberately engineered by the Thatcherites to restrict the freedom of interventionist governments in the future, will be another significant constraint on Labour's power of action.

The determination and ruthlessness of the Thatcher governments in tearing up the tacit conventions of two-party government also affects the confidence Labour could reasonably have in the durability of any reforms it might introduce. The post-war context, in which extended claims of citizenship were more-or-less willingly met by successive governments, and there was a consensual approach to class relations and to the dealings between government and opposition, gave Labour some good reason to trust in the existing constitutional arrangements, and indeed to claim this as grounds for its own trustworthiness. But, short of a catastrophic failure and discrediting of Thatcherism, what confidence can Labour now have that a future Conservative government will leave more-or-less unchanged anything that a new Labour government has done? The powers of a majority in Parliament having been already used by the Thatcher governments with such striking results in pursuit of their chosen interests, why should one expect greater forbearance from Conservative governments in the future?

There is also the critical problem of how Labour is to get itself elected under the present constitutional rules, and especially under the now unusual (for Western Europe) first-past-the-post electoral system. Note that Neil Kinnock's acclaimed election campaign of 1987 only notched up 31 per cent (3.3 per cent more than in 1983) of the national vote; that Labour holds only 3 seats in the south of England, outside of London; that Labour needs if it is to be returned with an overall majority, a larger percentage electoral swing against the government than has been achieved in any election in Britain since 1945; that Boundary Commission changes in constituencies, reflecting population movements, will soon make matters still worse; that under the present electoral rules the Thatcher governments have been able to re-write the political agenda even though obtaining a smaller percentage of the vote (43.3 per cent) than the Conservatives received in 1951, 1955, and 1959 as mandates for their 'consensus' programmes (the percentages then were respectively 48, 49.7, and 49.3 per cent. In 1970 Heath won 46.4 per cent).

Admittedly this sorry picture has been the result in large part of the division of anti- or non-Conservative votes between Labour and centre parties, to a greater degree than occurred in previous decades. The recent near-suicidal splitting of the Liberals and the SDP seems likely to change this prospect for the better, from Labour's point of view. But although voters for the Alliance must be extremely disillusioned with the centre parties after their post-election performance, it seems more doubtful that the underlying social and ideological base of the centre has been significantly eroded. Considering the relative growth in professional, white collar, and service sector employment, and the continuing shift of population out of the inner cities, and towards the South-East, one would rather expect to see a secular growth in the centre's political support. It seems not unlikely that after time has elapsed in which the post-election debacle can fade from memory, the centre vote will again revive especially in the south of England, and expose the demographic vulnerability of Labour's base of support.

Britain has been virtually unique in Western Europe both in the fierceness and unimpeded power of its neo-conservative governments' reaction to the social and economic pressures of the 1970s, and in the centralising and power-amplifying effects of its electoral system. In West Germany, France, and Italy, and in several smaller nations, the moves to the right which generally took place during the late 1970s and in the 1980s (France being somewhat later in the phasing of this than elsewhere, but not otherwise exceptional) have all been relatively contained by the tendency to consociation or power-sharing encoded in their proportional electoral systems, and in the multi-party parliaments and governments which result from them. The devolution of power in federal or otherwise decentralised governmental systems has in the case of West Germany and Italy had a similar 'braking' effect on neo-conservative initiatives. The same restraints on government would probably have been effective in Britain if a democratic tier of quasi-federal government had existed for Scotland and Wales, and if the powers of local government had any constitutional entrenchment. Labour Party leaders must retain an extraordinary sense of the innate superiority of British constitutional arrangements if they still think these matters are unimportant after the disasters their party has recently suffered, by comparison with their sister parties (or their equivalents) elsewhere in Europe. (There are now at last signs of a change of attitude towards regional government and the reform of the second Chamber).

Not only governments of the Right are subjected to restraint by a multi-party system which usually forces governments to maintain a fairly wide spectrum of support.[1] This limitation affects any government, and also has implications for the restraint of executive power in general. There is a combination in Britain of an absence of entrenched local or regional powers (as in the federal arrangements of the United States, Canada, and West Germany), and a first-past-the-post system; this is what, from a constitutional point of view, has produced the astounding centralisation and overbearing weight of the Thatcher government, and its capacity for unprecedented control of institutions hitherto funded by central government but mainly left to run themselves.

Weakness of central governments in the face of the legislature, and the sectional interests and the pressure groups that can influence it, can no doubt be a problem. Such criticisms are made of the American political system, where the executive branch cannot always get its way in Congress, and where a good deal of parcelling out of power and resources takes place through sectional and local pressures on members of the legislative branch. Criticisms have also been made of Italy's political system, in which the power of the state and its institutions is divided between the parties, who have, so to speak, colonised the state apparatus, to an unusual degree (see, for instance, Sassoon 1986). Weak government, however, is not now a British problem, and many might think that one of the first things a radical government should do is to build some greater protection, for both individual citizens and public institutions, against the overweening power of the central government, especially where its majority is formed by a single party.

Constitutional issues are usually seen in Britain as peripheral to the economic and social issues basic to the Labour Party's intended appeal. While the emphasis in the party's economic thinking is shifting from its traditional focus on the means of production, towards issues of social and individual consumption (see *Marxism Today* 1988 and 1989), political and constitutional questions may still seem to belong in the liberal rather than the socialist field of preoccupations.[2]

A 'Left' Individualism?

Certainly there is something surprising about attempts to revive the socialist project through advocacy of political conceptions, such as republicanism or citizenship, which effectively pre-date socialist politics, and seem more consistent with the tradition of collectivist liberalism. A tacit assumption of this approach is that class is no longer available as a major principle of affiliation and division; universal claims of rights or membership are proposed as an alternative. The new republicanism is an alternative to 'classism' even though one influential element of this approach (Anderson 1987, Nairn 1981 and 1988, Barnett 1982) derives from a Marxist analysis of the historical failure of the British bourgeoisie.

The difficulty of making democracy and democratisation the centre of a radical or socialist programme in Britain is that in practice the British don't seem to care much about these as abstract principles, at least so far as their own internal affairs are concerned. (These rights seem to matter more when they are being denied to other peoples, as in South Africa, or Eastern Europe.) As Hugo Young has pointed out, the British seem in the majority to care more for strong government than for democratic government.

Nevertheless, whether or not it is obvious to the populace at large, these issues are now quite central to any feasible strategy for Labour. Class conflict and class relations are conducted through political institutions and according to political conventions. To pay no regard to the form and consequences of these is to be blind to the real conditions of political action. Denial of the relevance of these constitutional issues can amount to an unspoken class reductionism, whether of a social democratic or Marxian variety. Labour has to develop a programme on these issues, if it is to have any chance of achieving anything else. And it has to do this even if the publics which care most about these issues are at the outset relatively small ones, composed of those already involved in the political process. The debate about constitutional reforms is in part a debate about instruments and means for doing other things, and its importance is not to be assessed only by the potential of 'democracy' and 'democratisation' as a basis for mass mobilisation, which may well at first be limited.

The bourgeois revolution of Thatcherism has speeded the arrival of an era of pluralist politics and class relations. This is, as Max Weber saw (see, Weber 1948; Beetham 1974), and as modern Weberians like Ralf Dahrendorf (1988) continue to argue, the natural condition of mature capitalist societies. Groups share life-chances defined by their resources of labour power or capital or land, and will naturally organise themselves politically to advance their common interests. Such groups are increasingly various and differentiated, owing to the (partial) economic revolution of 'post-Fordism', and to the break-up of the dominant class culture from above, and of the oppositional working class culture from below (See for instance Stedman Jones 1983). The solvent effects of prosperity, mass communications, universal norms of consumption, and citizenship, tend to create a more classless culture, even where differences of material life chances between classes are increasing.

However, in Britain, conflict-groups retain important affiliations and continuities with the older class structures of the past, as they do in all West European societies. The relatively 'pure' individualism and universalism that characterises the capitalism of the United States, which lacks a collective memory of an *ancien regime* except in the South, does not easily transplant to West Europe, despite the best efforts of capitalist 'modernisers' to make it do so. A viable radical or socialist politics has to maintain connection with, and spiritual roots in, pre- and post-individualist traditions of class and community, while no longer expecting that a socialist hegemony can simply be extrapolated from this by sheer force of working class numbers.

The idea of the strong nation state (Gamble 1988) and the

rights of the individual, enunciated as the twin principles of Thatcherism, are in contradiction with one another, and there is scope for those who oppose Thatcherism to argue the claims of the individual against the state, in demands for the protection of civil rights, for example to information, or to belong to a trade union. It is also necessary to argue the claims of individual social and economic rights against the effects of the market, for example in the fields of health, employment, housing, and minimum decent living standards. This is the basic socialist case for de-commodifying basic human entitlements (See Rustin 1985; Offe 1984). One political difficulty here is that the Thatcherites have been asserting the rights of the individual against a different enemy, namely the oppressive institutions of government. Since these institutions (local government, for example) often operate in conditions of acute scarcity, and in a rigid or overbearing way, there have been real dissatisfactions for the Right to exploit. (Self-criticism by would-be defenders of public provision can go too far, however: see, for instance, Corrigan *et al* 1988.)

An additional problem for the Left is to distinguish those market principles which it is now prepared to endorse, and those which it holds are inimical, or should be subordinated, to social rights prescribed by constitution or legislation. The Labour Party's state of confusion on these questions, brought about by the contradictory need both to come to terms with the necessity and indeed benefits of markets, and to direct its main political thrust against them, is now extreme. It is not possible for a party of the Left to succeed by being more individualist or a better guardian of the market economy than the Right. Its primary orientation must be one which defends the rights of the citizen and his/her quality of life against the baneful effects of markets, whatever may be also said or unsaid about the good which markets do.

Whilst some arguments against the Right can be made in terms of individual rights and entitlements, there are limits to the credibility or desirability of an individualism of the Left. There is more potential resonance in British society for claims and values that derive from social memberships of various kinds. These social identifications must include those of class, though not exclusively those of the working class. British society is not merely an aggregate of individuals united by nationality and common subordination to the sovereign state, but consists of a dense network of communities sharing values of different kinds. These include several national or quasi-national identities; a sense of belonging to region, city, and neighbourhood; religious affiliation; ethnic tradition; professional communities (the doctors, or the military for that matter); other vocations and commitments such as those of sport or culture.

Resistance to a wholly capitalist or bourgeois social order, and the damage it does as it ceaselessly transforms the material and social world (see Berman 1983) comes usually from particular communities and social selves, and not only as the claims of abstract individuals. Once, resistance was centred above all in communities of class. Increasingly, we see other sources and axes of opposition, sometimes refracting life-situations based on class (such links are evident in some aspects of green politics, for example, where a particular status group's property or way of life can be defended in the language of conservation (See Hewison 1987 and Wright 1985), but often based on different principles of identity and difference (gender, for example).

Both 'old' (ie, class-based) and 'new' social movements are critical to constructing a political force which could mitigate the effects of the ongoing process of capitalist transformation, the bourgeois revolution of which Britain has been recently suffering a militant phase. It is impossible to state with any confidence what the balance between class and non-class identities and appeals – the old or the new politics – needs to be in constructing an effective challenge to the Right. What is certain is that the institutions, values, and interests of class retain importance for any viable politics, and that proclamations of a post-class era are premature (See Hall 1988).

Constitutional reforms are not peripheral to these issues of class, social divisions, and political agency. They are central if a viable alternative to Thatcherite conservative rule is to be built. The Thatcher governments have sought to transform the political system, by strengthening on the one hand the power of the state, and on the other, certain powers of the individual. These are mainly, in Hirschman's illuminating terms (1970), those of 'exit' (the consumer's power in the market), though they sometimes include some elements of 'voice', when this can be expressed in the aggregative form of ballot against trade union or local government bureaucracies. (The Right is much less enthusiastic about more collective and discursive expressions of 'voice', or its deployment against the power of property, for example through public inquiry or broadcast report or debate.) As has been argued above, a system of government which had been mostly used in the past to negotiate and maintain long-term compromises between highly unified class blocs (and incidentally to allow a good deal of incidental autonomy in civil society), has been seized and reshaped in order to enforce the dominance of a single class.

Labour's response has been to ignore the institutions which have been thus legally hi-jacked. Imagining that nothing has really changed, its objective is simply to recapture office and use the institutions in the old ways. The left-wing Bennite version of this takes Thatcherism as a positive example in showing what could be changed by a determined government. 'If only we could do for our class what she has done for hers,' leftists say to themselves. But this seems a hopeless cause, taking into account the weakening of Labour's electoral base, and the vast differences between the options practically open to governments of the radical Right, and those of the Left.

The present party leadership's strategy is different. It is moving to accept some assumptions of Thatcherism (the value of markets, the importance of defending individual rights, the rhetoric of British nationalism) as non-contestable in present circumstances. It has less consciously accepted other Thatcherite tenets, such as the definition of voters as merely political consumers (hence the emphasis on market research in determining the shape of the policy review, and on media presentation in the last election campaign), and the view that corporate interests and structures (especially those of the unions) are a liability – a force for conservatism and against modernisation. The weakening of Labour's local and trade union base, deliberately effected by the Thatcher governments, has to some degree forced this choice of a market-oriented political style on Labour, since it has fewer human, institutional, and material resources for any other approach to the people. (Consider by contrast, for example, how the GLC was able to use its tenure of metropolitan local government to promote and encourage alternative views of society.) This weakening of Labour's roots in civil society (always somewhat thin, in truth)[3] also reinforces its conservativism on questions of the state. Labour politicians may understandably feel that the resources of the state are all they are going to have if and when they take office. There is no vantage point outside of the state from which the reconstruction of its institutions could be imagined.

Proportional Representation and Constitutional Reform
Another factor in all this is Labour's continuing idea of itself as the only legitimate opposition to the Tories, a survival of the two-party hegemony (or sometimes 'good loser' situation) of the first part of the century. Constitutional reform, if it is considered at all, will have to include proportional representation as a central proposal. Serious consideration by Labour of PR would signify that there was no longer a strong probability of its winning an outright majority, that it accepted the legitimacy of other potentially anti-conservative parties, and might in principle be one day prepared to share office with them. Even the issue of national or regional devolution has implications of this kind for power-sharing, since it might provide secure regional bases of office not only for Labour, but also for nationalist or centre parties. The Labour Party is so attached to the idea of the unified national state, and to the idea of itself as its alternative government, that it still seems unthinkable to many Labour Party members to put these ideas in question.

What alternative strategies are available? Clearly, since it is the division of opposition parties which keeps Thatcher in power on a minority vote, it makes sense to aim for the widest alliance against Thatcherism. There is a greater diversity of interests and values on the Left and centre of British politics than can now be contained within a single party, and especially inside a party with the Labour Party's history and traditions. In order to defeat Thatcherism, and to construct a base for a different politics, Labour must achieve some positive relationship to political and social forces that it seems unable to incorporate within its own party structures.

Constitutional reforms are central to the alternative strategy of building the broadest possible alliance against the Right. This is because they are an indispensable means of implementing a shift of power away from a single dominant bourgeois class fraction, and towards a greater plurality of social interests. Nationalists, liberal democrats, Greens, and Labour should be able to agree on a programme to change the constitutional system, which now puts them in permanent opposition, and which is being used to weaken many institutions in civil society (eg, local government) on which their strength depends. Tactically, this might be accomplished by means of a limited electoral pact, justified by the aim of constitutional and electoral reform.[4]

Constitutional reforms could be a means of defending both individual and social rights, against both state and market. Rights of the individual could be defended against government by means of a Bill of Rights and a Freedom of Information Act. They could be defended against markets by instituting statutory protection of rights to work, education, health care, and basic income. It is possible, as Mrs Thatcher has now recognised, that the developing European Community may be more responsive to the idea of such constitutional and legislative guarantees of rights than a British Parliament dominated by Conservatives. Social rights – that is to say respect for the autonomy of different institutions and communities in society – would be protected by a political system which dispersed rather than concentrated power between parties and geographical areas, and which redressed the balance of power between Parliament and Executive back towards the legislature.

One benefit of a proportional electoral system is that it allows a greater diversity of political opinion to be expressed and represented. Even with 'threshold rules' that require a party to gain 5 or 10 per cent of the vote to gain Parliamentary representation[5], the road would not be blocked as it is now to new forces such as the Greens. It is also important for the Labour Party to show that it does not seek a coercive monopoly of power like Mrs Thatcher's, if it is to rebuild public confidence. By support for constitutional changes which would limit its own power as well as that of the Right, Labour would indicate a pluralist good faith in a way that muscle-flexing by a party leadership cannot possibly do.

In a proportional system, the pressure for convergence on the centre within political parties is lessened. Since the full range of opinion, including opinion in the centre, is likely to be represented fairly, there would be more scope for representation of the positions of the Left. Given the deepening of class and regional divisions in British society in recent years, this would be no bad thing for democracy, and for the resolution of social tensions. It is plainly inconsistent for Labour to be seeking the democratisation of its own party structures, yet still wishing to benefit from its over-representation by the electoral system. If the centre vote recovers, this position will again become indefensible.

The British constitution has provided means for negotiating compromises between two opposed coalitions of economic, social, and religious interests, over a very long period. It also served to maintain a unified nation state (at high cost, especially to Ireland) during the period of Empire. The first-past-the-post electoral system amplified the power of the two major parties against any competitors, and thus helped to impose the compromise of opposed social blocs, with especial benefit to the Conservative bloc. But now that this system is being used to promote not a balance of social power, but the domination of a single party, social class, economic system, and ideology, it is time to look for other constitutional ways forward. Balance and compromise has now to be effected between many contending interests, not two antagonistic blocs alone.

The power of capitalism and the Right can only be contained if the political system admits more voices, and acknowledges diversity and pluralism as its positive principle, as federal constitutions do elsewhere, and fair voting systems do by implication. While there may be tactical benefits to Labour and the other opposition parties in seeking electoral reform and limited alliances with each other to bring it about, more important issues are at stake than this. A constitutional system descended from monarchy, and from the ruling class's tactical compromises with emerging classes, is not fit for a democratic society which must reconcile and balance the interests of many classes and other social interests. A pluralist society needs a constitution which supports and defends diversity and freedom, as ours now manifestly fails to do.

At this point, it is most important that the issues of the constitution and its effects should be fully included in the Labour Party's policy review process. As so often with developments in party policy, the precondition for this is probably the emergence of a large and independent movement of radical opinion outside the party. It is hoped that this movement will emerge from *Charter 88*, which has received unexpectedly strong support and attention since its publication.

Charter 88 called for

A new constitutional settlement which would:
Enshrine, by means of a Bill of Rights, such civil liberties as the right to peaceful assembly, to freedom of association, to freedom from discrimination, to freedom from detention without trial, to trial by jury, to privacy, and freedom of expression
Subject executive powers and prerogatives, by whomsoever exercised, to the rule of law
Establish freedom of information and open government
Create a fair electoral system of proportional representation
Reform the upper house to establish a democratic, non-hereditary second chamber
Place the executive under the power of a democratically renewed parliament and all agencies of the state under the rule of law
Ensure the independence of a reformed judiciary
Provide legal redress for all abuses of power by the state and the officials of central and local government
Guarantee an equitable distribution of power between local, regional and national government
Draw up a written constitution, anchored in the idea of universal citizenship, that incorporates these reforms

Changing the constitution is a much more substantial task

than passing a single Act of Parliament. Since it sets the rules for the conduct of the whole political process, it requires a large degree of agreement, by which all major parties would feel themselves bound.[6] Issuing a programme such as the above is only the first stage of what needs to be a deep and extensive debate, whose fruition could only come after many years, once many arguments had been won. A major omission from the Charter is the issue of Northern Ireland, a solution to whose problems is vital for the defence of civil liberties in Britain as a whole, as well for the welfare of its own population. The debate on constitutional rights and liberties should become central to Labour's policy-making process, following the limited initiative it has now taken on the issue of regional government and the reform of the Lords. It may turn out that the defeat and supercession of Thatcherism will turn on the development of such a constitutional programme, for enshrining civil, political and social rights. This could be the foundation for the broad alliance of the Left which might recapture the initiative in British political life after this long period of demoralisation and retreat.

Notes

[1] Obstruction of radical change has been a particularly marked feature of the Italian system of government. Recent laws to abolish the secret ballot in votes within the legislation are designed to increase the power of the governing parties over their dissident minority fractions.

[2] The *Charter 88* initiative, launched by a group close to the *New Statesman and Society* in December 1988 represents an important attempt to change this priority.

[3] This weakness is reflected in the growth of social movements outside the party structure (the anti-nuclear campaign, green politics, the third world aid campaigns etc) and the difficulties of the Labour Party in relating to them. And also in the preoccupation of local parties with factional power struggles whilst organisations like Parent Teacher Associations get on with maintaining the social fabric of the welfare state, and even organising in its defence.

[4] The logical form for a limited electoral pact would be agreement by Labour and SLD parties not to put up candidates in about fifty constituencies each. Each party would 'offer' constituencies in which it deemed it had little chance of success, but where the alternative non-Conservative party would have some prospect of victory if it stood alone.

⁵ The advantage of 'threshold' rules of this kind is that they limit the proliferation of small parties, and make stable governments more likely.

⁶ Vernon Bogdanor in the *Observer*, 8 January 1988, has proposed that a referendum might be the most effective and appropriate way of deciding the issue of proportional representation. This proposal might, he suggests, be a way of making progress which avoids the difficulties of electoral pacts under the present system. The referendums on devolution and European Community membership are relevant precedents, since they were also used to determine constitutional issues.

References

P. Anderson, 'Figures of descent', *New Left Review* 161, Jan-Feb 1987.

A. Barnett, 'Iron Britannia', *New Left Review* 134, Jul-Aug 1982, reprinted Verso 1983.

C. Barnett, *The Audit of War*, Macmillan 1986.

D. Beetham, *Max Weber and the Theory of Modern Politics*, Allen and Unwin 1974.

M. Berman, *All That is Solid Melts into Air*, Verso 1983.

N. Boyle, 'Thatcher's Dead Souls', *New Blackfriars*, Summer 1988, abridged in *New Statesman and Society*, 14 October 1988.

P. Corrigan, T. Jones, J. Lloyd, J. Young, *Socialism, merit and efficiency*, Fabian Society 1988.

R. Dahrendorf, *Modern Social Policy: An Essay in the Politics of Liberty*, Weidenfeld and Nicolson 1988.

A. Gamble, *The Free Economy and the Strong State*, Macmillan 1988.

S. Hall, *The Hard Road to Renewal*, Verso 1988.

R. Hewison, *The Heritage Industry: Britain in a Climate of Decline*, Methuen 1987.

A. Hirschman, *Exit, Voice and Loyalty*, Harvard University Press 1970.

D. Marquand, *The Unprincipled Society* (especially part 2), Cape 1988.

Marxism Today, articles on 'new times' in October 1988 and January 1989.

T. Nairn, *The Break-Up of Britain* (new edition), Verso 1981.

T. Nairn, *The Enchanted Glass*, Radius 1988.

M. Rustin, *For a Pluralist Socialism*, Verso 1985.

C. Offe, various essays in J Keane (ed), *Contradictions of the Welfare State*, Hutchinson 1984.

D. Sassoon, *Contemporary Italy*, Longman 1986.

G. Stedman Jones, 'Why is the Labour Party in a Mess?' in his *Languages of Class: Studies in English Working Class History 1832-1982*, Cambridge University Press 1983.

M. Weber, 'Class, Status, Party', reprinted in H Gerth and C Wright Mills (eds), *From Max Weber: Essays in Sociology*, RKP 1948.

P. Wright, *On Living in an Old Country*, Verso 1985.

Roland Petchey

The Politics of Health

Partly because of their vagueness, partly because of the clandestine nature of the prime minister's review of the NHS, and partly because of their refusal to accept the popular definition of the 'crisis' as one of underfunding, the Tories' proposals for the health service have not, in my view, been clearly understood on the left. The response to them has been a knee-jerk rejection, which is regrettable, since a more considered evaluation of them might have led to a more careful analysis of the alternatives that are available to us, given the difficulties which are peculiar to the health service, compared with other areas of social provision. To some, health policy has presented itself as the Achilles heel of the Tories. This would not however be the literary allusion of my choice. I prefer Matthew, vii, 3: Why beholdest thou the mote that is in thy brother's eye, but considerest not the beam that is in thine own eye?

The over-rapid rejection of the Tories' answers has prevented us from appreciating that they have, in fact, asked some extremely valuable questions about the health service. The weakness of the Labour policy review, by contrast, is that it doesn't appear to have done so. It would therefore seem prudent to devote a little time to consideration not only of the Tory proposals, but also to the underlying issues they address.

The Internal Market

It has now become something of a commonplace for commentators to remark that although the Tory review was prompted by what was generally perceived as a crisis of underfunding, it attempts to redefine the crisis as one of organisation. It studiously refrains from considering the level of funding; instead it addresses itself exclusively to the organisation of the health service. As is by now well known, the organisational innovation on which it is pinning its hopes is the 'internal market'. The intellectual origins of this 'marketisation' of health care can be traced back to a number of papers published by various right-wing pressure groups (eg, Butler and Pirie 1988a, 1988b; Goldsmith and Willets 1988a, 1988b; Whitney 1988; Brittan 1988) and ultimately to Alain Enthoven (1985), who is an American health economist, the designer of the 'Consumer Choice Health Plan' (Enthoven 1989a and b represent the latest stage in his thinking) and an advocate of Health Maintenance Organisations (HMOs) as the mechanism for promoting competition and regulating health costs. In a number of respects, however, the government's proposals are even more radical than Enthoven's. Indeed, he has expressed a number of concerns about them (1989c). First, his proposal was for experimentation only (initially at any rate) with the concept of the internal market. Second, he envisaged District Health Authorities (DHAs) as participating in the internal economy, whereas the government has gone much further down the road of plural provision. Accordingly Enthoven has voiced his anxieties over the introduction of wholesale change without prior experimentation and evaluation, and the possibility of fragmentation of services and the loss of co-ordination. This disagreement between Enthoven and the government might serve as a timely reminder that 'the market' is not necessarily a unitary phenomenon and that we may need to develop a more sophisticated analysis than has been traditional on the centre-left – one which is perhaps capable of discriminating between different forms of market.

It would be a mistake, in my view, to regard the internal market simply as an expression of right-wing dogma, or as a straightforward prelude to privatisation. It is being advanced as the solution to a number of structural weaknesses which have been identified (and not just by the Tories) in the NHS. Chief among these is the lack of incentive for economy in the provision of health care. The effect of the existing system of funding, it is claimed, is to insulate providers from the necessity of considering the economic consequences of their behaviour. The resulting inefficiency is demonstrated by wide variations in performance as measured by bed occupancy rates, theatre utilisation, length of hospital stay, and so on. Further than that, the funding system is seen as constituting a positive disincentive to efficiency, in that hospitals and districts which provide services to others have to wait for up to two years before their budgets can be adjusted to take account of these 'cross boundary flows'. Consequently, hospitals and districts which 'lose' patients thereby enjoy a windfall gain. The internal market, by (in effect) attaching resources to patients rather than to districts, is intended to address this problem of perverse economic incentives.

It is, as yet, much too early even to begin to work out how such a market might operate in practice, or even the extent to which the government would be prepared to allow it to operate. Virtually the only point on which there is agreement among commentators on the white paper is that there is a lamentable lack of detail, which the subsequent working papers have done little to supply. Nevertheless, some informed speculation might be possible. At the moment, units and districts have little incentive to consider how efficiently they provide various services compared with other units and districts. American studies, however, suggest that substantial improvements in efficiency may be achieved if services are transferred from low volume, high cost, low efficiency units. It is important to note that these appear to be *genuine* efficiency improvements. Not only are costs reduced – by 24 per cent according to one study of heart surgery (Finkler 1979) – but quality is also increased: Luft, Bunker and Enthoven (1979) report substantial reductions in mortality following heart surgery. In these ways it is at least arguable that the internal market is potentially capable of enhancing efficiency, enabling the NHS to utilise the same quantum of money to provide more and better quality care for patients.

If this represents the upside of the internal market, it must be recognised that there is a potential downside also, which the government so far has signally failed to acknowledge (at least in public). First, as low efficiency providers are forced to withdraw from the marketplace, it is inescapable that some patients will be required to travel in order to obtain some treatments. Even though the cost of providing those treatments may have been reduced to the NHS (as a result of the efficiency gains already mentioned), the costs incurred by the patients and their relatives in terms of additional travel time and expense, work-time forgone, and so on, are certain to be increased. One of the clear lessons to be learned from recent American experience is how easy it is to make the error of mistaking a cost which has simply been shifted outside the system (or section of it) for a genuine cost saving (see Petchey 1988 for a general review of this phenomenon, or Fitzpatrick, Moore and Dittus 1988 for a specific and graphic instance). The increased costs just referred to will not appear on the NHS balance sheet, but they are real enough and need to be allowed for in any cost benefit analysis of the internal market.

The second possible cost of marketisation is the possibility of interference with the rational strategic planning of services, with a consequent loss of co-ordination – an anxiety voiced, among others, by Enthoven (1989c). As a consequence of the internal market, health authorities are likely to become increasingly reliant on revenue derived from contracts with other authorities. As this happens, they could well lose effective control over the resources they currently manage, placing long-term planning in jeopardy. The potential for contradiction between the rationality of the market and the rationality of planning is graphically illustrated by consideration of the possible outcome of the government's decision to terminate the Resource Allocation Working Party (RAWP). This was the mechanism devised by the last Labour administration to redress regional inequalities in the distribution of NHS funding, essentially by diverting resources from 'overfunded' regions (mainly in the South East) to the 'underfunded' ones. As I have argued elsewhere (Petchey 1989), this historical concentration of medical capital was not accidental. Rather, it was a consequence of the geographical distribution of the hospitals taken over by the NHS in 1949, a pattern which was a product of the investment decisions made by private providers. The internal market and the abolition of RAWP, in conjunction with wider inter-regional inequalities and the strategic position of the metropolitan regions in terms of the national transport network, could well result in funds flowing from the regions back to the South East, aggravating the North-South divide. The ability to plan the distribution of resources is not something which should be surrendered lightly – whether at district, regional or national level. Admittedly the record of the NHS in this respect is far from perfect, but it is significantly better than other countries which are more reliant on private medicine, where the geographical distribution of medical resources tends to mirror the geographical distribution of income to a much greater extent. France is a good illustration of this tendency. In 1975 Paris had more than twice as many doctors per head as Picardy (216 doctors per 100,000 population as against 98). Nor is it just medical personnel whose distribution may be thus 'distorted' (in relation to social objectives) by the operation of market forces. In America, Hampton (1987) has identified what he terms a 'medical arms race' between hospitals, fuelled by public demand (mis)led by medical equipment manufacturers' advertising, which has resulted in unnecessary duplication of sophisticated and expensive technology for which (often inappropriate) use subsequently has to be found to prevent its under-utilisation and to justify the investment in it.

The third potential cost of the internal market as it seems currently to be conceptualised is its potential impact on the quality of care. This is because costs are much more amenable to quantification than the extremely elusive concept of quality, which requires the measurement of the outcomes of medical interventions. As a result, there is a danger that management of the NHS might be biased towards cost minimisation at the expense of quality of service. This could easily give rise to the adoption of policies which simply shift costs between sectors (eg, the acute and community), or encourage the neglect of the longer-term consequences of short-term cost saving initiatives (eg, reductions of length of stay in hospital).

As has already been observed, the foundation on which the internal market rests is a shift in the mechanism of funding. Instead of funds being allocated to providers, they will be attached to consumers: as the government puts it, 'money will travel with the patient'. As we have seen, this measure is intended to address one set of perverse economic incentives, but the danger is that in so doing it might serve simply to erect an alternative set. The problem is that, while for a large population capitation might be an adequate basis for funding, as the size of the population decreases (in other words as we descend from regional, to district, and ultimately to general practice level), so there is an increase in the risk that capitation could constitute an economic disincentive to the enrolment of high cost categories of patient (the elderly, for example, or the chronically sick). The difficulty confronted by capitation in health provision, as opposed, for instance, to education, is that medical expenditure is not readily predictable on an individual basis, and is moreover extremely concentrated. In other words, the vast majority of expenditure is accounted for by a tiny minority of the population. For instance, in France in 1981, 5 per cent of the population consumed 63.5 per cent of medical care, while 40 per cent consumed only 0.4 per cent and 23 per cent consumed no services at all. This means that, in practice, it is far from easy to devise a capitation system that fairly reflects variations in expenditure between categories of patient. Any mismatch between fee and expenditure could result in 'windfall profits' being made from some categories of patient, while others face restrictions on access to the care they require.

Consumerism – Or Patients' Rights?

Given these difficulties (and others which will be discussed below) I believe that Labour is correct in its rejection of marketisation as a remedy. However, as has already been stated, it must also be recognised that the proposals to marketise health care do not necessarily derive in any simple and straightforward way from Tory ideology; they are also informed by a diagnosis of structural weaknesses in the NHS – of bureaucratic inefficiency and professional rigidity. While the merits of the remedy may (and must) be disputed, the merits of the diagnosis require careful evaluation. I am far from convinced that the party's policy review process has, so far, paid adequate heed to the peculiarities of healthcare in general and the NHS in particular. Regardless of the size of the NHS budget, it is incumbent on an administration of any political hue to attempt to ensure that investment in the health service is used as efficiently and effectively as possible. In order to do this it has to achieve an appropriate balance of power between the three crucial political forces in the health arena: patients, doctors and managers. Certainly, the policy review demonstrates an awareness of this problem in its repeated references to the need to make an efficient and effective use of resources, and in its proposals for Health Quality and Health Technology Commissions, for instance, or 'quality audits'. However it is disconcertingly vague (to the point of total silence even) on how, and by whom, day to day resource allocation decisions will be made. Who, in other words, is going to manage? and, perhaps more pertinently, in whose interests?

Market theory offers the Tories a ready 'solution' to this problem, which is essentially economic. It is the market itself which determines the allocation of resources, and consumer sovereignty ensures that it does so in a way that furthers the interests of consumers. A succession of Tory health policy documents has paid lip service to the sanctity of patient choice and of the delegation of decision making as mechanisms for creating a system of provision which is responsive to local variations in need. In this respect, as Pollitt (1989) points out, the NHS is little different from other sectors of the public services. The proposed reforms correspond closely with what he terms 'the standard package of developments', which includes:

> new budgetting systems aimed at giving managers a clearer picture of the costs of the activities for which they are responsible; sets of performance indicators; closer definition of individuals' tasks, frequently accompanied by new forms of staff appraisal, and by merit pay; an emphasis on greater delegation of decisions; and pressure to pay more attention to the wishes of consumers of the service.

Running through this standard package, he identifies a 'clear line of stress' resulting from the pull between stricter *upward* accountability to top management and politicians, and responsiveness *downwards* to consumers. In his view, despite the rhetoric of consumer sovereignty, the reality, at least so far, has been a tightening of control by top management. Few of the consumer initiatives which have been undertaken are any more than superficial, consumerism being so far equated with 'customer relations', rather than with any kind of genuine empowering of patients.

What then are the specific obstacles to consumerism in health care? The logical precondition for consumer sovereignty is a marketplace, and Siminoff (1986) identifies a number of logical objections to the whole concept of a 'health-care market place'. Even in the US, she argues, health care has never conformed to the ideal of the competitive market. What is more, she claims that it can never do so unless or until a number of features distinguishing it from other markets are removed. These distinguishing features include: obstacles to rational consumer behaviour such as difficulties that consumers face in acquiring medical knowledge, or the life and death nature of decisions; and the impossibility of consumer sovereignty in a 'market' where the actual decisions are made not by the consumers (the patients) but by agents (the doctors). Given these peculiarities of the medical 'market', it is not surprising that even in the US fewer than 40 per cent have been found to engage in consumerist behaviour – willingness to obtain information, exercise independent judgement and make quality comparisons when selecting a doctor (Hibbard and Weeks 1987). A recent survey of the British literature on consumerism and health care concludes as follows:

few people behave in the way implied by the classic market model. Surveys show that convenience and tradition rather than an evaluation of available alternatives largely determine the choice of general practitioner. Most people either inherit their doctor or simply choose the nearest practice. Only a minority take into account a recommendation, and this is usually from friends, relatives or neighbours. Once registered there is little incentive to change ... four out of five adults had been with their present practice for five years or more and during a year only 4 percent had registered with a new doctor. Most people change doctors only when circumstances force them to do so rather than for positive reasons, such as the possibility of obtaining a better standard of service.

(Leavey, Wilkin, Metcalfe 1989)

Undoubtedly there are aspects of the NHS about which patients are perfectly competent (and indeed entitled) to make judgements – the efficiency of appointment systems, the quality of the hospital or surgery environment, the attitudes of staff, and so on. These are sometimes (somewhat dismissively) referred to as the 'hotel-keeping' functions of the NHS, but they *do* need to be taken seriously – not only because it is the deficiencies of the NHS in these areas which are the strongest attractions of private medicine, but because of the significance of such social-psychological factors for the effectiveness of the healing process itself. So far, the left may have been able to comfort itself with the repeated opinion poll findings of widespread public loyalty to the NHS, but this apparent bedrock of support should not be taken for granted. Expressions of satisfaction with the NHS might indicate not a high standard of provision but the low expectations of patients. As more people experience private medicine via the internal market, expectations and satisfaction might shift significantly.

While these 'hotel-keeping' functions should not therefore be neglected, it would be a misfortune if they were to be elevated above clinical quality, or to become the limits of patients' rights. Although the policy review makes reference to a number of devices which are intended to enlarge patients' rights (the 'Charter of Patients' Rights', 'user-panels', 'patient-satisfaction surveys', for example), these proposals are, in my view, flawed by the failure to analyse the internal politics of health care. Any significant shift in the direction of increasing the rights of patients requires a corresponding shift in the locus of power in the triangular relationship referred to earlier – between managers, doctors and patients. Alford's (1975) analysis of this relationship might prove helpful at this point. He conceptualises health care in terms of a number of broad interests which are distinguishable according to the extent to which they are served (or not served) by the basic logic underlying the health care system. These interests may be 'dominant', 'challenging', or 'repressed'. In the forty years since its inception, the dominant interest in the NHS has been the doctors, with their basis of professional monopoly unchallenged (and possibly even strengthened) by the socialisation of medicine. It is at least arguable that patients have hitherto been the repressed interest. Since the Griffiths Report (National Health Service Management Inquiry, 1983), however, the government has been mounting a sustained challenge to the medical profession's forty-year domination of the NHS, by means of a radical transformation of the role of health service managers. Whether this process is sufficiently advanced that we now need to identify managers as the dominant interest, rather than as mere challengers, is not really relevant. The point is, as Harrison (1988) has shrewdly observed, that any amount of shifting the frontier of control back and forth between doctors and managers will not of itself necessarily produce any benefits for patients – as long as they remain the repressed interest.

The policy review's silence on the manager-doctor relationship is therefore puzzling and worrying. Admittedly, as has been mentioned, it does propose bodies such as the Quality Commissions, which will presumably have the remit of monitoring medical practice, but there would be difficulties in ensuring that they perform a real, rather than a cosmetic, function. Two such difficulties may be identified. The first is that by the nature of their terms of reference, such commissions will either consist largely of medical professionals, or else will inescapably be reliant on the testimony and advice of such people. The monitors, in other words, will not be genuinely independent of those whom they are supposedly monitoring. The second reason is that, compared with other countries, the NHS so far has a very good record when it comes to the evaluation and introduction of new treatments. There is no evidence that NHS doctors have been profligate in their use of untested drugs, or over-eager to embrace new technologies. Where their record has perhaps not been unblemished is in their attitude towards patients as people. It is an indictment of the neglect by the NHS of this aspect of its operations that it has taken till now for research to be carried out into the reasons for non-attendance at out-patient clinics (Frankel, Farrow, West 1989). Its findings? The major cause of non-attendance was the inadequate notice that patients were given of their out-patient appointments. Prior to that, non-attendance had been arrogantly attributed to the failings of patients rather than of the system.

Resource Allocation

To return, then, to the question posed earlier – who is going to make decisions about the allocation of resources? I do not believe that we have the option (not that it was ever realistic) of ignoring the necessity of making resource allocation decisions – even in health care. Yet the policy review shows no signs of having addressed this (in my view) central issue. Decisions about the rationing of resources have, after all, always been made in the past, but covertly, and by doctors, according to undefined, largely unscrutinised and frequently non-clinical criteria. My concern is that, through its failure to analyse the doctor-patient-manager relationship, the policy review could well result in simply tilting the balance back in favour of the medical profession. There has been a tendency on the left to dismiss management (of any kind) as a tool of capital; but to do so in the context of the NHS is to run the risk of discarding some of the benefits which have derived from the budget restraints and the introduction of general management. One of the most significant gains has been to persuade the medical profession finally to abandon its shibboleth of absolute clinical freedom. Doctors are, at last, beginning to show signs of taking seriously their responsibility for evaluating their care and treatment practices (clinical audit) and – even more importantly – for addressing themselves to the financial implications of their clinical practice (the 'Resource Management Initiative'). To be sure, this is something which is at a very early stage of development, and the response to it has been extremely uneven within the medical profession. Moreover, the prospects for these initiatives are under serious threat currently as a result of the disputes between doctors and the government. Nevertheless, Harrison (1988) may be right when he concludes that these developments 'would represent a scenario more desirable than any other organisational changes within the NHS'. The important lesson though for the policy review is that these concessions have been extracted from the medical profession only after prolonged pressure. Any relaxation of that pressure will lead to a rapid professional retrenchment.

In this context it might be pertinent to draw attention to

apparent inconsistencies in the policy review's approach to patients and doctors, as compared with users and providers of other services. If we look at education, for instance, we find there a proposal for a General Teaching Council 'to determine, enforce and enhance professional standards' and to ensure 'a higher degree of external accountability for the delivery of those standards'. If we look at local government, we find a proposal for enforceable 'quality contracts' with compensation for breach of contract. There are no comparable proposals in health care: no binding contracts on health authorities (only a 'local contract with the community'), no proposals for medical education. This latter, in my view, is a serious oversight, since clinical decisions by their very nature, have to be made by clinicians. It would require a very long-term programme, but if in the long term we want medical services which are patient-centred and socially responsible, it requires that we at least attempt to re-shape the medical profession. We should be looking at ways of diversifying recruitment to medical schools (perhaps by facilitating the entry of mature students, or developing 'top up' courses for other qualified health workers). We should also be looking at ways of altering the content of medical education in order to increase awareness of the social determinants of health and illness, and the limitations of the bio-medical model.

There is one final structural weakness in the NHS which successive governments have neglected and which is likely actually to be aggravated by Tory health policy. I refer to the tripartite structure of the NHS, in which responsibility for the acute sector and for general practice is divided between District Health Authorities (DHAs) and Family Practitioner Committees (FPCs) respectively, while responsibility for social and public health services, and for certain community nursing services, rests with the local authorities. This structure has been identified as a major source of inefficiency and must also be regarded as responsible for encouraging the development of the NHS as a hospital-biased sickness service. To its credit, the policy review has recognised this structural defect and proposes to rectify it by merging FPCs with HAs, and aligning these new administrative units more closely with the boundaries of local authorities. The aim of these proposals is the thoroughly commendable one of integrating more effectively the various health services, but they are not without their difficulties. For instance, both organisationally and financially, FPCs are much weaker than the HAs with whom they are to be merged. It may not be easy to prevent them being absorbed into the existing pattern of health provision, rather than acting as a catalyst for change towards a community-focussed pattern. Again, how are integration and co-ordination to be achieved without creating an additional tier of administration which will have the effect of removing policy making one stage further away from patients and workers?

Extension of democratic accountability in the health services is an objective of several policy review proposals. For instance, it proposes that the new health authorities will have a majority of members appointed from local government, health workers and voluntary agencies, and that there will be stronger, better-resourced and more democratic Community Health Councils. But will these proposals ensure that patients cease to be (in Alford's terms) the 'oppressed' interest? While user involvement and democratic accountability are wholly commendable as abstract principles, the obstacles to their implementation in the NHS are even more considerable than in other sectors of public provision. The first of these, which has already been discussed, is the difficulty for non-clinicians of judging the quality of service, and the potential contradiction between provider-defined 'needs' and user-defined 'demands'. The second is that roughly 90 per cent of the population are totally reliant on the NHS from birth to death for the entirety of their health needs. Perhaps 99 per cent will at some stage use the service. How do we ensure that the whole population can play a meaningful part in setting priorities and making decisions about how resources are to be allocated? Clearly, consumerism is inadequate for the reasons discussed earlier, even though it would be wrong to leap to the opposite conclusion. There *are* aspects of health care provision on which patients as consumers are currently competent to pass judgement, which is why the policy review proposals for user panels and patient satisfaction surveys are welcome (even if they only adopt current best practice in the

NHS). Elsewhere vouchers are suggested as a possible means of empowering consumers but, because of the highly concentrated nature of health care consumption referred to earlier, and the potential for unpredictable and catastrophic costs, they do not seem appropriate to health care.

The objectives that the policy review has set itself in this context are thoroughly laudable, but I have reservations about the suitability of the mechanisms which have been proposed for achieving those objectives. Elected representation on health service management bodies is all too easily subverted into a bureaucratic formalism which serves to keep control and choice of services remote from individual citizens. While we are acutely attuned to the deficiencies of the Tory market model of health care, based on consumer demands, we may be less aware of the deficiencies of the alternative that is being proposed, namely participation by citizens in a political market. As Klein (1983) succinctly puts it:

> The imbalances of the political market ... are very similar to the imbalances of the economic market. Not only is there an imbalance between the concentrated interest group of health service producers and the diffuse and heterogeneous interest group of health service users, but within the health service user group, the distinctions made in the context of the economic market carry over into the political market ... encouraging political demands would run counter to policies designed to favour the most vulnerable: those with the least political resources.

Health For All

This latest consideration leads on to discussion of a further potential inconsistency in the policy review group's proposals. The health priorities it has set itself (derived from the World Health Organisation's strategy for 'Health for all by the year 2000') correctly emphasise the promotion of good health, the prevention of illness and the reduction in health inequalities. These are to be national priorities, and they imply a significant redistribution of resources – from the acute sector to prevention and promotion, from middle class areas to working class areas and so on. If such a national plan is to be successful, it requires that there should be clear constraints on the ability of local interests to impede implementation of national policies. Not only does the policy review ignore this requirement, it also appears to be putting forward proposals which could actually run counter to it: 'Local authorities will be given more powers in relation to NHS decision-making'. 'Local is beautiful' may be superficially appealing as a principle, but in practice 'local' is as likely to be conservative as socialist. Localism could easily become parochialism, mobilising against attempts to redistribute resources away from high visibility, high. technology specialties to the low visibility 'Cinderella' services. It would not be wise for a future Labour government to rely on the voluntary co-operation of local authorities in the implementation of its health policies. Although it is likely that a great deal will be achievable through exhortation, it may still be necessary to contemplate the possible use of statutory imposition of the local targets referred to in the policy review. The Tories have not scrupled to employ all the means of leverage at their disposal – legislative as well as financial – in pursuit of their social policy objectives, so the apparent failure of the review to consider the full range of such forms of leverage is all the more surprising. Only one mechanism of national resource allocation is referred to (but not specified in detail) – 'activity-based' budgetting. This is described as a 'logical extension of the case-mix accounting system currently being developed within the Resource Management Initiative'; from this it might be reasonably inferred that the review group is contemplating some system of nationally-determined prospective prices for different cases (based, no doubt, on US-style Diagnosis Related Groups (DRGs). If this is so, then perhaps it is as well that there is a commitment to develop it initially on a pilot basis, for American experience with DRG-based prospective payment is far from happy (see Petchey 1988). Unless careful heed is paid to this American experience, the kind of payment system which appears to be envisaged by the policy review group could well turn out to have consequences quite different from those intended. Rather than systematically rewarding effort it could have the effect simply of producing haphazard gains and losses. In general practice also, the review group has set itself a number of targets for the improvement of quality, but without specifying the means by which it will achieve its objectives. How does it propose to sanction doctors who are unwilling or unable to practise in the manner desired? The only concrete proposal is to reduce list sizes, presumably based on the belief that there is an inverse relationship between list size and quality of care. But it has been argued that the main beneficiaries of reductions in list size have not been patients (in terms of increased consultation time) but GPs (in terms of increased leisure)!

What then, to coin a phrase, is to be done? Undoubtedly in the short term there is political mileage to be gained at the Tories' expense by playing up the issue of under-funding and playing on public fears about 'their' doctors and 'their' NHS falling prey to faceless accountants and managers. In the longer term, however, this tactic brings with it the danger that the Labour Party will get itself locked into a (perhaps uneasy) defence of the status quo ante 1979. And this, it seems to me, is precisely the direction of the policy review proposals. They are essentially conservative; the model of the health service which they advocate is the traditional 1949-79 NHS. Obviously, this criticism does not apply to all the proposals. Some are genuinely radical (I have in mind particularly the proposed amalgamation of FPCs and HAs, although, as I have argued, this is not without its attendant difficulties). Others are innovative and welcome (such as the proposal for local health targets, although I suspect that these would have to be given teeth if they were ever to be effective). Others are innovative but of doubtful utility (the Quality Commissions for instance). The majority, however, represent embellishments of ideas which have not proved noticeably successful in the past (Community Health Councils, for example). The proposals, in my view, fail to hang together in a coherent and logical way because there is a hole in the centre of the analysis which underlies them. The Tories, to give them credit, have recognised the need to ask questions about how health priorities are to be set, how decisions about the allocation of resources are to be made, how the efficient and effective utilisation of the available resources are to be ensured. It is my belief that the review group has ducked those questions. We might want to argue against the Tory *answers* to those questions, involving as they do the disciplining of medical practice by market forces, but we cannot afford to ignore the questions themselves, because to do so is likely simply to let the medical profession off the hook and return us to the not-so-good old days of a provider-dominated, user-friendly NHS. The Tory proposals for a health-care market quite clearly imply a continuation of the recent shifting of the balance of power between doctors and managers. The review group's proposals are likely to result in the reversal of that process. Simply changing the identities of the 'dominant' and the 'challenging' groups is unlikely to alter significantly the 'repressed' status of patients, for the reasons that have been discussed. The elements of consumerism incorporated into the Tory proposals are superficial; the representative structures which the review group proposes are likely to reproduce existing political inequalities in the health arena, unable to serve either as an effective counter-balance to the power of the medical profession or as an effective vehicle for the articulation of the interests of subordinate users.

Empowering Patients

The problems in health care that will be encountered by an incoming Labour government will not be the result simply of a decade or more of Tory underfunding or Tory policies; they will be the product of contradictions which have been inherent in the NHS since its inception. It could be argued further that it is not just four decades of the NHS which need to be analysed, but three centuries of western medicine, and that what is needed is not just a new kind of medical practice, but a new kind of medical practitioner and a new kind of doctor-patient relationship. The policy review group has specified quite clearly the kind of medical service it requires: prevention rather than cure; patients put first; quality prioritised; efficiency and appropriateness of services; user involvement. I am, however, unconvinced that the proposals it has put forward will be effective *except in the context of a reform of the medical profession*. Certainly some of the administrative and regulatory structures it suggests may be effective at the level of general policy formation, whether nationally or at district level, but it is difficult to see them being effective in *empowering users* whether individually or as members of communities, creating a health service that is genuinely popular, in the sense of belonging to the people who use it.

How might this be done? There are two dimensions to the problem I believe. The first of these is empowering users relative to the health service as an organisation. The review group, as we have seen, has suggested a number of mechanisms, but it strikes me that although appropriate at the policy level, these are unlikely to achieve a significant increase in the rights of individuals where it matters – at the level of daily usage. In other areas, the policy review has been prepared to contemplate the introduction of statutory, enforceable rights for service users. Why are these deemed inappropriate as a means of making health authorities answerable to patients – for unacceptable delays in treatment for example? It is the second dimension of the problem which is the more difficult, and this is the empowering of patients *relative to the medical profession*. Some of the panoply of regulatory and advisory bodies suggested by the review group might just prove necessary for this task (although I have my doubts) but it is extremely improbable that they will prove adequate for the reform of a profession, which is what I am advocating. It goes without saying that any such programme will require a sustained and long-term commitment from government drawing on all resources at its disposal, but in my view it is essential if patients are to cease to be the repressed interest. Nor should we overlook the fact that the Tories have already shown themselves prepared to engage the medical profession not just on a series of fronts (limits on prescribing, advertising, demarcation with other health professions) but also by a variety of means. The review group's proposals appear timid in the extreme by comparison.

The prospects for any such reform are not easy to evaluate. Certainly, as it is currently demonstrating, the medical profession is capable of mounting determined resistance, but in the past decade it has shown itself ready to contemplate change, albeit under intense pressure. There are other steps that could be taken in addition to the ones already being employed; I have already referred to the possibility of changing the profession (admittedly in the longer term) by altering medical education and the pattern of recruitment to it. Whatever happens, these pressures for reform must be maintained because, otherwise, the prospects of escape from paternalism and professionalism will be bleak.

Involving the Community in Community Care

There is one final element which I believe is absent from the review proposals. A finding which emerges clearly and consistently from a variety of studies throughout the world into the implementation of the WHO 'Health for all' programme is that the most significant factor contributing to success is the degree of local participation. Where policies have been imposed from the top down, they have tended to fail; where they have emerged from the bottom up they have succeeded. Local health targets are a welcome step in this direction, but the manner in which they are determined and the extent to which local communities are genuinely involved in their determination are likely to be crucial if those targets are to be meaningful. We should not overlook the obstacles to this involvement, not least a cultural tradition in which health is regarded as something which is 'done' to people by 'experts'. There are, nevertheless, encouraging local initiatives which serve to indicate what can be achieved when a community and health workers, *working as a team*, attempt to develop an approach which challenges the medical model of health and the dominant individualised concept of health care.

There are numerous instances which could be described, but I propose to concentrate on one such initiative discussed by McShane (1986). This is not exceptional; rather it serves to illustrate an approach which is beginning to be adopted elsewhere on a local basis and often in isolation from other projects. What is significant about this initiative is that it involves genuine 'out-reach' – much more than simply parking a mobile clinic on an estate for a day and waiting for patients to refer themselves. The Health Profile of a West Belfast Estate, decribed by McShane, involved interprofessional co-operation across the health service/local authority divide, but much more importantly the professional Health Profile Team worked with the Housing Action Committee, PTA, the church and other community organisations. Open meetings for residents allowed the expression of anger and frustration, and were followed by visits to all who had attended, and invitations to a second meeting to initiate the project. Drafting and re-drafting the questionnaire, interviewing households on the estate, writing the report, all of these were shared activities. Aside from the empirical findings of the Health Profile, four other features of note emerge from this exercise. The first is the extent of the involvement and co-operation which such genuine collaborations seem capable of achieving; there was a phenomenally high – 95 per cent – response rate on the estate. The second is the high degree of congruence between the residents' perceptions of the factors influencing health, and the professionals'; unemployment, housing and smoking were cited by three quarters of the sample. The third feature was the high level of demand for greater contact, more time and more information from professionals across the services. The final feature is the extent to which the professionals who participated in the project found themselves compelled to examine closely their own attitudes, values and working prac- tices and, above all else, to listen and take seriously the views of service users. What this and other similar initiatives reveal is a hitherto largely untapped interest and enthusiasm for pursuing health issues in local communities. This source of communal energy and commitment is a potential benefit which cannot readily be drawn on by the Tories or by commercial medicine, whose model of health promotion is individualised and commodified. The superiority of the Left's analysis of health derives from its insistence on the importance of the structural determinants of health and illness – something explicitly and bravely acknowledged by the policy review. Such community initiatives are likely, though, to reveal not just untapped enthusiasm but also unrecognised need. Are we able and ready to tackle the structural inequalities they bring to light?

References

R. R. Afford, *Health Care Politics*, University of Chicago Press 1975.

L. Brittan, *A New Deal for Health Care*, Conservative Political Centre 1988.

E. Butler and M. Pirie, *The Health of Nations*, Adam Smith Institute 1988a; *The Health Alternatives*, Adam Smith Institute, 1988b.

A. Enthoven, *Reflections on the Management of the NHS*, Nuffield Provincial Hospitals Trust 1985; A consumer-choice health plan for the 1990s', *New England Journal of Medicine*, 320:1, pp29-37;2, pp94-101, 1989a and b; 'Words from the source', *British Medical Journal*, 1989c.

S. Finkler, 'Cost Effectiveness of Regionalisation', *Inquiry*, autumn 1979, pp264-70.

J.F. Fitzpatrick, P.S. Moore and R.S. Dittus, the case of 'elderly patients with hip fracture', *New England Journal of Medicine*, 319:21, pp1392-7, 1988.

S. Frankel, A. Farrow and R. West, 'Non-attendance or non-invitation? A case control study of failed outpatient appointments', *British Medical Journal* 298;pp1343-5, 1989.

M. Goldsmith and D. Willetts, *Managed Health Care: A new system for a better health service*, Centre for Policy Studies 1988a; *A mixed economy for health care*, Centre for Policy Studies 1988b.

J. Hampton, 'MRI and Hospital Politics', Hospital Update, November 1987, pp889-90.

S. Harrison, *Managing the National Health Service*, Chapman and Hall 1988.

J.H. Hibbard and E.C. Weeks, 'Consumerism in Health Care – prevalence and predictors', *Medical Care*, 25:11, pp1019-32, 1986.

R. Klein, *The Politics of the NHS*, Macmillan 1983.

R. Leavey, D. Wilkin, D.H. Metcalfe, 'Consumerism and General Practice', *British Medical Journal* 298, 1989, pp737-9.

H. Luft, J. Bunker, A. Enthoven, 'Should operations be regionalised', *New England Journal of Medicine* 301, pp1364-9, 1979.

L. McShane, 'Health Services in Working Class areas', *Critical Social Policy* 14, 1986, pp1986.

R. Petchey, 'Health Maintenance Organisations: Just what the doctor ordered?', *Journal of Social Policy*, 16,4, 1988, pp489-507; 'The Health Service White Paper: The politics of destabilisation', *Critical Social Policy*, 25, 1988, pp82-97.

C. Pollitt, 'New wave public service reforms', *Health Service Journal*, 27.4.89 (supplement), pp4-5.

R. Robinson, 'New Health Care Market', *British Medical Journal* 298, 1989, pp437-9.

L. Siminoff, 'Competition in primary care in the US: Separating fact from fantasy', *International Journal of Health Services*, 16:1, pp57-69, 1986.

R. Whitney, *The National Health Crisis*, Shepheard-Walwayn 1988.

Charlie Leadbeater
Popular Social Ownership

The political, economic, and cultural conditions for old style nationalisation have gone, probably for good. The disintegration of what was for many a touchstone of post-war socialism is the product of two linked developments, which will mark off the 1990s from earlier decades of post-war development.

The first and most obvious is the Thatcher governments' privatisation programme, sweeping apparently unchecked from companies like Cable and Wireless to British Telecom, the telecommunications utility, British Gas, and on into the electricity supply industry, the water authorities and the coal industry. It is a remarkable transformation, which only started in earnest during the second Thatcher government. Should it win another election and carry out its pledge to privatise the coal industry, close to a score of corporations, which for many were emblematic of the achievements of post-war socialism, will have been transferred to private ownership.

But it is not merely an enormous institutional achievement. It has been underpinned by an equally significant political and ideological shift. Privatisation has taken on a crucial symbolic importance within the ideology of Thatcherism. Private stands for choice, efficiency, flexibility, self-sufficiency whereas public stands for lack of choice, inefficiency, inflexibility, and subsidy. By winning popular support for privatisation through its wider share-ownership policies, the government has widened support for private property – not merely as an economic instrument to achieve higher efficiency, but as a source of authority, order and stability. It widens the constituency which has an incentive to defend the rights and powers of private property. Thus economics, politics and culture cohere and combine. Privatisation is simultaneously a cultural and an economic policy: it has proceeded by intensifying, and modernising capitalist culture. This cultural policy has been vital to the success of the political project to dismantle the great lumbering state corporations, which towered over people as part of the corporatist state. Both have contributed to the economic goals, to reintegrate public corporations within the profit-seeking, market economy.

Thatcherism's strength in this is that it has worked equally effectively within the state and within civil society. Its aim has been to redraw the line between the two and to transform them both.

It has used the power of the state in a direct, strategic, and ruthless way to achieve its goals. Even when the programme has faced opposition – for instance over electricity privatisation – it has ridden on. It has weathered mistakes and miscalculations, for instance over the sale of the second tranche of shares in BP, which got caught up in the aftermath of the stock market crash of October 1987. Privatisation share issues have been underpriced so they will rise to a premium after the sale, thereby attracting small investors. Privatisation has been one part of Thatcherism's repertoire of determined actions by the state against the rusting infrastructure of the post-war settlement. Thus privatisation has been part of Thatcherism's recomposition of the state from an embracing, spreading, managerial corporatist state into a limited, authoritative, strategic state.

But its strength is that it has also worked within civil society. Privatisation has not been a purely instrumental state policy, it has been aimed at renewing capitalist culture. It has coalesced disenchantment with the distant, disempowering corporatist state within a modernising Conservatism. Private companies are not merely a source of wealth, but a source of values. While the large state, the big unions, the tower block, symbols of the overpowering scale of the corporatist era, have been systematically attacked, the large company has escaped unscathed. Indeed privatisation has further de-politicised corporate decision making. Large corporations are more than ever beyond political reach as unquestionable components of the economic order of a civil society which is constituted by markets, companies, and private individuals. It has been an exercise in heightening capitalist consciousness among the public, making people realise that when they are saving, investing, working, buying, they are participating in a capitalist economy. Thus privatisation, by withering public ownership does not merely redraw the line between the state and civil society it is also an attempt to reinvigorate civil society within a New Right image – to further limit civil society to a domain of markets, companies and individual workers and consumers. The role of the state is limited. But so too are the possibilities of transformation within civil society. As narrow capitalist values become more entrenched, so society becomes a meeting place for companies and individuals as workers or consumers, brought together through markets, prices and contracts. A civil society which is defined by markets, and private ownership, is one which systematically excludes interests and concerns which cannot be expressed through the cash register, the nexus of profit and loss. It rests for instance on the exclusion of the domestic sphere, of the family, and patriarchal power, from civil society, as a sort of pre-political domain.

Thus privatisation has two key elements. First, the transfer of ownership of corporate assets from the state to the private sector. Second, the intensification of privatisation and marketisation within society itself.

The power of Thatcherism's programme, then, is its sweeping range, from the high ideological goals, through the programme of government, its fiscal policies, and its attempt to nurture a cultural transformation within civil society. It is strategic not merely because it has used the state's power to hit clearly defined targets. It is strategic because it works at all levels of its politics.

The second development which has undermined traditional social ownership policies is the intensive and extensive restructuring of the British economy. The 1930s were a decade when the Western advanced economies adapted from the 19th century technologies of coal and steam, to the new core technologies of electricity and oil, which spawned new products, patterns of consumption, production processes and patterns of corporate power. It was upon this technological transformation that the core sectors of Fordist production were built – cars, steel, electrical appliances, and consumer durables. The 1980s are a period in which the economy is adapting to the new core technology of information technology, linking telecommunications and micro-electronics. Computers, facsimile machines, robots, are already the currency of work. The full impact of information technology on production and work, products and consumption are yet to be felt.

But while new technology is the most tangible aspect of this restructuring, it neither defines it nor explains it. New technology is just one aspect of a much wider corporate restructuring. Simply put, the advanced Western economies are moving into a new phase of development because companies are changing how they operate. Companies are altering what they produce, how they produce, how they are organised internally, where they produce, where they sell, how they sell, and how they compete. The economic core of the shift from Fordism to post-Fordism is not new technology, but fundamental changes in corporate strategy.

Within the economy as a whole there is a shift from manufacturing to services. Companies are changing how they produce by introducing new technology – in service sectors, manufacturing, and primary sectors. Manufacturers are talking of not merely introducing new technology to automate existing processes but of moving towards computer-integrated manufacturing, or 'total manufacturing flexibility'. But, as importantly, production is being fundamentally reorganised around new technology – with the abolition of traditional demarcation lines between skilled and unskilled, blue and white collar workers, the growth of teamworking, quality circles and sub-contracting. Fordism was classically associated with core industrial regions, the manufacturing belt of the Northern USA, the English Midlands, the Ruhr, and Northern France. Industry massed within these regions; workers and consumers massed with Fordist cities, and conurbations. Post-Fordism is associated with new growth corridors – Route 128, Orange County, the Cambridge-Reading-Bristol corridor, Toulouse, Grenoble and southern Bavaria. It is also associated with new industrial towns, the international corporate headquarters of Swindon, a former railways town, the mass service sector employers of Basingstoke, the electronics assemblers of Dundee and the science park companies of Cambridge.

This restructuring of how goods and services are produced and where they are produced is the product of changes in the scope and character of competition between companies. Under Fordism the key to competition was the economies of scale, of mass, high volume production, to cut the price of standardised output. Economies of scale are still vital in many sectors, but economies of scope have become much more important – the scope to switch production much more quickly between products to meet shifting market demand. Product differentiation, niche marketing and innovation have become more important with the saturation of traditional mass markets. Competition has intensified and internationalised. Many companies, for instance the computer manufacturer ICL, see themselves not as national exporters but as global producers, competing equally effectively in a range of markets. The predictable national market has been destabilised by rising international competition, and a wave of international restructuring.

Post-Fordism and Social Ownership

This restructuring carries important consequences for social ownership policy. Social ownership seeks to transform power within the economy, so it must be conditioned by the character of the power exercised by companies. In seeking to match and transform the power of companies, social ownership is also shaped by that power. The nationalisation programme of the post-war years syncronised with Fordism, a distinctive phase of capitalist development based on large, vertically integrated producers, selling standardised products into stable, largely predictable national markets. Manufacturing production was the commanding height of the economy; the male, manual, organised working class was the commanding force of socialism's advance.

Nationalisation was deeply influenced by the character of capitalist production, and an assumption that capitalism would develop in a linear and predictable way. The centralisation of economic control within large, vertically integrated companies, in which the division of labour was organised through scientific Taylorist management techniques, set the conditions for nationalisation. The assumption that capitalist companies would increasingly develop towards this model of integrated, consciously planned and co-ordinated centralised control, meant that capitalism itself would lay the basis for socialist planning and nationalisation. The centrality of nationalisation was in some sense guaranteed because the capitalist economy would develop in this linear way: the whole economy would gradually become more and more like a giant, planned, ordered Fordist factory.

Nationalisation was part of a much wider political settlement between capital and labour, to regulate the economy, provide a stable framework for economic growth, and ensure some of the benefits of economic growth were delivered in the form of welfare benefits, and full employment. Nationalisation was a component of the Keynesian-welfare state regulation of the Fordist economy, to match mass production with mass consumption. With the restructuring of the 1980s and 1990s those economic conditions for the old, Morrisonian style of state corporation nationalisation have gone. Social ownership will now have to confront and be shaped by a very different kind of economy, in which ownership, production and competition have further internationalised.

The 1990s will see the widespread emergence of multinational service sector companies. New relations have been formed between companies. Multinationals increasingly exercise their power through joint-ventures, technology transfers, marketing agreements, collaborative research and development, as well as direct investment. Production has lost its old predominance – marketing and retailing have become more dominant within corporate strategy, as intensified competition has meant that it has become more important to be close to the consumer. Production is no longer the pre-eminent commanding height. Global companies have become more important, but so too have small companies as innovators, and sub-contractors. Many large companies control suppliers not through vertical integration of ownership but through long-term supply contracts. Competition has intensified and is taking new forms, which means companies are having to work in much more unstable, uncertain and unpredictable environments.

Whether governments pursue an interventionist or a free-market industrial policy, they will confront two common problems.

First, companies designed for the mass production of standardised products to compete in stable national markets have to be transformed into companies capable of using new technology and flexible production techniques to create new products for intensely competitive, uncertain international markets. Companies may survive by doing well what they have always done. It may be enough to plan for the future by extrapolating from past experience. But if companies are to be successful they will need to do more than what they have always done. They will need to create and exploit the opportunities of new technology, new products and new markets. Doing that requires more than planning effectively for the predictable. It requires something most British managers still do badly, if at all: acting strategically within uncertain markets to minimise vulnerability, and maximise strength.

Second, there is an intensification of competition, and a new web of inter-company relations which are building up through joint-ventures, sub-contracting, the internationalisation of production, marketing and ownership, and the importance of marketing and retailing in determining what is produced. This means that increasingly it will not be enough to seek to control single companies. It will not be possible to control a single company without influencing the environment – the sector – in which that company operates. Old style nationalisation was based on the idea that ownership of production was vital to control. If the great production sites of Fordism could be controlled then much of their economic hinterland could be controlled as well. Production was the commanding height; ownership guaranteed the power to change production priorities. But increasingly it will only be possible to create the room for new corporate strategies by influencing how companies interact with one another, how they compete and collaborate. To alter the options open to a company will require changes in the environment within which it operates. Changing the owners of the company will only be one, and not necessarily the most important, part of changing the constraints within which a company operates.

These two developments, the rise of Thatcherism and the restructuring of the economy, combine into a dual revolution. Thatcherism's policies are aimed at freeing the economy, not to create free markets, but to free corporations to restructure. The economy has been further opened to international capital. Thatcherism is attempting to appropriate and mould economic restructuring, to synchronise its politics – popular capitalism, privatisation and enterprise culture – with the transition to post-Fordism, to create a conservative modernisation, a reactionary restructuring of economic life. This dual revolution has undermined the conditions for traditional nationalisation policies. The political coalition which supported nationalisation in the 1940s and 50s has gone. The economic conditions which supported it have faded. The cultural conditions which led people to accept state corporations as a form of social ownership have also gone, with the turn against the power of the corporate state, and the spread of individualised ownership of assets through home-ownership, savings, and pensions. The building society and the bank are now the central social institutions of popular, mass forms of individualised ownership.

This creates two fundamental questions for the Left. First, how can large international companies be controlled? This question of method – 'how can social ownership and control be achieved?' – has been the main focus for rethinking social ownership policies. It is a real and troubling question. But it has obscured a second question which the Left also needs to rethink. Why should these companies be controlled, in whose interests, to what ends? It is not enough to show that policies can be dreamt up which would deliver control over large companies. The Left has to also win the argument that they should be controlled.

The two questions are linked. The task of controlling large companies has become more difficult with the internationalisation of ownership. How is it possible to control companies which are owned in Japan, South Korea or the United States? The intractability of coming up with credible answers to this question means that it becomes academic to think about why large companies should be controlled. Why bother to think about what you want, if you can never think of a way to control these companies to achieve your goals? Equally the depoliticisation of corporate decision making, and the establishment of narrow notions of efficiency, profitability and competitiveness as the guides to economic policy, undermines strategies aimed at social control. Why bother thinking of how you will achieve control if at the end of the day there is no escaping the constraints of the international market? Support for social ownership, a belief that social control can be exercised, in part depends on winning support for the idea that it should be exercised. If there was greater support for the goal, the question of how it could be achieved should become less politically problematic. So if social ownership is to be renewed it must answer these two questions; how can control be exercised, and for what ends?

Popular Social Ownership

What might make up a dynamic, radical, popular, social ownership policy, which matches the immense power of multinational corporations and the wave of restructuring ushering in post-Fordism by offering an alternative vision of the modernisation of the British economy? Why should socialist strategy seek to change the way companies, both large and small, operate, and how will that change be achieved? The key to tentative answers to these questions will be found in four issues.

First, the most immediate issue which has to be confronted is the relationship between social ownership and the market. How far can social ownership depart from market criteria of efficiency and competitiveness? This question in turn resolves into a series of questions about social ownership and markets, for there is no single market that socialists should be concerned about. With some companies the primary concern may be their relation with the financial markets – for instance, how can social ownership promote investment which the capital market, left to its own devices, will not provide? With others it will be the market for goods and services, or their approach to the labour market. These markets differ in their characteristics, their internationalism, and the speed with which they respond to changes. Nevertheless there is a common set of questions which need to be answered about the relationship between social ownership and markets. Should social ownership be part of a strategy to introduce more strategic planning, or more detailed planning into the economy? How far can socially owned companies depart from market criteria of profitability and efficiency? How far can social ownership be used to promote different kinds of market outcomes? How much is social ownership about ensuring companies respond to market pressures in a different way from privately owned companies?

Second, the question about the relationship of social ownership and the market is really part of a much larger question – the relationship between socially owned companies and civil society. The relationship between socially owned companies and the market is really just one aspect of their relationship to civil society. Social ownership strategy must be based on a recognition that companies are central institutions in civil society. They affect how people work, whether they work, when they work, where they work, what they consume. Bringing companies under social ownership is a vital component of a strategy to socialise civil society. Society cannot become more democratic, more plural, more egalitarian, unless the institutions of civil society are transformed. Companies are among the most important institutions in civil society. Bringing companies under social ownership must mean opening them to pressures and demands within civil society which they can currently resist, if not ignore – for instance pressure for environmentally responsible production. At the end of the day this is what social ownership must mean – making companies fully socialised institutions, accountable in some measure to society rather than just to shareholders.

Third, this clearly raises questions about how social ownership should be achieved. If the goal is to socialise and democratise civil society, should social ownership proceed through state ownership of companies? Can socialism be inserted into society by the state? The right to own property is central to the rights guaranteed by liberal democracies. But in practice this has meant the right to own private property, and this in turn has meant that large parts of the population are excluded from owning their per capita share of the nation's assets. The British workforce is not without assets in the form of savings, pensions and housing. But it certainly lacks the power to control the productive assets of the economy. As traditional Marxists have argued, it is this inequality in ownership of productive assets which means that a society in which people are formally equal becomes a society in which they are actually unequal.

One response to this is to call for the abolition of private property by its negation, through vesting ownership of productive assets in the state. Disposition over productive assets becomes a question of political power exercised through the state. This argument has underlain many traditional approaches to social ownership. It must be emphatically rejected.

This is because people no longer trust the central state to be able to represent their interests, and thus the social interest. It is not just a question of how democratic the state is. The plurality of interests which go to make up the social interest are shifting. They certainly cannot be reduced to a single, national antagonism between capital and labour, for they include demands of consumers, environmentalists, national and regional movements and coalitions, feminists and others. To take property into state ownership does not socialise civil society, it negates it, by subordinating civil society to the state. This is why in Eastern Europe economic reforms to free enterprises from the rigid controls and luxurious inefficiency of central planning go hand in hand with a resurgence of political movements within civil society. Both are a rejection of a system in which society has been subordinated to the state. If social ownership means state ownership, one unequal contract, between workers and employers, is replaced by another, between individuals and the state. Privatisation has not merely redrawn the line between the state and civil society. By doing so it has further privatised civil society. Any central state involvement in moves towards social ownership must also be aimed at achieving a change in civil society. The measure of social ownership should not be how many enterprises are returned to state control. It should be how that process helps to socialise the economic life of civil society.

Fourth, social ownership strategy has to confront difficult questions about large companies, and especially large international companies. To some extent this is the same as the question of the relationship between socially owned companies and the market. How is it possible to change how companies behave if it is impossible to change the competitive environment which conditions their actions? But with international companies this takes on an added dimension. Even if international companies are UK owned they will be competing in markets outside the UK, which any national strategy will find it impossible to influence. But in addition many of the larger companies in the UK are foreign owned, and operate as parts of an integrated international production system. Ford's UK plants are entirely dependent upon supplies from continental plants. So social ownership would be significantly constrained in achieving changes in Ford's operations in the UK. But on top of that it would be largely impossible to take Ford into social ownership, because it would be next to impossible to buy shares in the company. Indeed these problems apply, in some degree, to large parts of the car industry. Every car producer in the UK is internationally constrained in some way. Jaguar is heavily dependent on sales in the US; Austin Rover is heavily dependent on its links with Honda for engine development; Peugot Talbot with its parent in France; Vauxhall Motors with the rest of General Motors' operations on the Continent. The names tell the story: Renault Trucks, Leyland-Daf, Ford-Iveco, GM-Izusu, Volvo Trucks, and most notoriously Nissan.

The most important company to control in the vehicle industry is Nissan, because it sets the pace which other companies have to respond to. Even if the other companies could be taken into social ownership, the room for manoeuvre would be severely limited if Nissan was running free, able to set the standards for efficiency and costs. But taking Nissan into social ownership would be next to impossible. It would involve buying shares in the parent company in Japan at great expense, for dubious gains.

So there is an enormous problem here. The assets controlled by international companies are vital to the future strength of the UK economy. If social ownership is to mean more than a new investment policy in small firms it must confront the question of how to influence large, international, often foreign owned companies. How should we set about attempting to answer these questions?

Hard Questions – Hard Choices

At the end of the day the Left will only build a credible case for social ownership if it comes up with a credible argument for its benefits. What will socialisation of civil society mean? How will it benefit people, empower them, provide them with higher standards of living, a higher quality of life? If market assessments of values are not to be the sole guides as to how the economy should be organised what are the other criteria to be used? These questions will only be answered by confronting directly the predominant notions of consumerism and efficiency, for these are at the root of Thatcherite arguments about the central role of the market in organising the economy. The Left will have to be clear about what it accepts of these dominant images of consumer choice, efficiency and value for money and what it seeks to change.

Some of the dominant definitions of consumer choice and efficiency should be accepted. The days when socialism could be predicated on the idea of infinitely expanding social needs and infinitely expanding resources are over, if they ever existed. If you are providing for people's social wants and needs, whether it is with their money through the welfare state or your own, there is nothing essentially capitalist about asking what the comparative costs of different strategies are, or what is the best way of spending the money. Efficiency is not an idea produced by the capitalist class to enslave workers. It is an idea which people use in their everyday lives as they decide how best to allocate their time, energy and money. There is something in this basic notion of doing things efficiently which socialists should embrace, and would reject at their peril. Increasing efficiency is, after all, the foundation for socialist ideas of a society of abundance. It is not the market which creates winners and losers, successful companies and unsuccessful companies. Any economic choice creates winners and losers, if you have to choose between one option and another, but cannot have both. Any preference, whether expressed by a consumer, a manager, a state planner, or a democratically convened planning authority, will create winners and losers, those who survive and those that do not. The criteria used in the choices may differ. But there is nothing essentially capitalist about making hard choices, between mutually exclusive possibilities. That is just an economic choice. If socialists reject those notions, they are not rejecting capitalist notions of efficiency and choice – they are rejecting economics – the economics of everyday life as much as the economics of major corporations.

Indeed the argument can be taken a step further. Social ownership strategy should in part be aimed at increasing competition in some areas of the economy which are dominated by cartels, oligopolies and monopolies. One thing unites British Telecom's (BT) poor performance before and after privatisation – it is a monopoly. It is that, not its ownership, which means that it fails in its chief commercial and social task – to provide consumers with a decent telephone service. Simply taking BT back into social ownership will not persuade people that it will provide a better service. The key is to restructure the company, and indeed the entire telecommunications sector, via a change in ownership. BT, whether publicly or privately owned, can dominate its consumers because there is no penalty for it, no competition. The key is to put management under some competitive pressure to improve services. This could be achieved quite simply. BT could be broken up into a set of decentralised regional companies, which lease lines from a central telecommunications authority. Every five years the managers of these, say twelve, regional telecommunications companies would have to submit themselves for re-election by a ballot of the consumers in their region. Different management teams would compete on different management manifestos to run the service in the area. Competition (management competition), consumer accountability, decentralisation, democracy and social ownership would be brought together, under the aegis of a regulatory body which would be responsible for licensing the lines. The important thing is not just to change the owners of a company but to restructure it. Similar approaches could be applied to other utilities.

In other markets, such as the credit card market, and the petrol pump market, which are characterised by oligopoly control, increasing regulatory powers to enforce greater competition and weaken the power conferred by concentrating ownership would be necessary.

So social ownership should be founded upon a recognition of the importance of basic notions of efficiency, and choice, as well as embracing the usefulness of competition. In part social ownership strategy should be aimed at promoting different sorts of market outcomes through strategic investments. For instance, higher spending on training, education and research and development should be aimed at raising the competitiveness of the economy over time, to set the economy's development on a higher path. But again the strategy and the market have to come together. Japanese industrial policy has been successful not just because it has led to higher investment in these areas, but because that investment has, in turn, to be linked to the development of growing sectors. The key in these areas is not to plan outcomes, but to act strategically to influence market outcomes, to guide the economy onto a high income, high skill, high productivity path. Neither planning nor markets, will achieve that. What could are strategic actions to shape how markets develop.

Social ownership will also be about ensuring that companies respond to market pressures in a different way. It should, for instance, mean greater worker involvement in decision making. But this will not wish away or dramatically alter the pressures which companies are under. It will mean that companies respond to those pressures in a different way. If under a future strategy an international engineering company were taken into social ownership, there would be no justification whatsoever for it being less efficient than its international competitors. What should differ is the way that it becomes internationally competitive – for instance, through worker involvement in decision making over training, product development, and investment.

Efficiency, Markets and the Left

Thus far this has been a fairly limited account of the relationship between social ownership, markets and notions of consumer choice and efficiency. The Left needs to accept, indeed embrace, some basic arguments about the importance of efficiency and markets. However what this amounts to is an argument for changing our ideas about social ownership, rather than about how social ownership will change the economy. Take the following five ideas about how a modern vision of social ownership should seek to socialise the economic life of civil society, in a popular but potentially radical way.

1. The utilities should be based on a notion of consumption which is different from companies in the competitive trading sector, because they provide essential services. This not only means that these services should be universally available. It also means that utilities under social ownership should cultivate consumer constituencies. This was the great attraction of the Greater London Council's fares fair policy of the early 1980s – consumption was politicised. It built up a constituency in support of a London transport policy. Social ownership of utilities should aim to do the same thing, through, for instance, providing rebates on telephone calls for single mothers, or cut-price gas at weekends for pensioners. Part of socialising civil society through social ownership should be the use of social ownership to politicise and socialise consumption decisions. Some of the aims traditionally confined to the welfare state should be pursued through social ownership; the line between the social and the economic should be broken down.

2. A renewed socialism should be informed by a range of social movements organised around a range of social antagonisms, not merely a supposedly all embracing social antagonism between capital and labour. Social ownership should not just be a policy to empower workers against employers, it should aim to socialise economic life. Thus vital to social ownership should be the green agenda. The

green movement has mounted the most sustained, popular, and biting attack on capitalist values of recent years. It directly and comprehensively challenges narrow notions of efficiency and profitability as guides for what should be produced. What is efficient for a company may not be 'environmentally efficient' for this or future generations. So a vital goal of social ownership should be to move the economy onto an environmentally efficient path of production.

3. The Thatcher government's privatisation programme is aimed at a limitation of civil society to a set of activities which companies and individuals undertake as workers and consumers, which can be co-ordinated through the market. That is the core of the Thatcherite view of society. It rests on an apparent exclusion of the domestic sphere, of domestic labour and responsibilities, from society. The domestic sphere is pre-political, pre-economic, a domain that workers return to after work, bringing home their hard earned cash to make the home more comfortable and secure.

One of the aims of social ownership policy should be to lay bare and alter the links between the domestic sphere and the economy. Thus one of the clearest goals for social ownership strategy should be to ensure the economy of work is reorganised around domestic responsibilities, around the responsibilities for child care, care for the elderly and the sick, as well as leisure. This is a very concrete example of what social ownership should mean: an economy which is organised around the needs of the domestic sphere as well as the needs of production in the formal economy. Social ownership should thus be conceived as partly an investment through industrial policy in the family, in child rearing, in welfare provided through the home. Thus policies on child care for all parents who are workers, more flexible working time fashioned to the need of parents and carers, should be central to social ownership policy. It should put companies under much stronger social obligations to meet the social needs of their workers, for instance by providing improved health care at work. The campaign for an improved health service should not be confined to the NHS, it should inform social ownership policy. Some may argue that this amounts to a privatisation of welfare. It should rather be seen as a socialisation of the company.

These remarks suggest two interim conclusions. First, social ownership strategy needs to be clearly integrated with other elements of socialist strategy, covering the environment, child care, women's rights, health care. It cannot be conceived as just an economic strategy. Second, if there is to be a new settlement with capital, it will not be between capital and labour in the old corporatist model. It will be between capital and a range of social movements, campaigns and interests. It will be a much more plural settlement – or series of settlements – than the post-war settlement.

4. Vital to the post-war settlement, in which nationalisation played a central role, was the commitment to full employment. How can this be resurrected within a new strategy for social ownership? Given the internationalisation of the economy and the scale of unemployment, it is unlikely that Keynesian policies for raising employment, through higher growth, stimulated by a period of higher public borrowing, will succeed for long, if at all. The Keynesian, national route to full employment is closed. The focus should shift to the micro-economic route, to employment security. The national political settlement between companies and organised labour, at the level of the national state, should be replaced with a set of micro-economic industrial settlements at the level of industries and companies. The aim should be to ensure that socially owned companies treat labour as another of their *fixed* costs. Unions and companies should be encouraged to sign security agreements, where more flexible working practices, flexibility within the company, is traded off for employment security. The union's primary aim should not be to pursue industrial settlements, covering training, employee involvement in decision making, changes to working practices, in return for employment guarantees. This suggests a third interim conclusion. A national settlement between capital and labour should not be the goal, but rather a set of micro-economic industrial settlements between workers and companies.

5. It is also vital to understand the links between social

ownership, industrial policy and national, regional and local politics. Take Scotland as an example. The future of the Ravenscraig steel plant, the future of the Scottish coal industry, the closure of Caterpillar's plant outside Glasgow, Ford's ill-fated investment in Dundee, were not just industrial questions, they became 'national' questions. National coalitions can form around industrial issues. So too can regional coalitions about the future of the North-East or South Wales. This suggests that the sites at which coalitions in support of social ownership can be built will not be at the UK level, but at those of Scotland, Wales, and regions within England. Social ownership questions will often simultaneously be issues of regional and national identity.

Equally it is clear the local state has taken on a new role in economic development in the last decade (see Cochrane and Massey in this collection). The pressures of restructuring are forcing cities to act in more creative, innovative, comprehensive ways to attract international capital. Many more cities are now directly competing in the international market for investment, to attract some form of growth sector whether it be the science park companies in Cambridge, the international corporate headquarters of Swindon, or the electronics assemblers of South Wales. This means that in some ways local politics are more constrained by the demands of capital. But it also means that local politics are upgraded, made more important, for it is the local state which is directly confronting international companies.

Nor is this competition simply a matter of tax breaks, free factories, and looser regulations. Cities are consciously investing in their cultures; consciously reinventing a new model urban culture to attract high income workers. New towns repeatedly stress the cleanliness of their environment, both natural, social and architectural. Clean efficient new technology goes with a non-racist culture in which Australians, Japanese, Germans and Americans can mix, and a clean natural environment of, for instance rolling Scottish forests, or Wiltshire fields. This means that municipal politics has to develop not merely new economic agencies to attract capital, but in addition new cultural agencies to create a model, clean urban environment.

It also means that the local political arena is vital to the interaction between society and major corporations. In California for instance recent local elections have seen the emergence of low growth, slow growth and planned growth coalitions to regulate corporations. In some prize Californian locations councils have started charging high taxes on big corporate buildings to finance low income housing. The local political arena can be the site of unusual coalitions between investors and community groups, both concerned about the quality of the urban environment; or between investment agencies, unions and companies over investment plans. The local state is the vital point of contact between civil society and the corporation. It is at this level that interventions need to be made, and coalitions in support of those interventions can be built (eg, the community concern in St Helens over the recent take over bid for Pilkingtons).

This suggests a fourth interim conclusion. Social ownership cannot be part of a national settlement because of the importance of the politics of towns, cities, regions and nations in relations with companies. In future social ownership will have to be pursued through a much more socially plural settlement, between companies and a variety of social movements and organisations, rather than just capital and labour. A national settlement between capital and labour needs to be replaced with a set of industrial or corporate settlements, aimed at ensuring employment security. A single national settlement needs to be replaced with a set of local, regional, and national settlements between companies and coalitions organised in these different locations. The goal of social ownership as part of a single, overarching, comprehensive macro-economic, macro-political, macro-social settlement between capital and labour needs to be replaced, by an intersecting set of micro-social, micro-economic, micro-political settlements.

Delivering the Goods

If that gives some indication of how the core goals of social ownership should be conceived, what of the means of achieving them. How is it to be done? The central goal should be the socialisation of ownership in civil society. Social ownership should not be conceived as an instrumental state policy to dispossess nasty capitalists. It should be conceived more as a cultural economic policy, to spread a culture of social ownership through economic life. The central'state may play a central role in organising, targetting and financing strategic decisions. But the implementation and design of these decisions should be decentralised. Thus if a strategy to improve companies' investment in training is to have a tangible effect in improving skills that can be used in production, it must be locally delivered through, for instance, training agreements within companies. Part of social ownership strategy then should be to give workers some 'ownership' of their training provision, through legislation forcing companies to set up training funds jointly controlled with their workforce. If the state takes strategic stakes in companies, control over these stakes should be devolved either to local authorities, or local regulatory bodies set up to regulate companies' activities. In short the aim should not be to insert the state more into civil society. The state should work in collaboration with unions, councils, other groups in civil society, to empower them, to socialise civil society. State ownership should be a means towards the socialisation of economic decisions, not a substitute for it.

Socialisation of ownership should concentrate then on tangible collective forms of workers, consumers, and citizen share ownership, through employee share ownership plans, wage earner funds, regional investment boards, and greater industrial democracy within companies. If social ownership is to be tangible ownership, it will have to match the concreteness of home-ownership or building society accounts. Thus, for instance, one step that a future Labour government could take is to pass legislation forcing say the top 200 companies to make over between 10 and 15 per cent of their shares to local regulatory bodies, which could then devolve the shares to worker share trusts, or local authorities. That would be the equivalent of taking between 20 and 30 large companies into state ownership. A policy of state ownership of 20-30 major companies is extremely unlikely to win popular support. A policy which led directly to decentralised empowerment of workers and communities would stand a much higher chance of winning popular support. These policies would have to work in tandem with policies on wealth taxation and inheritance taxation, as discussed elsewhere in this book, to alter the distribution of ownership. Social ownership should be conceived as part of a wider policy towards social capital ownership, rather than merely as an instrumental state policy to change the status of corporations.

In addition there are three economic criteria which a policy of social ownership needs to meet. It needs to match the internationalisation of ownership and control. It must take account of the shift in corporate power away from production as the commanding height, towards retailing and marketing. Controlling access to the market is the key power in the economy, rather than productive capacity. Finally, it needs to recognise that to influence a single company it will be necessary to influence the development of entire sectors. In other words, relations between companies, as competitors or suppliers and customers, are more important than the relationship between a single company and its owners. Many companies' room for manouevre is limited, not by the imperatives of their owners, but by their position within their market sector – whether they can dominate or whether they are dependent upon other companies.

Social ownership could in time spread through entire sectors, changing the way that companies interact. But this will be an inadequate strategy for two reasons. In the short run, which could be at least twenty years, this would mean there was little social control exerted over sectors. But even in the long run there is no guarantee that a set of socially owned companies will interact in a different way from privately owned companies. It could for instance mean that in a sector like the motor industry there would be cut-throat competition between socially owned producers. Social ownership might mean common interests are established *within* companies. It is no guarantee that mutually compatible interests will be established *between* different socially owned enterprises.

The traditional socialist answer to this problem is to say that social ownership has to include measures for democratic planning. Social ownership and industrial democracy ensure socialisation of decision making within the enterprise;

democratic planning ensures socialisation of decision making between enterprises, about how their activities are co-ordinated. This argument still has much to recommend it, but with one vital qualification. Democratic planners need information to make their decisions. If that economic information is not to be provided by a vast, inefficient and unsuccessful bureaucracy collecting data, it can only come from one other source: the market. If there is to be a form of democratically accountable decision making within the economy, which avoids the pitfalls of repressive, unwieldy bureaucracies collecting information about supply and demand for hundreds of thousands of products, which is then fed into the central planners' computer, the information upon which democratic decision making will be based will come from prices in the market, from consumer preferences expressed through consumption decisions. In other words a non-repressive, non-centralised, flexible form of democratic economic decision making actually requires the market to reveal what people's choices and preferences are.

So democratic decision making over the coordination of the economy will need to be combined with the market. It cannot be democratic planning, which would be unwieldy, inefficient, bureaucratic and possibly repressive. So it would have to be democratic regulation of markets. Forms of regulation would be vital to influence relations between companies across entire sectors. Thus sectoral or local regulatory bodies could be vested with statutory powers to regulate businesses over a certain size to ensure they met certain minimum standards – covering training, investment, purchases of supplies locally, environmental standards, etc.

Regulation of sectors would allow policy to influence single companies through intensive regulation, over pricing for instance, but also entire networks of companies. The key power which regulatory bodies would hold over companies would be the power that marketing and retail companies hold over producers: the power to deny access to the market. This is the key economic power to control. For instance it means it is much more important to have control over the Central Electricity Generating Board than the coal industry. The coal industry is entirely dependent upon the

CEGB, which controls the market not just for coal but for other energy producers. The CEGB controls the coal industry's access to its market.

Thus access to the market could be linked to investment and other decisions. Companies wishing to locate in the UK could be regulated this way – the key power the UK government could have over companies it cannot control through ownership is to deny them access to British consumers. To win that access they would have to offer something in return. As control of access to markets is such an important power, the strategy would have to command the support of consumers. Only with their support would it be possible to credibly deny companies access to the market.

Regulatory boards could not be mechanistic technical institutions, they would have to be democratic. They could form democratic rallying points within the economy, through which a variety of social groups could press their interests. Thus democratic regulatory bodies could have a democratic dynamic within them which statist models of social ownership lack. This democratic involvement would also be vital to prevent the regulators becoming ensnared, and eventually entirely captured, by the companies they seek to regulate.

Regulation could also have an international dimension, often though not always lacking in traditional social ownership strategies. It should be Labour's aim to get common European regulatory codes to govern the operation of multinational companies. Indeed the social dimension of the creation of the single European market has already opened up this avenue, although other aspects of the programme would limit national regulatory powers. In addition to regulation, social ownership itself should increasingly have an international dimension. Many industrial policy questions within the UK, for instance the future of the UK consumer electronics industries and defence industries, can only be sensibly addressed within a European strategy to build up European industries. This should involve the British state in joint-ventures, and agreements with other European states. But at a grass roots level for instance, worker share ownership schemes in multinational companies should develop an international dimension; local authorities in different countries which are hosts for the same multinational companies should be encouraged to collaborate over policy.

Social ownership cannot be a sudden, dramatic, 'left' strategy. It has to be a strategy which rolls through the economy, gathering momentum and support as it goes. It must generate and arise from real popular concerns and demands. In the next few years there will be considerable potential support for such a strategy. Even the limited regulation of BT has mobilised consumer disenchantment with the company. The wave of hostile take-over bids which is threatened by the restructuring in the run-up to the creation of the single European market will led to demands for state intervention. The growing saturation of traditional forms of savings – pensions and housing – will lead to widespread demand for more direct forms of investment in the economy. The Left needs a strategy which articulates these demands within an economic strategy which is aimed at a socialisation of the economic life of civil society.

The means will be a variety of forms of decentralised, collective, social ownership, combined with democratic regulation of major companies and sectors. The goal will be to establish an interlocking set of micro-economic, micro-social, micro-political settlements, which reflect the plurality, diversity and dispersion of interests which make up the social interests, which should be expressed through social ownership.

Chris Pond

Socialism and The Politics of Taxation

Amongst the more remarkable achievements of the Conservative governments of the 1980s was that they maintained throughout a reputation for cutting taxes, when in reality the opposite was true. During the ten years of Mrs Thatcher's rule so far, the overall burden of taxation has increased as a proportion of national income, from 34 per cent of GDP to 38 per cent. At each election, meanwhile, the Labour Party found itself in the dock of public opinion, accused of being in favour of high taxation, while the guilty party in this regard smirked on the sidelines. The confusion was compounded by the fact that Labour, eager to disprove the allegation, offered the electorate an ambitious programme of public investment and social spending which seemed to have no visible means of support. While the public in general approved the objectives of spending programmes, the proposals lacked credibility by apparently offering something for nothing.

The challenge for the Labour Party in the run-up to the next election is to present a taxation policy which is credible, economically efficient and fair. Taxation cannot be seen merely as a means of financing spending programmes. As the Tories have shown, the tax system is a powerful machine for shifting resources from one sector of the economy and from one social group to another. Too often on the Left, tax is considered as a technical matter, best left to economists and accountants. Yet the politics of taxation will be of central importance in determining the outcome of the next election. If once again the Labour Party allows itself to appear muddled and uncertain on the issue, or worse still sinister and evasive, the consequences could be severe.

Taxes: the Tory record

Ten years of Mrs Thatcher, as we have noted, have resulted in a higher overall burden of taxation. Income tax, the most visible part of the edifice, has been reduced. But national insurance contributions, an equally important tax on earned income, though less obvious as such, has increased sharply. For every £1 raised in income tax in 1988/89, national insurance contributions raised 76p; in 1978/79 they had raised only 53p for every £1 collected in income tax. While income tax retained at least some element of progressivity, national insurance contributions are unashamedly regressive in their effects: for the very lowest income groups NI contributions impose a harsh 'poverty trap', because contributions are payable on all earnings once the basic exemption limit is crossed. Meanwhile, the upper ceiling on the contributions means that above a certain level of earnings, no additional contributions are payable. So not only are NI contributions virtually invisible to the casual observer; they also impose a heavier burden on the poor than on the rich. Both characteristics might be considered likely to endear them to the present government as a convenient form of tax.

Taxes on spending have also increased, more than offsetting the cuts in income tax. The Prime Minister and Chancellor Lawson seem locked in struggle against the forces of the EEC who wish to extend VAT in Britain as part of the harmonisation of taxes across Europe. The struggle might have been greater still had Mrs Thatcher not almost doubled VAT herself in 1979, except on luxury goods. The standard rate was increased from 8 to 15 per cent; that on luxuries from 12½ to 15 per cent.

Overall, the burden of indirect taxes has increased by £22 billions in real terms since 1979. Whereas central government expenditure taxes raised slightly less than income tax in 1978/79, they now raise one third more than income tax (*Hansard*, 29 July 1988, cols 737-738). Again, the burden has fallen most heavily on the poor: according to the Central Statistical Office, the poorest households pay almost a quarter of their income (23 per cent) in direct taxes, while the richest pay only 16 per cent.

The table opposite, taken from the answer to a

parliamentary question tabled by Nick Brown MP, shows what has happened to the tax burden of a family on the average wage, and three quarters of the average, since 1978/79. The small cut in income tax has been outweighed by a rise in national insurance contributions, VAT and local rates. The table takes no account of other 'hidden' taxes, such as the extra charges imposed by the Treasury on electricity and gas prices as a means of adding to central government revenue.

Table 1: Taxes as a proportion of gross earnings of a married couple with two children, 1978/79 and 1988/89

	75 per cent average earnings		100 per cent average earnings	
	1978/79	1988/89	1978/79	1988/89
Income tax	8.1	7.1	14.4	11.5
NIC	6.5	9.0	6.5	9.0
VAT	2.6	4.8	2.6	5.2
Other indirect	10.1	8.9	8.6	7.9
Domestic rates	3.4	4.2	3.0	3.7
TOTAL	30.7	33.9	35.1	37.3

Source: *Hansard*, 10 January 1989, cols 635-642

For the household on a relatively low wage, the cut in income tax has been miniscule. The increase in national insurance contributions and in VAT are almost five times as large. Local authority rates hit low income groups hard (although not nearly as hard as the poll tax which is to replace them). Restrictions in local authority grants and on their borrowing powers have been responsible for a large part of the increase in domestic rates, which alone almost wipes out the small income tax cut for the lower earning family in the table. Overall, this household is paying 3 per cent more in taxes than ten years earlier.

The household on the average wage has fared little better. The cut in income tax left them with less than 3p in the pound more in the pay packet. This was almost wholly offset by the increase in national insurance contributions. Domestic rates and other indirect taxes (such as taxes on alcohol, petrol and tobacco) took exactly the same proportion of average earnings as it had ten years earlier.

Meanwhile, the amount of earnings taken in VAT doubled.

While the overall burden of taxation has increased, the distribution of that burden has shifted, from the rich to the poor, from companies to the individual and from wealth-holders to wage-earners. The main beneficiaries of income tax cuts were the already well-off. The starting rate of tax was exactly the same in 1989 as it has been in 1979 – 25p in the pound. But the rate on the highest investment incomes was cut from 98p to just 40p (and from 83p to 40p on earnings). Of an estimated £20 billions awarded in income tax cuts between 1978/79 and 1987/88, almost a quarter (24 per cent) went to the 1 per cent of taxpayers with an income in excess of £50,000 a year. Each of them enjoyed a tax cut on average, of £20,760. One in a thousand taxpayers have an income in excess of £70,000 – they enjoyed 18 per cent of the tax cuts.

The Prime Minister expressed her concern about the burden on the lower paid in an interview for BBC *Newsnight* on 30 July 1985: 'I do feel very strongly indeed that people on comparatively low wages and pensioners pay too much tax. You see 41 per cent of our income tax comes from those who earn average male earnings or less.' This concern seems to have failed to communicate itself to the Chancellor of the Exchequer. Of the cuts in income tax awarded since 1978/79, only 2 per cent went to people 'on comparatively low wages' of less than £5000 a year, even though they represented one in eight of all taxpayers.

Mrs Thatcher's three governments have created a tax system that is both unjust and inefficient. Nineteen out of twenty taxpayers are subject to the same rate of income tax; but those at the lower end of the income scale also pay national insurance contributions. The burden of taxation on the poor, already unacceptably high ten years ago, is now greater still. Meanwhile, the system is riddled with anomolies and loopholes which both distort economic activity and increase the unfairness of the system.

This presents a considerable challenge for Labour. It must devise a tax system which is able to raise sufficient revenue to meet its commitments on public spending and social investment, but in a way that is fair and efficient. Moreover, Labour paid a heavy price for the substantial increase in wage taxation during the late 1970s, which Thatcher was able to exploit to the Tories' advantage (see Day and Pond 1982). A new tax regime must ensure that the burden on the average and below average wage-earner is not further increased.

Supply-Side Mythology

The Conservatives are unashamed about the shift in the burden of taxes from the rich to the rest, although they are grateful for the continuation of the public myth that taxes overall have been reduced. They believe inequality to be functional to the efficient operation of the economy. While the wealthy are further enriched, they argue, the rest of society benefits from the stimulation that tax cuts create for enterprise and investment. Hence, the benefits of tax cuts for the rich eventually 'trickle down' to the rest of society. J K Galbraith, the American economist, finds the theory amusing. He likens the idea of trickle down to the notion that, if you feed sufficient oats to a horse, there will eventually be something left for the sparrows. Just as this notion is more readily accepted by horses than sparrows, he observes, so the idea of trickle down is more attractive to the rich than to the rest.

Ministers also collude in the myth (perhaps because they believe it) that tax cuts generate beneficial incentive effects. The logic of the argument requires some agile intellectual acrobatics. A tax cut may encourage people to work harder because they can keep more of the extra income they earn; alternatively, they may decide to work less, since the Chancellor has given them additional income without the need for additional effort or risk. After the 1988 Budget, some of the wealthiest individuals found themselves £50,000 to £100,000 better-off. No-one would suggest that winning the pools was an incentive to work harder; why should windfall tax gains have this effect? Many of these people might have been encouraged to work harder had their tax burden *increased*; they would then have needed to expend more effort to achieve their ambitions for a certain lifestyle or level of expenditure.

It is important in rebuilding the tax system to disentangle the truth about incentives from the myth. The effect of tax cuts will depend on the balance between the average and the marginal rate of tax. The marginal rate is the rate of tax payable on additional income: for 94 per cent of British taxpayers it is (in 1988/89) 25p in the pound. The average (or 'effective') rate of tax is the amount that is payable as a proportion of an individual's total income. This will vary according to the taxpayer's circumstances, whether s/he can offset a mortgage or a pension against tax, whether s/he is married, and so on.

The higher the marginal rate of tax in comparison to the average rate, the greater the disincentive effect. This is because the marginal rate of tax determines whether an individual finds it worthwhile to work extra hours or take on more responsibility. On the other hand, the average tax rate determines what a taxpayer has left to spend after paying tax. A cut in the marginal rate of tax may encourage extra effort; but a cut in the average rate of tax will leave the taxpayer with more to spend, without the need for extra work or responsibility.

In the tax system created by Thatcher and Lawson, the greatest disincentive effects are faced by those on the lowest incomes, who face the same marginal rate of tax as everyone else, but whose average rate is lower because the personal allowances account for a bigger proportion of their total income. Since the total amount of revenue raised is equal to everyone's tax contribution added together, the sum of the average tax rates, it follows that the most efficient tax system (in terms of incentive effects) is one which raises the required amount of revenue with the lowest marginal rates of tax.

As Galbraith, again, has observed, this is of little concern to the enthusiasts for supply-side economics:

> Let us take supply-side theory at its face value, however modest that may be. It holds that the work habits of people are tied irrevocably to their income, though in a curiously perverse way. The poor do not work because they have too much income; the rich do not work because they do not have enough income. You expand and revitalize the economy by giving the poor less, the rich more.
>
> (quoted in Hemming 1984)

Those facing the highest marginal rates of tax, of course,

are those caught in the poverty trap of taxes and means-tested benefits. Their numbers have increased dramatically under Thatcher, to reach a record half a million in 1988/89. These are households facing marginal 'tax' rates in excess of 60p in the pound. However, these are the very people who have least opportunity to adjust their work effort and earnings to take account of the disincentive effects, since hours of work are determined by the employer and not by the employee.

A major study of incentives at Stirling University was commissioned by the Treasury at a record cost of £600,000. The study took seven years to complete, but when the research was completed the findings were never published. The conclusions were not pleasing to a government whose economic strategy rested on the assumption of incentive effects which proved more myth than reality. The study revealed that four out of five of those in work had no opportunity to work longer hours in their main job. Among those not in work, four out of five were either unable to work at all or unable to find a job. In these circumstances, tax cuts can have little effect.

The study predicted that the cuts in the standard rate of tax from 29p to 25p in the pound between 1987 and 1988 would have no effect on hours worked for 98 per cent of households. Of the rest, half were expected to work more, and half to work less as a result of the tax cuts. The study also predicted that an increase in tax rates from 29p to 40p in the pound would still have no effect on the hours worked by 92 per cent of families, while 5 per cent would work fewer hours and only 2 per cent would work more. The most effective means of encouraging people to work harder, the research showed, would be to reduce mortgage tax relief, since additional effort would then be essential for people to maintain their commitments. Paradoxically, it appears that the more powerful influence on work effort in the 1988 Budget was not the tax cuts provided, but the increase in interest rates which followed as a result (Brown 1987).

Lawson maintains, despite the evidence, that cuts in the higher rates of tax are justified in economic terms. In support of this assertion he cites the fact that more revenue is now contributed by the rich towards total taxation. This, he claims, is an indication of the supply-side effect, encouraging the better off to take risk and increase their efforts. The explanation for this phenomenon is rather simpler: since 1979 the share of both income and wealth enjoyed by the better off has increased. Since their share of the nation's economic resources has increased, so too has their share of total taxation. But the amount of tax they pay as a proportion of their income has fallen.

Fairness and Efficiency

There is no trade-off between fairness and prosperity, as the Tories would have us believe. The 'economic miracle' achieved since 1979 represents no more than an old-fashioned credit boom, enhanced by a large element of negative redistribution and financed by North Sea Oil and privatisation receipts. There has been hardly a period since the War when incomes on average have *not* increased. What distinguishes the 1980s is that the widening disparity between rich and poor renders that average less meaningful than ever before. Mrs Thatcher boasts that 'Everyone in the nation has benefited from the increased prosperity – everyone' (*Hansard*, 17 May 1988). The Prime Minister seems to have lost her grip on reality: the numbers in poverty have increased by 55 per cent since 1979; the numbers of homeless are at record levels. Even those who have gained from tax cuts find the enjoyment of their private prosperity tarnished by public squalor.

Central to Labour's future economic and social policy is the belief that economic efficiency and prosperity are damaged by inequality and injustice, not enhanced by it. Inequality is a drain on the nation's resources and a source of waste and inefficiency. It deprives people of the chances necessary to meet their potential and to make a full contribution to economic activity.

It is against this background that a new tax structure must be devised. Reform must recognise that taxation is itself an instrument of social policy. In the past lack of co-ordination between tax and social policy has created the poverty trap, the result of the clash between a tax system which imposes too heavy a burden on the poor and a social security system too heavily dependent on means-tested benefits.

The interaction between taxation and social policy is evident also in the 'dependency culture' (to borrow a phrase from John Moore) generated by tax reliefs and allowances. Just as public spending provides an element of public welfare through the social security system, the health service and education, so the tax system encourages a (sometimes more generous) system of private welfare, albeit one which is financed from public funds. The dependency of the middle class on tax relief for housing, pensions and life insurance is treated differently from that of the population as a whole on the visible welfare state. Indeed, a further shift from public to private welfare in the health service is now taking place, with the extension of tax relief to private health insurance. The Left must recognise that taxation is more than a collecting box for public spending. Taxation must be given a central role within both economic and social policy. It cannot be the only mechanism for redistribution, but it has an important part to play in working towards a fairer and more prosperous society.

A New Tax Strategy

Tax changes over the past decade have accelerated a trend that had taken place over the previous thirty years, shifting the burden of tax towards the poor. By 1988/89, almost seven million taxpayers had an income below the Council of Europe's 'decency threshold'. They represented almost one in three of all taxpayers, and more than two in three of the low paid.

The tax system is no longer an effective means of redistributing income from rich to poor. Indeed, its effect is sometimes in the opposite direction. The lessons of the past forty years are that taxation and social spending cannot be the only means of redistributing income. We need to tackle inequalities at their source, to treat the disease and not just the symptoms. This means we have to intervene directly in the processes that generate poverty and inequality, by tackling unemployment and low wages, fighting discrimination on the grounds of race and sex and providing adequate child care facilities to enable parents to compete on equal terms in the jobs market. Nevertheless, taxation will continue to have an important role in helping to redistribute incomes and wealth. It can only fulfil this role if the tax system itself is progressive. How is this to be achieved?

The first step is to lift the poorest out of tax altogether. The poverty trap is witness to the absurdity of taxing people on an income which is considered so low that they are entitled to claim means-tested benefits such as Family Credit and Housing Benefit. About three quarters of all those entitled to Family Credit are also subject to income tax. If they also claim Housing Benefit they stand to lose up to 97p in each extra £1 they earn as a result. The table below shows how the poverty trap operates:

Table 2: *Components of the Poverty Trap, 1988/89*
Loss of income for each £1 increase in wages

Income tax	25p	
National Insurance	7p	
Family Credit	47.6p	
Housing benefit	17.3p	
Overall loss	96.9p	in the £1

Source: Low Pay Unit, 1988

Shortly after the war, tax was not payable at all until earnings reached the average wage (for a family of four). Now those on incomes below the average contribute more than 40 per cent of all tax revenue. Removing low income households from tax would not solve the poverty trap, but it would certainly alleviate its effects. There are several ways of doing this which we need not discuss in detail here (such a discussion is included in Hills 1989). We need only note that the poor now contribute so much to total revenue that taking them out of tax will be expensive: the cost of exempting those with an income below the Council of Europe decency threshold is about £4 billions, although it would be much higher than this if an increase in tax allowances were used to take the poor out of tax. The reason is that much of the revenue lost would be enjoyed as tax cuts by people well above the tax threshold. Indeed, those paying tax at the higher rate would gain most; those just above the tax threshold least.

We should not assume that all of the low paid would welcome being lifted out of the tax net. There are two reasons for this, the first of which is practical: many of the poor cannot afford to be taken out of tax, or at best would gain little from this generosity. This is because means-tested benefits such as Family Credit are now assessed on the basis of net income. A tax cut automatically triggers a cut in benefit eligibility, leaving the poor no better off and the Exchequer no worse off. For every £1 in tax cut a family in the poverty trap would stand to lose 96p in benefits. This problem does not arise if the increase in tax-free income is given in the form of increased child benefits. The Tories have reduced the real value of child benefits (a universal benefit payable to the parent responsible for the children) in order to boost means-tested Family Credit. Substantial increases in the benefit would be an efficient means of helping families with children.

The second reason why the low paid may be less than overjoyed about their removal from the tax system is that citizenship and taxation are closely linked. The phrase 'no taxation without representation' can take on a sinister ring when expressed in reverse. Exemption can look like expulsion from the tax system, and from the rights and privileges that taxpayers can legitimately demand. Many of the low paid would see it as a matter of dignity to be able to contribute to collective provision, as long as taxes are levied fairly and as long as they received a wage which, even after tax, left them with a decent minimum income. This is further reason why tax cuts are no alternative to policies such as the minimum wage.

Progressive Taxation

The British tax system is now one of the least progressive in the world. The starting rate of tax on the poor is higher than in most other countries, and the top rates on the rich are lower. Most people, as we have noted, pay tax at the same rate. Why should it be otherwise? Some argue that, because most of the incomes of the poor are exempt from tax altogether (as a result of the personal allowances) their average rate of tax is still much lower than that imposed on the rich. That is no longer the case. In 1988/89, a single person on the average wage, earning £254 a week, paid 29 per cent of their income in direct tax; someone earning £5000 a week (twenty times the average) paid *at most* 39 per cent of their income, even on the unlikely assumption that they had no mortgage, no pension scheme and no life insurance contributions to offset against their tax liability. Ten years ago, the average earner paid a very similar proportion of her/his income in direct deductions; but the richer taxpayer contributed 75 per cent of her/his income. Having twenty times the income, the richer taxpayer contributed 2.4 times the amount of tax; he still has twenty times the income, but now contributes only 1.3 times as much tax.

A tax system which takes so much from the poor in comparison to the amount taken from the rich has rather limited potential for redistribution. Inequalities have increased sharply since 1979 and the tax system, instead of compensating for this, has tended instead to reinforce the widening divide. Redistribution is not, however, the only reason why a Labour government should replace the current, virtually flat-rate, tax system with a more progressive structure of rates. Even if the aim were only to ensure that the burden of taxation was equally shared, higher rates of tax should be levied on the rich than on the poor. A certain level of income is necessary to provide a minimum standard of living appropriate to allow full participation in the society and period in which people live – what North American tax experts like to describe as 'non-discretionary' expenditure. Above this level, income provides the means to choose between different forms of non-essential spending. Since by definition, the rich have more non-essential (or 'discretionary') income than the poor, depriving them of part of it will impose less sacrifice than taking the same amount from someone at or below the poverty line. Critics may argue that such comparisons are invalid: what the poor consider luxuries, the rich may consider necessities. No doubt there are some who would argue that possession of a Porsche is essential for those living in Docklands: one estate agent even provided one free with each flat sold in the area. But few would disagree that failure to acquire a Porsche is less of a sacrifice than failure to acquire an adequate diet, warmth and housing.

Highlighting the extremes in this way serves, perhaps grotesquely, to illustrate the need for a progressive structure of tax rates simply to ensure that the burden of taxation is fairly shared. There can be little doubt that tax imposes considerable sacrifice on the poor. Few claims of that sort are nowadays heard on behalf of the rich. A progressive tax structure is therefore necessary both to allow for an element of redistribution and to ensure equality of sacrifice in the distribution of the tax burden itself. There are also sound economic reasons for requiring a progressive structure of rates. In our earlier discussion about incentives, we drew attention to the fact that incentives are not simply related to the level of tax paid by an individual but to the marginal rate of tax in relation to the average rate. In a tax system with very few rates, as with the present UK tax system, the marginal rate is the same for most taxpayers. Yet the average rate of tax is lowest for those at the bottom of the income scale. It follows that the greatest disincentive effects are felt by those on the lowest incomes.

For some, this may mean a disincentive to earn more, especially for those in the poverty trap. For others, the decision may be whether to enter the labour market at all. In practice this is largely theoretical, since the poor have little choice about the hours they work or whether they work at all. The choice to remain unemployed, even for a short period while looking for an appropriate long-term job, has now been withdrawn. An unemployed person refusing a job because of the level of pay or the conditions of work now faces disqualification from benefit for up to six months. The carrot of tax incentives, under this government, has been reserved for the rich; for the poor, the Conservatives prefer to use the stick of benefit withdrawal. Setting aside the selective way in which the theory of incentives is used by the present administration, the theory leads to the conclusion that only a progressive structure of rates, imposing lower rates of tax on the poor, will maximise efficiency.

A more progressive structure of tax rates has been proposed by John Hills. His proposal is compared with the current tax structure in the table below. The important thing to note is that the new structure raises the same amount of revenue as the present one, and makes 55 per cent of families better off.

Table 3: A more progressive income tax structure

Taxable income (£ pa)	Tax rate (p in the £)	
	Proposed	*Present*
0-8400	22	25
8400-16,400	34	25
16,400-19,400	40	25
19,400-24,400	45	40
24,400 and above	50	40

Source: Hills, 1989

The table assumes the current level of allowances. It provides an illustration of one alternative and more progressive structure of tax rates that would increase fairness in taxation, while also improving incentives. Under this regime, most people earning less than the average would face a lower marginal rate of tax, improving incentives. Yet there is no loss or revenue and most families would be better off. Hills calculates that only 13 per cent would lose.

The maximum rate of tax suggested by Hills is no more than 50p in the pound. This is very much less than the rate of 83p in the pound (98p on investment incomes) which the Tories abolished in their first Budget. Yet such high rates of tax are not necessary to ensure an element of fairness and redistribution. The very high marginal tax rates on the rich which existed at the end of the 1970s presented a facade of progressive taxation which was quite misleading. Very few individuals were subject to the highest rates, but their very existence soured public attitudes towards progressive taxation, creating an atmosphere of sympathy for the rich in general. Yet the reality behind this facade was of a tax system which was ineffective as a mechanism for redistribution. Even with nominal tax rates at this level, the richest 10 per cent of taxpayers effectively paid no more than a quarter of their income in tax (Field *et al* 1977). The reason was that the rich, although nominally subject to high rates of tax, were provided with numerous escape routes from their full effects.

Reform of the system need not herald the return of such high rates of tax at the top, which serve only to encourage the rich and their accountants to devote more energy to tax avoidance than to productive activity. All that is required is that the actual amount paid in tax bear a closer resemblance than at present to the nominal rates of tax. This highlights the need for an extension of the tax base, an issue which we examine in the next section.

A Comprehensive Tax System

The foundation of radical tax reform is the extension of the tax base through the development of a Comprehensive Income Tax (CIT). It is both inequitable and inefficient to tax different forms of income in different ways. Yet in the present system earnings, self-employment incomes, fringe benefits, investment incomes and capital gains are all taxed in different ways and often at different rates. The effect is to distort economic activity, by encouraging taxpayers to make decisions on the basis of the tax relief available. For instance, an income of £10,000 taxed as earnings would attract tax of £2376.25 in 1988/89, unless part of it was paid in the form of fringe benefits which are wholly or partly exempt from tax; if it were taxed as investment income it would attract tax of only £1476.25, since the 'employment income surcharge' of national insurance contributions would not apply; and if it were taxed as a capital gain, it would attract tax of only £1250 (Low Pay Unit 1988).

This means that there is a considerable incentive for people to adjust their affairs to minimise tax liability. If they are able to convert their investment income into capital gains, for instance by buying an asset which is likely to increase in value rather than investing in a firm, the taxpayer can increase her/his return substantially. This is nonsense in economic terms. To the extent that wage and salary earners are subject to disincentive effects, the effect on those receiving investment incomes or capital gains is certainly smaller still. A government that presents the disincentive effects of taxation as an economic imperative ignores the principle when it suits its purposes. National insurance contributions, the tax on earned incomes, have been increased, while investment income surcharge has been abolished, increasing the relative burden of tax on earned income and therefore the disincentive effects.

Over a period of four decades, the tax base has been further eroded through the growth of tax reliefs and allowances. Because only about half of all household incomes are subject to tax at all, marginal tax rates – the element of the tax structure most likely to create disincentive effects – are higher than they need otherwise be to generate a given level of revenue. This further encourages taxpayers to seek refuge in tax reliefs or forms of income that are more lightly taxed than earnings. The escape routes available for the poor, however, are few.

The distortions which the reliefs create in relation to incomes are further compounded in their effect on savings. Most personal savings are channelled into owner-occupied housing, pensions and life insurance, the three main forms of tax-exempt saving. Mortgage interest relief cost the Exchequer approximately £5,500 millions in 1988/89, equivalent to 4p on the standard rate of tax. This subsidy has had the effect of forcing up house prices, leaving the average home-owner little better-off in terms of net housing costs.

The additional revenue required for social spending and investment under a Labour government should be raised, not by increasing marginal tax rates but by extending the tax base, treating all forms of income and saving in the same way wherever possible. In economic terms this makes good sense, because it would remove the distortions to economic activity described above. It would also be fairer. The exemptions and reliefs provide a tax shelter for the better off, helping them to sidestep their proper contribution to public resources.

Tax reliefs and allowances are the welfare state of the rich. They have the effect of shifting the tax burden from the better off, who are able to make most use of them, and towards those with the lowest incomes. In their social effects, the reliefs are highly regressive: the types of spending, saving or income which they exempt are mainly those of higher income groups, and the value of the reliefs increases for those paying tax above the standard rate.

Because the existence of tax reliefs creates an element of dependency, their abrupt withdrawal could cause considerable hardship. Mortgage tax relief is the most difficult example. The Treasury would like to see it withdrawn, for sound economic reasons. Indeed, by forcing up interest rates, Lawson has effectively withdrawn the mortgage interest subsidy in a covert way, since most people's net mortgage repayments are the same as they would be if interest rates had remained the same and the tax relief no longer existed. Rising interest rates have hit low income home-owners hard. Repossessions are running at a level ten times that registered ten years ago. Yet mortgage tax relief gives twice as much help to those with an income above £25,000 as to those on a low income who need the help most.

Sudden withdrawal of mortgage tax relief would add to the hardship that the Tories have created, but the subsidy could be more carefully targetted at first-time buyers and those on below average incomes. The first step is to allow the relief only at the starting rate of tax, rather than at the higher rates. Restricting mortgage interest and pension relief to the basic rate would have saved more than £1.5 billion in 1987/88 (*Hansard*, 8 February 1988, cols 93-94). Over time, the tax relief should be allowed to wither away by maintaining the ceiling at its 1988/89 level. The impact of this would be reflected in lower house prices, so that most households would be no worse off.

No less contentious are the tax concessions to the private pensions industry, but the resources drawn into public funds through the tax relief make it still more difficult to maintain a properly funded public scheme. Taxing pension fund income would yield an estimated £4.1 billion; the exemption on employee contributions costs a further £3 billion or more, and much of this benefits the already well-to-do. Private pension schemes often offer poor value for money to the individual contributor as well as to the Exchequer, but withdrawing the tax concessions in the absence of a properly funded public scheme would create justifiable concern. However, the concessions cost the equivalent of 4p on the basic rate of income tax. If these resources were directed towards a national pensions scheme, the prospect of being able to offer people real security in their retirement would be less elusive than is presently the case.

These are the most sensitive of the tax reliefs. In total the reliefs cost £25 billion in revenue foregone, a substantial element of public expenditure, administered through the tax system mainly for the benefit of the better off. This figure includes the cost of the basic personal allowances which exempt the poor from tax altogether. So at least £4 billion of this sum must be considered a structural element of the tax system rather than a tax 'concession'. Many of these reliefs and concessions are fondly treated, and their removal will inevitably elicit protest. Yet a package of tax reforms which reduced tax rates at the same time as phasing out the tax reliefs, and which was seen to be fairer and more efficient as well, might command considerable public support.

Taxing Wealth Inequalities

Inequalities in wealth are greater even than those in income. One per cent of the adult population owns between a fifth and a quarter of the nation's personal wealth, and the concentration of wealth ownership has changed little in half a century (Pond 1989). Wealth inequalities are a matter of concern to democratic socialists, not only because they represent extreme differences in material well-being and resources, but because the ownership of wealth brings with it considerable social, economic and political power. Democratic processes and institutions are undermined if wealth and the power which attaches to it are heavily concentrated in the hands of the few.

The past ten years have witnessed a worsening of wealth inequalities, partly because of the effects of tax changes, which have virtually eliminated the effective taxation of wealth. Estate Duty, which was the main form of wealth taxation between 1894 and 1975 came to be considered as a form of 'voluntary taxation', paid only by those 'who disliked their heirs more than they disliked the Inland Revenue'. The replacement of Estate Duty with Capital Transfer Tax in 1975 under the last Labour government was intended to close major loopholes through which vast estates escaped like a camel through the eye of a needle. Although CTT closed many loopholes, it provided generous exemptions in their place. The most important of these was the tax-free transfer of wealth between spouses. Nevertheless, CTT was a more effective tax than Estate Duty and, over a period of generations rather than years, would have made some impact on wealth inequalities.

It was not to be given this chance. CTT was abolished by Nigel Lawson and replaced by Inheritance Tax, effectively reinstating the loophole that gifts during the wealth-holder's lifetime would be exempt from tax. In 1988, the top rate of Inheritance Tax was cut to 40p in the pound, the same as for income tax. This compared with a top rate of tax under CTT of 75p in the pound. As a result, somebody unfortunate enough to die before the 1988 Budget and fortunate enough to leave £2 million would have paid £343,000 more tax than if they had lingered until after the Budget.

There is no economic justification for this cut in Inheritance Tax. As a result of the revenue loss, the burden on household taxes generally is increased, and tax rates on earned income are higher than they need otherwise be. Since the main justification for Tory income tax cuts is the need to encourage incentives, this appears a distorted set of priorities. The disincentive effects to inherit wealth must surely be rather less than the disincentive to work additional hours or to take on an extra job. And as Cedric Sandford, a specialist on wealth taxation, wrote recently in the *Financial Times*:

> It is argued that an important incentive to enterprise is the desire to hand on a business to one's children. Yet many successful entrepreneurs do not have children or have children uninterested in the business. The incentive of these entrepreneurs does not seem to be impaired.
>
> (*Financial Times*, 25 January 1989)

As the Bolton Committee on Small Firms also warned 'it should not be assumed that the children of a successful entrepreneur will necessarily inherit his acumen and energy'. Under the Tory tax regime they will, nevertheless, inherit his wealth unhindered.

Inheritance is the main engine of inequality in wealth. Most of the wealth owned by the very richest individuals is inherited, rather than earned or saved, and inheritance serves to regenerate and reinforce the existing inequalities.

For economic and democratic reasons, the Labour government needs to reinstate an effective tax on inheritance, preferably one which is payable by the recipients of the wealth rather than, as now, by the donors. It needs to be sufficiently progressive to ensure that the largest concentrations of wealth, over time, are dispersed (see Pond 1983).

About half the OECD countries – a dozen in all – have some form of annual wealth tax. Individuals pay a tax each year assessed on the value of their property, above a certain level. No such tax exists in Britain, but its time is overdue. Most of the countries currently operating annual wealth taxes do so for purely economic reasons: if investment incomes are taxed, but wealth itself is not, this encourages people to hold their wealth in 'unproductive' forms which yield no income and attract no tax. The expensive cars that litter the streets of our cities are rather glamorous forms of tax avoidance. A car costing in excess of £100,000 when new, unlike the average runabout, is unlikely to depreciate in value. Yet any increase in its value is not subject to tax (as long as it is classed as the owner's main vehicle) whereas the income from the same sum invested would be taxable.

A future Labour government should introduce an annual wealth tax on economic grounds alone, to remove this type of distortion. The revenue yield from such a tax is unlikely to be large: despite Tory scare stories, most of the wealth of the bulk of the population, including owner-occupied housing, would be exempt. Yet an annual wealth tax could also be helpful, alongside an effective tax on gifts and inheritance, in breaking down wealth inequalities. The two types of tax could be linked together: instead of valuing wealth on an annual basis, an additional levy might be applied when wealth changes hands, representing an advance payment of wealth tax over a period of perhaps ten years. If the property changes hands more quickly, a rebate would be payable against the next advance payment; if it was held for longer, an extra tax would be levied transfer. The Meade Committee (1978) on tax reform proposed a number of other ways in which an annual wealth tax and transfer taxes could be linked together.

Tax Policy: the Way Forward

A programme of reform designed to make Britain's tax system fairer and more efficient could command widespread public support. Attitude surveys suggest that a majority of the public feel the cornucopian tax cuts awarded to the rich during the past decade to be unfair. They also suggest that people are willing to pay more for public spending and social investment, as long as they feel they are getting value for money. This should not lull us into a false sense of security about taxation. The increased burden of tax felt by those on below average earnings could actually increase resistance to Labour's programme if those affected feel their tax burden will increase still further.

In this chapter I have argued that taxation should represent a central element of future economic and social policy. Tax policy should be recognised explicitly, not only as a means of financing social policy objectives, but as a means in itself of achieving those objectives. The tax and social security systems need to be properly co-ordinated to prevent the collision between the two which has resulted in the poverty trap. Meanwhile, we need to recognise the role of tax reliefs and allowances as a form of private or 'fiscal' welfare, alongside the public provision of the welfare state. The cost of such reliefs should be treated as 'tax expenditures' and treated within the same mechanisms of planning and control that apply to other forms of public expenditure. Finally, tax policy has an important role to play in helping to achieve a fairer distribution of income and wealth. Tax and social security reform will help to reduce the impact of poverty and inequality, even though a solution to these problems will require more direct intervention to tackle their root causes.

For ten years the Thatcher governments have sought to justify injustice with the excuse that inequality is necessary for economic growth. Socialists should not collude with this mythology. There is no trade off between fairness and prosperity, between equity and efficiency. In no area of public policy is this clearer than in the field of taxation. Thatcher has created a tax system which is both unfair and economically inefficient, one that is riddled with anomalies that distort economic activity and create inequities. It is possible to devise a tax system which is more progressive, yet which increases the opportunities and the incentives of a majority of the population. Poverty and inequality destroy people's opportunities to fulfill their own potential and to contribute fully to society. It is a source of waste and economic inefficiency which should have no place in modern economic policy. Tax policy cannot alone tackle inequality; but it is a beginning.

References

C.V. Brown, *Taxation and Family Labour Supply in Great Britain*, University of Sterling unpublished mimeo 1987.

L. Day and C. Pond, 'The Political Economy of Taxation', *Socialist Economic Review*, Merlin 1982.

F. Field, M Meacher and C Pond, *To Him Who Hath: A Study of Poverty and Taxation*, Penguin 1977.

R. Hemming, *Poverty and Incentives*, Oxford University Press 1984.

J. Hills, *Changing Tax*, CPAG 1989.

Low Pay Unit, *The Eye of the Needle: the 1988 Budget and the Low Paid*, March 1988.

Meade Committee, *The Structure and Reform of Direct Taxation*, Allen and Unwin 1978.

C. Pond, 'The Changing Distribution of Income, Wealth and Poverty', in C. Hamnett *et al* (eds), *The Changing Social Structure*, Open University Press 1989.

C. Pond, 'Wealth and the Two Nations', in F Field (ed), *The Wealth Report 2*, RKP 1983.

Allan Cochrane and Doreen Massey
Developing a Socialist Urban Policy

For a long time there seemed to be a deceptively easy agreement across the British political spectrum that our inner cities were in an appalling condition (see, for example, Harrison 1983 for a graphic summary). They had become the homes of the poor, the disadvantaged and the black. Housing was decaying, poverty and social divisions increasing, and industry was in a terminal state of decline. Unemployment levels were high. The urban environment was a depressing mix of dereliction, graffitti, and drabness. Crime, particularly burglary and street crime, was out of control. Many women were afraid to leave their homes after dark because of the threat of mugging and violent attack. Inner urban schools were almost universally perceived as failures, incapable of being policed or providing adequate basic education to their pupils.

Elements of common experience combined with the prejudices of 'common sense' to create an immensely powerful set of images about the inner city as a place of despair, failure and fear. In a sense it became a metaphor for the wider condition of British society, bearing only an incidental relationship to the problems of those actually living *in* the inner cities (or in other marginalised parts of urban areas). It was almost irrelevant to point out that there was a very healthy market in expensive houses and flats in many inner cities (particularly in London), which helped to generate dramatic differences in lifestyle, income and wealth between near neighbours. Irrelevant, too, to point to the equally dramatic concentrations of poverty in the vast post-war peripheral council estates which ring our major cities.

Yet in recent years, these images of the inner city seem to

have become more and more dated or at least have come to coexist alongside other ones. Now, the inner cities are apparently in the process of transformation into suitable sites for luxury housing, office and retail development. Victorian canal basins and derelict docks have metamorphosed into leisure marinas. Even Brixton has its brasserie and wine bars. The key problem for policy-makers has become not how to tackle the problems of poverty and social inequality, but rather how to remove the human and physical obstacles to development. The ease with which this change has taken place and the lack of reflection on its implications confirms the lack of clarity which has always surrounded debates about the inner city, even on the Left.

The 'inner city' became an object of government policy without its ever becoming clear what (or even where) the problem was. Urban policy – in practice in Britain simply another way of saying inner city policy – has acted as a chameleon, changing its colours to fit with the wider economic and political priorities of governments. The 'problem' itself has been redefined to fit these priorities. In the late 1960s – in a pale reflection of the US experience – the urban programme was presented as a means of avoiding race riots and in response to the rhetoric of Enoch Powell. It was accompanied by the tightening of immigration controls. The term inner city was used as a more or less explicit proxy for race. By the 1970s, it had been reinterpreted as a problem for the professionals. Communities were expected to pull themselves up by their bootstraps with the help of professional community workers. Local government bureaucrats talked of corporate planning and the 'management of urban change'. It was the period of area management and the self-help welfare state. In the late 1970s, the emphasis shifted again. Now the problem was defined as one of manufacturing decline and the failure of councils to respond to the needs of industry. Community was forgotten about – now the partnerships were with big business rather than play groups, and the official maps of the inner city were redrawn to cover industry as well as housing. In the 1980s the problem has been redefined yet again.

The Thatcherite Assault

The inner cities and inner city policy have in the past been seen as Labour's property. It was Labour local authorities which ran these areas and Labour governments which introduced policies to deal with their problems. In many ways Labour continues to take this view. In Parliament Labour MPs regularly accuse their Tory opposite numbers of being callous and uncaring, and seize on every opportunity, from *Faith in the City* to the latest comments of Lord Scarman and Prince Charles to show how much more they care. Their arguments are easily caricatured by the Right as offering more of the same – 'throwing money at the problem' – but, more important, they also fail to engage either with the new, post-1987, political agenda for the 'inner city' or with the changing forms of urban crisis in the late 1980s.

When Margaret Thatcher announced, immediately after winning the 1987 election, that the inner cities were to be a central focus of her government's attention, she was announcing a new political onslaught rather than a revived urban programme. The inner cities are to be key sites in the battles to confirm the new terrain of politics for the 1990s and beyond – the intention is that even if a Labour government is elected it will only come to power on terms bequeathed by the Thatcher 'revolution', with no chance of reverting to the policies of the past. For the government, the inner city is not merely a place – or set of places – but a syndrome: a disease to be eradicated by the fire of Thatcherism. The survival of the 'inner city' threatens the Thatcherite vision of the future while helping to reinforce the political ideology on which that vision depends. In the rhetoric of the new right, the inner cities are presented as monuments to the failures of post war collectivism and they have become a remarkably powerful parable for the 'British disease' as a whole. They combine images of decline, in the form of derelict land and buildings, the scars of Victorian industrial and commercial success and post-war economic failure, with those of bureaucratic state intervention in dilapidated council estates, 'loony' left councils and their dependent welfare recipients, and a dread of social disorganisation, reflected in concentrations of the black population, a fear of rising crime and 'riots'.

There are three main, interrelated, aspects to the government's policies linked by the objective of making urban areas safe for capitalism – replacing the image of decline with one of opportunity. First, they have the straightforward political aim of undermining the local bases of Labour support which have caused a few hiccups to the onward progress of the Thatcherite juggernaut. The local welfare state, particularly in housing and education, is being ripped apart, and is set to be further dismantled. Second, there is the wider issue of managing the existing population of the inner city – the black, the poor and the 'dangerous classes' – the people who cannot be accommodated into the new Tory utopia. Parts of the inner cities may be 'regenerated', but other parts will be more clearly identified as homes for those who need to be kept under control. Third, there are the policies which are aimed at bringing the inner cities (or, at least, some of them) back into profitable use for capitalism. The 'success' of urban regeneration like that achieved in London's Docklands is important to the Tories not just as a symbol of dynamism and enterprise in solving the 'inner city problem', but also as a model for the revival of British capitalism, based on the identification of new opportunities for profitable investment fuelled by state subsidy.

The political attack on Labour councils is an important part of government strategy. It is for this reason that housing and education – by far the biggest components of local authority spending in urban areas – have become targets for attack (see Cochrane 1985). The proposals for breaking up the housing stock of the major municipal landlords, particularly in inner London, if successful, will both substantially reduce the power of councils, as measured in their capacity to spend, and break the link between tenant and municipal landlord which the new right believes has kept inner city residents tied to Labour through subsidised rents. Similar arguments lie behind the proposals for a poll tax and unified business rate which are intended to force the poor to pay for local services and will also incidentally increase central control over local spending.

Underlying this directly political attack is a more insidious one, in which the inner city problem continues to be used as a code for problems of 'race', or, more accurately, ways of dealing with Britain's black population (as well as troublesome sections of the white working class). There are two main elements in the developing Tory strategy – first is the continued commitment to strengthening the powers and increasing the numbers of police in urban areas, and second is the range of proposals for ensuring that social – and racial – segregation is further encouraged, so making it easier to police certain delimited areas and contain 'trouble' within them. The proposals for breaking up council housing also have the implication that tenants on better estates will be able to exclude groups, defined as 'problems', while those estates left to be managed by the council will be occupied by the 'undeserving' poor. Social housing will be clearly stigmatised as housing for 'problem' groups. If this division can be made effective and reinforced by an education system in which some schools are similarly identified, then segregation can consign whole sections of the population to internal reservations, to be supervised by police, teachers and social workers.

There may still be some support for the old community-type approaches associated with the failures of the social democratic past, but only as forms of charity passed through voluntary organisations. Unlike Labour's leaders the government has little interest in proposals arising from worthy reports like *Faith in the City* or the inner cities research industry within Britain's universities. These are still stuck in an urban programme timewarp somewhere in the early 1970s. The government's subsidiary commitment to the creation of a class of black small businesspeople is unlikely to be successful in terms of numbers but will be more useful ideologically. The prosperity of the few will be used to justify the marginalisation of the many, because it will confirm that they can be blamed for their own 'failure'. It will be easier to justify an increased authoritarianism to maintain control of the failed, as well as presenting a harsh warning for those who do not walk the Thatcherite straight and narrow of economic success.

Since the 1987 election the programme of urban development corporations (UDCs) has been expanded significantly, and new stress has been placed on the need for public-private development partnerships through urban development grants and other means. Local enterprise boards and councils – particularly those controlled by Labour – are often bypassed in this process because of the fear that they might seek to gain concessions from developers. The proposed partnerships are based on the state's taking an explicitly secondary role, in which it provides extensive infrastructural support to make private development profitable. Property development is to be the basis for renewal, with the public sector doing the dirty work of land assembly, reclamation and the provision of infrastructure, while private developers cream off the profits. Although their promotional hype clearly exaggerates it, there can be no doubt that in their own terms the development corporations, most noticeably, but not only, in London's Docklands, have been remarkably successful in beginning to transform the areas in which they have been set.

The most recently proposed development corporations (including Sheffield) are to have much less financial support than the earliest ones, such as Docklands and Merseyside, or even the second wave of Trafford Park, Tyne and Wear, the Black Country, Teesside and Cardiff Bay. Instead of having hundreds of millions of pounds to spend they only have around £15 million a year for five years. And, of course, much of the money allocated to them is not 'new', it includes sums which would otherwise have been channelled through local authorities. But like the others the new ones carry important messages with them: first that the power of local councils needs to be bypassed by actively oriented development agencies, with their own planning powers and powers to negotiate with private developers; and secondly that urban regeneration should be defined in terms of property development, new build and refurbishment, and the attraction of a new class of resident, in luxury homes, effectively forcing out the old. In Scotland, similar messages have been transmitted for a longer period through the Scottish Development Agency and its more localised agencies, such as GEAR (Glasgow Eastern Area Renewal), set up in 1976, from which many of the lessons underlying the UDC programme have been drawn.

As the basis of a strategy for a more general economic revival throughout urban areas, the UDC model is an illusion. Despite the massive subsidies offered in terms of infrastructure and cheap land prices, profits have generally been distributed to property companies, and not produced by new enterprises. It is clear, too, that the UDCs will only succeed because other areas are left to rot – so far there have been no proposals for a second UDC in London because of the concentration on Docklands. Unlike the now politically less important enterprise zones, the urban development corporations are not being proposed as sets of universally applicable panaceas, or even as ones which might be relevant to all inner cities. On the contrary their selectiveness is clear and their main beneficiaries in the world of property development clearer still. But it is as part of a political strategy that 'Action for the Cities', the urban development corporations and all the other paraphernalia of the Thatcherite assault need to be judged, and not as technocratic solutions to a set of agreed problems. Their urban programme offers the possibility of genuinely 'spectacular' change, most obviously in Docklands, but also in shopping malls, riverside developments and retail complexes outside London. Instead of reducing inequality it glories in it, with stark symbols of success, but equally obvious badges of failure for those trapped in the wrong sort of housing and the wrong sorts of jobs (or none at all).

The Changing Urban Context

But it is not enough to place the Conservative government's urban policies in the context of its broader political programme. Their significance is reinforced by their interaction with major changes already taking place within Britain's cities. It is barely an exaggeration to describe this process of change as an urban crisis, in which the old sets of social relations which sustained urban communities lose their force, to be replaced by others whose implications remain uncertain. The urban system as a whole is being transformed in ways which mean that any focus on the problems of the 'inner city' alone is highly misleading. The nature of the problem is not one of decline, but of restructuring and change throughout the system.

The nature of this crisis cannot even be understood simply by looking at the symptoms which afflict British cities. One of the most obvious of these symptoms has been the dramatic loss of manufacturing jobs over the past twenty years, but deindustrialisation in the UK is only one consequence of a massive reorganisation of manufacturing industry on a world scale. There has been an increasing internationalisation of industry which has encouraged the growth of some forms of mass production in the Third World which have previously been important in the UK. Although there has rarely been any direct movement of production from a region of Britain to a third world country the change in the balance of investment over time has, nevertheless, been significant. The problems faced by British cities and towns are caused by processes which produce social conflict of a very different kind in many countries of the Third World.

The reorganisation of the economy has not brought decline to all urban areas in Britain, as a narrow focus on manufacturing might imply. A rise of new sectors within the economy has been noticeable, too, and it has served to reinforce the divisions between different cities, and even parts of the same city. During the 1960s and early 1970s the growth in service employment was within the public sector (particularly local government and the NHS) and tended to be relatively evenly spread across the country. Since the start of the 1980s, however, the expansion of service jobs in the private sector has been much more important – in banking and finance (a sector also undergoing a marked internationalisation); in professional services and in tourism; and in the bundle of cultural and leisure sectors, which also now includes retailing.

Nor has it only been services. Some parts of the manufacturing sector are healthier than others. Electronics is the sector most often referred to in this context – although it is important to note that there has been a significant decline in employment here, too. But the geography of these new sectors – in both services and manufacturing – is significantly different from the geography of the sectors which are in decline. They are overwhelmingly based in (parts of) London, in the regions of the South and East, and in less urbanised areas. Most new employment growth is taking place well away from those areas which are in need of jobs as a result of the process of deindustrialisation.

Alongside this sectoral restructuring there is, as others in this book argue, a whole set of changes in the organisation of production and the labour process in almost every sector of the economy. The buzz word here is 'flexibility'. As a term it is currently much overused, but there can be no doubt that significant changes are indeed taking place. There is increased sub-contracting; increased temporary working; more part-time and casualised employment; there are more smaller factories in place of the huge establishments of the 1950s and 1960s; there is evidence of flexible specialisation in some sectors, with different implications for different sections of the workforce; accompanying this are some signs of changes in the nature of competition, focusing more on design and quality rather than simply cost, with an emphasis on slightly up-market 'designer' products rather than on mass produced goods, reinforcing the importance of urban areas as centres of consumption.

This scenario, however oversimplified, has been accompanied by a further important change, namely a marked increase in the degree of inequality within the national labour market and in the British social structure. All three of the processes outlined above have contributed to this increasing inequality. The decline of manufacturing employment has taken away hundreds of thousands of relatively well paid and skilled jobs in the centre of the labour market. The new sectors have particularly highly dichotomised occupational structures. The spread of incomes and status within the banking industry, for example, is particularly dramatic, from the high paid speculators in the city to the clerical workers in the offices. Similarly, in electronics, there is clearly a big gap between the highly paid technicians and the very low paid assemblers in long lines in factories. The new labour processes are producing their own kinds of polarisation: this time between a core of relatively well paid, certainly more stable, forms of employment and a growing periphery of temporary, part-time and more casualised workers. Real incomes for the top 10 per cent of earners rose by 25.7 per cent (for women) and 22 per cent (for men) between 1979 and 1986, while for the bottom 10 per cent they grew by only 8.8 and 3.7 per cent respectively. There is a growing stratum of professional workers in the private sector, based in finance and professional services, in management and in science and technology – educated rather than skilled in the old sense – whose members are doing quite well in financial terms. There is little doubt that the structure of the labour market is becoming more unequal, even before we take into account the unemploymed at one end of the spectrum and the owners of capital at the other.

The Impact on Urban Areas

These various processes find clear reflections in the detailed restructuring of our urban areas. Most obviously, there has been a long-term decentralisation of population and production towards smaller towns and rural areas and away from big cities. This is the result of a combination of deindustrialisation, the fragmentation of production, and of the locational demands both of the new sectors of production, and of the new middle class which works within them. But – and this is important – the story of cities is *not* just one of decline. At one extreme, the internationalisation of all parts of the world economy, and most particularly of the finance sector, is leading to the emergence of a small group of world cities. Just a handful of these – such as New York, Tokyo, Zurich and London – are emerging as key centres of control. Slightly lower down the hierarchy there is another rung, including cities such as Los Angeles and Hong Kong. What is happening is a gathering in of control of the world economy into these top elite cities.

This has a number of very important implications for the structure of urban Britain. First it means that London's economy is increasingly oriented towards the international economy. With its dominance by the City, of course, this has always been the case, but now this characteristic is even further reinforced. Second, the rest of the United Kingdom is increasingly left to the mercy of major national and multinational firms. 'Local' economies are less and less local in terms of control and decision-making. Third, there are the effects on the internal structure of London itself. On the one hand there has been the all too well known influx of the young, rich and upwardly mobile ('yuppies'). There is a celebration of luxury consumption and (at least until late 1988) of a house price boom of obscene proportions. At the same time – and partly as a result of this – there has been the disruption of established communities and the ghettoisation of those who service this new 'booming' economy, and of the unemployed and unemployable. The inner cities have begun to be restructured as the poor are gradually cleared from some and concentrated in others. In some areas the marginalisation of the poor is emphasised by the proximity of council estates to the new 'gentrified' mansions of the rich.

Evidence of similar social polarisation can be seen in other British cities although London's special position in the international system of cities highlights the position particularly clearly. The processes of change and restructuring outlined above are also leading to patches of redevelopment in cities lower down the urban hierarchy. It is redevelopment for services, for complexes of shopping and leisure activities and, possibly, for up-market housing. Indeed it sometimes seems as if there is a band of property companies roaming the country in search of canal basins and wharves to develop. What is important about this phenomenon is that it may indicate that the inner city problem is beginning to change to the extent that the term cannot continue to be used in the careless way that it has been in the past. As recent Centre for Environmental Studies research on outer council estates has shown, the 'inner city' problem has never been a simple one of geographical location since many of its features are to be found far outside any narrowly defined inner city.

The poor can be just as effectively marginalised in purpose built ghettoes as those the market creates for them. The 'inner city' can be recreated in the 'outer city'. Indeed this may be one consequence of the break up of council housing proposed by the government. Some of the big northern industrial cities seem to be experiencing this phenomenon at the moment even without the help of the central government intervention. It would be a mistake to equate these changes with the London experience since the potential for development of these places as service centres is not the same and the decline of manufacturing employment as a result of deindustrialisation remains a crucial backdrop. But quite intense competition for commercial redevelopment of small parts of the central area, the ghettoisation of the poor within other parts and their expulsion to outer estates is more and more common. The cities of the Midlands and the North are increasingly competing to service growing hinterlands with massive shopping complexes – everybody wants a Metro centre.

Finally, there is a whole variety of different fortunes facing the range of smaller and middle sized towns of Britain. Historic towns, for instance, are experiencing on the whole a relative boom time, as they benefit from the growing trade in heritage tourism, and as their environmental attractions are traded on by the new sectors of the economy. In total contrast, the small manufacturing towns of the North are in many cases seeing the collapse of virtually the whole of their historic economic base, and often with very little to replace it. Meanwhile, some towns in the outer South East are becoming foci for the growth of the new sectors. A long list of towns doubled their employment either in finance, banking and insurance or in electronic engineering between 1971 and 1981. Yet alongside this, even in the South East, processes of decline also have an impact – there is deindustrialisation for instance in the ring of manufacturing-based new towns around London. Finally, tourism and the hotel trade is growing nationally and playing a part in the revitalisation of some areas, but in many of the smaller towns around the coast tourism is being replaced by private sector welfare provision in the form of residential homes for the elderly.

So, there is no *single* urban crisis. Yet all urban areas are imbedded in the same set of wider processes discussed above. And the uneven processes of development and redevelopment mean that most growth is taking place far away from areas where there has been decline. So on the one hand there are areas of decline which face great difficulty in attracting new growth, and on the other there are areas where growth is leading increasingly to problems of congestion. Most urban areas also share the problems of increasing inequality within the population as a whole, while changing hierarchies between and within urban areas are harshly reinforcing those inequalities with the help of state policy.

Responding to the Crisis

In the past the British urban crisis has generally been defined as a geographical problem – as a problem of *place*, a problem of the inner cities. This has made political argument relatively easy for the Right in recent years. The focus on particular areas has meant that evidence of progress can be presented in straightforward terms. If there is a little bit of development, if new buildings are put up, and if new people are brought into the area, and the social structure is changed a little (or a lot) then the problem has been solved. The area has been transformed. This fits in nicely with a strategy which wants to demonstrate success in a limited number of showcases as part of a battle for ideological supremacy. But the inner city problem is *not* a problem of place, at least in the sense that it can only be found now and forever in a ring around the centre of our major cities. It is a problem of poverty, unemployment and deprivation, of a declining industrial base and of increasing inequality which is reinforced by locational exclusion and marginalisation. Indeed, in that sense it is not an *inner* city problem at all, even if there has historically been a concentration of such features in the inner cities. One of the clear features of urban development in the late 1980s has been the extent to which the 'inner city' problem can be isolated and moved about.

The government's current policies will make a difference to the inner cities and the people living in them, but they will not solve those problems. Nor are they intended to. Yet at present it looks as if Thatcher's policies are going to set the agenda for the inner cities over the next decade, not least because most Labour controlled local authorities – their only obvious rivals – are trapped in a similar logic. They, too, are involved in putting together (and sometimes initiating) deals with developers for major retail and leisure schemes. Already, the language of public/private 'partnership' dominates the approach of both central and local governments. Indeed at local level it is often Labour councils which are most enthusiastic in seeking out financial partners in the private sector. As David Harvey has recently pointed out,

> For fiscally stressed and depressed cities there is no other choice except to like or leave the package on offer. A lot of political will and not a few concessions are required to attract developer capital and to capture some benefits for the disempowered and impoverished

> (Harvey 1989, p 21).

The worst possible, yet most likely, scenario for the future is the prospect of Labour councils squabbling over crumbs from the inner city cake – an enterprise zone here, a technology college there, and maybe even the 'plum' of an urban development corporation.

Two key points arise from our broad survey of urban policy in the 1980s. First, if any socialist initiative is to be launched, it needs to be able to build on *an alternative political vision*. An alternative is needed which can challenge the wider model of 'economic regeneration' underlying the new policies, and the general increase in inequality and social polarisation within and between urban areas which that model implies. As Charlie Leadbeater argued in relation to social ownership, repeating the nostrums of the past will not connect with the new political agenda. Just as Labour's attempts to reconstruct the economic partnerships of the 1970s with unions and big business have gone nowhere, so similar attempts to rediscover a consensual approach to the 'inner city problem' are doomed to failure. Secondly, a socialist initiative needs to relate to the changes which are actually taking place. There *is* an 'urban crisis', even if it is not quite the same as the one defined by Britain's policy-makers. Urban problems cannot be discussed as if they were isolated to the 'inner cities' and so susceptible to positive discrimination of one sort of another. The reshaping of our cities is at the heart of a wider process of economic and social restructuring which is also redrawing the boundaries around the 'inner city' and changing its meaning.

At national level, Labour has shown little sign of being able to respond to the political challenge which it faces. In the early 1980s the main alternatives to the policies of the government were developed not by the official opposition but through a small number of (left) Labour councils, notably the GLC and Sheffield among others. A whole series of articles and books has been produced which discusses the activity of these councils (for example, Boddy and Fudge 1984, Gyford 1985 and Blunkett and Jackson 1987; see also Wainwright 1987, Ch 3). These councils, each in its own way, and in ways not reflected or apparently understood at national level, set out to develop strategies for change. It is not necessary to support every initiative undertaken by the 'local socialists', nor indeed to believe that they succeeded in producing a coherent and worked out set of strategies, to see that they were involved in a different sort of debate from that which has recently dominated in the Labour Party. And a different sort of debate from the one being encouraged by the party's current policy reviews.

The 'local socialists' and the radical professionals they attracted to work for them at the beginning of the 1980s did not attempt to defend and repeat the accepted truths of the past. In fact they explicitly rejected central elements of the 'municipal labourism' of the post-war period, and presented themselves as searching for alternatives not only to the policies of Thatcherism, but also to the 'corporatist' practice of the Labour Party in government. They wanted to escape from the political and practical constraints of old-style, professionally based, bureaucratic 'reformism'. Implicitly, if not explicitly, they rejected the GEAR model, by stressing that the answer was not to search for ways in which the policies of the government might be improved in this way or that, but rather that it was necessary to develop an alternative set of political ideas, around which a new socialist political agenda could also be constructed. The 'urban policy' underlying the debates of the early 1980s (although it was not referred to in those terms) was one which brought together a concern for production with a recognition of the growing inequalities between different groups, an interest in the changing cultural requirements of the urban population and a commitment to wider democratisation.

It placed the changing realities of urban living within a wider context, not pretending that it was possible to improve matters simply by redistributing financial crumbs to the most disadvantage. Cities were understood as places in which to live as well as work, and which were being destroyed and divided by the *carte blanche* granted to developers with the support of central government. Socialist initiatives were needed to extend the arena of public space for collective and individual use rather than private and corporate use. The popular reaction towards the 'planners' and modernist architecture, was interpreted not so much as a longing for tradition and heritage, but as expressing a widespread feeling of alienation from those aspects of the urban environment from which individuals are often explicitly or implicitly excluded. At the same time the need directly to influence the process of economic change through 'restructuring for labour' was stressed. At their best, the campaigns and policies of the left authorities were political in the same sense as Thatcher's crusade against the inner cities. But where Thatcher sees the inner cities as a threat and as part of a legacy of collectivism to be excised by the surgeon's knife, they presented them as potential sources of richness and diversity and stressed the need for a renewed collectivism based not on the bureaucratic hierarchies of past state provision, but on the active involvement of those currently being managed through the state. In other words they wanted to construct an alternative vision instead of one which took its cue from the government.

It is perhaps hardly surprising that this alternative vision was not always clearly spelled out, partly because the initiatives were diverse and locally dispersed. And the initial rhetoric sometimes bore little relation to political practice. At first little attempt was made to develop any coherent theorisation and later there was little time to do so, although the first steps were taken in that direction (eg, in GLC 1985 and a number of other GLC publications; Mackintosh and Wainwright 1987, Blunkett and Jackson 1987; and Sheffield City Council 1987). But it is around these initiatives that the most fruitful debates about socialist urban policy have taken place, suggesting new possibilities for the 1990s, only some of which we consider below.

One crucial aspect of any socialist urban policy must be a commitment to making all the facilities of the cities accessible to those who live in them, including the poor and other groups often trapped in the home, including the disabled and women with children. At a most basic level this should include the provision of a well developed (and cheap) public transport system. At present in most British cities public transport is being run down, fares are rising, and the spread of networks is being reduced, while even car travel is becoming more difficult as roads deteriorate and levels of traffic increase. Against significant obstacles and opposition, in government, courts and often the Labour Party hierarchy, some councils (such as the GLC, South Yorkshire and Sheffield) did manage to develop popular alternatives, particularly with commitments to cheap fares, which were only finally defeated by the wholesale privatisation of bus transport. A commitment to an expanded role for public transport is not merely a technical question of (usually wrong) estimated passenger miles, to be left to the transport economists, but one of crucial political importance because of the impact it could have on the ways in which people experience urban life. It could play a part in ending the isolation of the inner cities and the outer estates and creating the possibility for a new urban culture. It would make it possible to present alternatives to the threat of heavy lorry traffic, and urban motorways which are clogged up as soon as they are opened, as well as proposals for a brand new network of toll roads. The development of the Docklands Light Railway shows that even Thatcherism is prepared to extend public transport when it is in the interest of developers and highly paid commuters. Labour needs to show a similar commitment to its supporters.

Policies aimed to improve mobility will themselves play an important part in transforming urban areas but several of the councils also explicitly directed their attention to cultural activities and access to them. The current process of urban change is creating new monuments to consumption in shopping complexes to which many have access, but often on strictly income related terms and under the supervision of armies of private police. The public infrastructure, however, is decaying to the extent that a large scale programme of public investment is needed. It is well enough known that the cities have been relying on Victorian sewers for too long, but they have also been relying on the Victorian parks for recreation, and they are equally in need of restoration and extension into new areas of cultural provision which are not hidden away behind the walls of overpriced leisure complexes. Sheffield tried to point in this direction in the early 1980s with its proposals for a mix of parkland, leisure facilities and innovative industrial development in the largely derelict Lower Don Valley. Attempts were made to implement these proposals through the decade, but resources have always been a problem, requiring compromises with developers despite a successful bid to host the World Student Games. Now the council's initiatives have largely been bypassed by the imposition of an urban development corporation. A socialist government should be expected to encourage the development publicly accessible space and other cultural facilities.

Some of the councils also challenged some of the key formulations of the government through the development of local economic strategies, because of the recognition that economic restructuring was itself a key element in determining the forms of urban change. In developing these strategies, the past failures of both the market economy and the social democratic strategies of the 1970s were acknowledged. If, as one GLC publication argued, profit was actually a misleading guide to investment, so was collaboration between big business and the state on the old National Enterprise Board model, and bureaucratic decision-making on the old nationalised industry model (see, for example GLC 1983, Murray 1987 and Leadbeater, above). Instead, a stress was placed on new forms of worker democracy (including co-operatives), a search for socially useful production, heavily influenced by the experience of the Lucas Aerospace Corporate Plan, and a commitment to equal opportunities both at work and in access to employment. The value of community influence on production, too, was emphasised, both in moves towards popular planning and in a general commitment to decentralisation. 'Local' economic policies were increasingly presented as being good in themselves because they made it possible to widen debate over economic decision-making (see, for example, Blunkett and Jackson 1987, Ch 6). In the early manifestos and programmes of the local socialists there was frequently reference to planning agreements and enterprise planning which implied a set of negotiated and continuing agreements over investment, marketing and employment policies between councils, employers and workforce.

The Labour Party leadership has been suitably timid in its interpretation of the local economic strategies and local enterprise boards developed in the early 1980s. Every official Labour statement which endorses the idea of enterprise boards and proposes their linking into a national system, also manages to remove any reference to their radical potential – they become agencies for increased local or regional investment with little consideration of attempts to use such investment to change and challenge the priorities of the market or to encourage wider political debates linking production and consumption. The GLEB experience before 1986, in particular, is explicitly ignored as if it might be too embarrassing precisely because of its radical implications. One is left with the overwhelming impression that what is wanted is a local version of the old NEB in its blandest form, and without any notion of planning agreements (see, for example, even sympathetic formulations such as Parliamentary Spokesman's Working Group 1982, s 3.5, Parliamentary Spokesman's Working Group 1985, s 3.2). What counts is the ability to 'lever' more or less money from the private sector; this, of course, is also the language of Thatcher, and fails to see matters from the other point of view: namely the extent to which the private sector is able to lever more or less from the public.

There is some justifiable controversy about the lessons to be drawn from the local economic policies developed by the left councils in the early 1980s. Some have argued that they offer a suitable model for wider development as part of a national strategy (see, for example, GLC 1985 Introduction, Murray 1987, Mackintosh and Wainwright 1987). Murray, in particular, suggests that the changing nature of production, distribution and consumption in the late 20th century – the shift from 'Fordism' to 'post-Fordism' – makes it possible for the state to intervene in ways which can maximise impact on economic decision making, while making it unnecessary to engage in bureaucratic mechanisms of control or nationalisation. He draws analogies with the power of major retail concerns (such as Marks and Spencer) over their suppliers and the power available to the state, if it can identify key, strategic, points of intervention. The importance of Murray's argument is twofold: on the one hand his approach confirms that urban change can only be understood in the context of wider economic changes, and secondly it suggests forms of intervention which can be undertaken within a more decentralised (and, he argues, democratised) system, involving local agencies rather than encouraging bureaucratic planning from the top down. It suggests the possibility of a series of planning networks, linking state, workforce and communities in economic decision making, instead of leaving them at the mercy of the decisions of developers and multinationals. A socialist programme for the 1990s based on this model would include a range of possibilities, from share ownership, to the negotiation of contracts for purchasing or loans subject to social and other conditions, to full ownership at local or national level. But all of them would include some notion of bargaining, and, potentially in some versions, an explicit attempt to empower key groups, particularly workers, but possibly also consumers (see, for example, Gough 1986).

Some have drawn more sceptical conclusions from the experience of the left councils with different implications for the development of a socialist urban policy. Most of those still working at local level would almost certainly now be more modest, and their emphasis has shifted to the development of investment partnerships with the private sector, rather than attempts significantly to influence its decision making. In some cases they have explicitly distanced themselves from more radical ambitions which they feel have made it more difficult to develop such partnerships. They have tended to stress the scope for increasing levels of investment in areas previously unpopular with the City and its major financial institutions, particularly in the inner cities, outside the South East and in manufacturing industry (see, for example, Marks 1987). Developing public/private partnerships is presented as one way of reorienting urban development away from the

narrow path it is currently taking. On this model, the role of
the state is to encourage a wider and less unequal dispersal
of growth.

Others have argued from rather a different point of view
that the local experience has merely confirmed the weakness
of the local state in the face of the power of the market, and,
in particular, the power of major capitalist concerns. Nolan
and O'Donnell, for example, argue that the operation of the
law of value makes it unlikely that local intervention can
ever have a significant part to play in the development and
implementation of economic policy (Nolan and O'Donnell
1987; see also Eisenschitz and North 1986). But the
implications of these arguments are of wider significance,
since they suggest a continuing weakness for any left
government attempting to manage the state within a market
system, whether at national or local level. Intervention at
the level of the enterprise or sector is likely either to lead
towards further intervention, possibly involving nationalisation and the need for wider political mobilisation, or else
may leave the Left trapped once more in the role of
underpinning the economic restructuring initiated by
capital.

The continuing debate over the socialist local economic
strategies of the early 1980s should not be an excuse for
ignoring them. By raising the importance of political power
and bargaining between different groups over change, some
of the local initiatives also began to revitalise the notion of
planning as part of a socialist programme, not as something
which was imposed from the top down but as a living process
of democratic debate. They had the potential to open up the
issue of production to political discussion, involving workers
and community. Maybe in retrospect it is obvious that there
was little hope that they could themselves reverse or even
channel the tide of capitalist change but it is a sign of the
state of political thinking on the Left that their ideas now
seem to have been repudiated as hopelessly utopian even as
the basis of a national political programme.

If a socialist urban policy is to be developed, it needs to be
set in a wider context of political and economic change, and
the importance of trying to influence that context needs to
be grasped. Just as Thatcher has placed urban issues at the

heart of her strategy for the third term, so they need to be at the heart of Labour's response. But that requires a radical leap of the imagination rather than an endless process of detailed criticism of everything that the Tories propose. Instead of criticising the government for taking a political initiative when Labour favours a more bipartisan (consensual) approach, with policies generated by professionals and experts, Labour needs a positive set of proposals based around a vision of the future which challenges instead of critically reflecting the privatised fantasies of the present government. The Left has some local experiences from which to learn and on which to build. But the Labour Party seems dead set on ignoring them in order to present itself, increasingly hopelessly, as a responsible alternative government. It is not so rich in political ideas that it can afford to do so.

Some of the material in this chapter was originally presented in a different form to a conference of the Centre for Local Economic Strategies.

References

D. Blunkett and K. Jackson, *Democracy in Crisis. The Town Halls Respond*, Hogarth Press 1987.

M. Boddy and C. Fudge (eds), *Local Socialism?* Macmillan 1984.

A. Cochrane, 'The Attack on Local Government: What it is and what it isn't, Critical Social Policy', 12, Spring 1985.

A. Eisenshitz and D. North, 'The London Industrial Strategy: socialist transformation or modernising capitalism?' International Journal of Urban and Regional Research, 10.3 1986.

Greater London Economic Policy Group, *Jobs for a Change*, GLC 1983.

London Industrial Strategy, GLC 1985.

J. Gough, 'Industrial policy and socialist strategy: restructuring and the unity of the working class', *Capital and Class*, 29, 1986.

J. Gyford, *The Politics of Local Socialism*, George Allen and Unwin 1985.

P. Harrison, *Inside the Inner City. Life under the Cutting Edge*, Penguin 1983.

D. Harvey, 'Downtown', *Marxism Today*, Jan 1989 pp.21ff.

M. Mackintosh and H. Wainwright (eds), *A Taste of Power. The Politics of Local Economics*, Verso 1987.

S. Marks, *Enterprise Boards. Their Contribution to Economic Development and Investment*, Centre for Local Economic Strategies 1987.

R. Murray *Breaking with Bureaucracy. Ownership, Control and Nation-alisation*, Report No 4, Centre for Local Economic Strategies 1987. (Also published as 'Ownership, control and the market', in *New Left Review* 164.)

P. Nolan and K. O'Donnell, 'Taming the market economy? A critical assessment of the GLC's experiment in restructuring for labour', *Cambridge Journal of Economics*, 11, 1987.

Alternative Regional Strategy. A Framework for Discussion, Parliamentary Spokesman's Working Group 1982.

Planning for Full Employment. Options for a Modern Employment Strategy, Parliamentary Spokesman's Working Group 1985.

Sheffield: Working It Out. An Outline Employment Plan for Sheffield, Sheffield City Council 1987.

H. Wainwright, *Labour: A Tale of Two Parties*, Hogarth Press 1987.

John Gabriel
Developing Anti-Racist Strategies

The ability of the Conservative government to capitalise on racist traditions and, in turn, to popularise its own racisms in 1980s Britain has left the Labour Party defensive and apparently ready for compromise. In the early years of the decade attempts by some local Labour boroughs to develop anti-racist programmes offered some hope to those active in anti-racist politics. However, in the wake of a third successive defeat at the national polls, Labour parties, both locally and nationally, appear once again in retreat.

In Birmingham, for instance, now the largest local authority, the Race Relations Committee has been abolished, and the administration of race relations has been subsumed under the Personnel Department. Other service departments are no longer requested to consider the equal opportunity implications of their policy proposals. Moreover, existing equal opportunity initiatives, including the funding of local community groups, appear especially vulnerable in the authority's cost cutting programmes. At a national level too, the Labour Party shows little sign of putting its poor record right. Its continued opposition to black sections in the party, its attacks on local anti-racist initiatives and its failure to develop a national anti-racist programme, hardly augur well for a future Labour government.

In the first part of this chapter I shall illustrate the importance of the term institutionalised racism with particular reference to Conservative government policies in the 1980s. These policies will be briefly examined in terms of their actual provisions, the assumptions on which they rest and their frameworks for implementation. I shall be arguing the need for this kind of analysis as a basis for an assessment of the Labour Party's response, which will be explored in the second half of the chapter.

The section on the Labour Party will begin with an overview of political developments in the party around race over the past decade. This will include an assessment of the most recent manifesto and policy review document. Then, through a more detailed case study of Wolverhampton, the paper will identify a number of factors which have weakened Labour's anti-racist challenge. Amongst these are: the problems of building an anti-racist consensus; a tendency to challenge racism without tackling the institutional context in which it is maintained; a resistance to acknowledge, and draw on, the collective discriminatory experience of black people, and finally problems with the process of making and implementing anti-racist policies. The overall aim of this chapter is to promote a debate within the party, out of which a more positive and effective programme on racial justice and equality might be developed.

A Note on Analysing Racism

One way to study racial inequalities is to investigate statistical evidence on unemployment, homelessness, incidents of physical assault and abuse and other similar kinds of data, in order to build up a picture of the experiences and conditions of black people of Afro-Caribbean and Asian descent. Whilst this kind of evidence is extremely valuable, as the various Policy Studies Institute reports have shown (see, for example, Brown 1984), such evidence on its own, without any underpinning analysis, can, and often does, get attributed to a number of factors which preclude a full consideration of the significance of institutional racism. For instance, inequalities have been attributed to innate biological and/or cultural differences between black and white people. In this case, the 'problem' becomes focused on black people's 'intelligence' or cultural 'deficiencies', rather than on white-dominated institutions.

However, pathologising the black community is not the only way of diverting attention from the problem of institutional racism. There is a strand of thinking on the Left which attributes social inequalities between black and white to world capitalist development. International movements in capital and labour are said to structure both these material differences and the racist ideologies which render such differences intelligible. Since, according to this argument, institutional processes follow inevitably from the inexorable logic of capital, there is no need to examine them in detail. It also follows that we should not be seeking to challenge racism on an institutional basis, but instead concentrating on industrial conflict and extra-institutional struggles, for example street uprisings, as a focus for analysis and intervention. In many respects, not least of all political, this perspective is quite incompatible with those forms of biological and cultural determinism referred to above. Nevertheless, the implications of this kind of analysis tend towards a limitation on the consideration of, and political response to, racism in institutions.

Furthermore, it is important not to restrict the resources for analysing institutionalised racism to the content of political speeches or policy documents, or to media coverage. Institutional racism is not just an ideology which can be understood by reconstructing the logic of racist discourse, important though this is. The significance of such reconstructions can only be fully grasped when they are examined in the context of a broader analysis of political processes, processes which accommodate not only a consideration of racism, but also anti-racist strategies and interventions. The material outcomes for black people in terms of jobs, housing and education at any given moment are the consequence of a balance, albeit an unequal balance: of progressive as well as negative political forces.

The economy is clearly very important in shaping these material outcomes, but it too can be accommodated within this broader political analysis. Both its distributive and allocative roles can be examined within a political framework into which can be inserted an analysis of the way such mechanisms work to disadvantage black people. As regards class formation, as opposed to class location, the evidence presented below will suggest that, far from supporting or complementing anti-racist struggles, class-based politics have served to undermine and deny the specificity of the black experience of racism.

The role of anti-racist forces is an integral part of this

analysis. It could be argued, for instance, that black unemployment and homelessness and incidents of racial assault, might well have been higher than they are at present were it not for the containing role played by black and anti-racist organisations and sections of the labour movement. The framework for analysing those outcomes would therefore have to examine not just the racist assumptions underpinning economic or housing policy or the content of policies themselves. It would require a political analysis of processes not just of policy formulation but of policy implementation and administration. It would then be possible to examine how these processes have provided openings (as well as closing down space) for interventions by black community organisations, trade unionists and local authorities. This is not to say that such challenges have necessarily been very effective, or that they are equal in strength to those they confront. Indeed, the nature of these political inequalities, and the conditions which make for more or less effective interventions, is an important focus in itself, and one which should form an integral part of the wider framework of analysis.

The aim of this chapter is to develop the kind of political analysis which, hitherto, I have discussed in general terms. I write as a member of the Labour Party, active in anti-racist politics throughout the decade of Thatcherism, through an involvement in anti-racist organisations in Wolverhampton as well as the local Labour Party. My commitment to the kind of analysis of political processes developed here is derived from this experience. Needless to say I have had uneven access to the various political contexts which provide the basis for this chapter. This is reflected in what follows: at times I use secondary documentation; elsewhere I rely more directly on my participation in political and community organisations in Wolverhampton.

Institutionalised Racism: the Legacy for the Labour Party

A number of writers have tried to identify and explain new forms of racism, peculiar to the last twenty years or so, which have supplanted the older, cruder forms, which had been tainted by Nazism (Barker 1981). The old racism distinguished groups on the basis of biological differences, and ranked these according to inferior and superior characteristics. It provided an important source of legitimation for black slavery and colonial annexation, as well as the Holocaust.

In contrast, there are a number of distinguishing strands to the 'new racism'. The first can be linked to the views of Enoch Powell, and to an intellectual tradition, sociobiology, which underpins his views. Accordingly, the 'scientific' basis of Powell's 'rivers of blood' prediction rests not so much on the idea that black people are biologically and mentally inferior, but on the inevitability of conflict between black and white. According to this argument, all of us have adapted genetically to a competitive, aggressive society in which conflict over scarce resources and discrimination against out-groups are inevitable. The 'new racism' thus offers a biological justification for discriminatory treatment, including repatriation. It also provides an argument against trying to outlaw discrimination via legislation, since such attempts fly in the face of 'human nature'.

Skin colour has been fused with national identity, to give additional potency to latter-day racism. This link was well illustrated by journalist Peregrine Worsthorne after the Falklands War with his claim that the indigenous white British had more in common with those living eight thousand miles away than with Asian or West Indian neighbours living next door. Such ideas dovetail with Enoch Powell's view of Britain, eroded and hollowed out by unassimilable alien wedges in the heartland of the state (cited in Gilroy 1987, p 43). It also links with Margaret Thatcher's speech in January 1978, in which she spoke of people's fears of being swamped by people of a different culture.

These views have found their most obvious expression in nationality and immigration legislation. In the government's own terms there may be firmness but there is certainly no fairness in its immigration policies. There can be no justification for making black people the reason for, and target of, control, whilst at the same time providing loopholes for largely white immigration and citizenship status (eg, the patriality principle), exemptions (eg, the countries excluded from visa controls), and actually increasing opportunities for largely white immigration (eg, as a result of EEC membership). A good example of the government's double standards on immigration can be found in a memorandum sent by the Home Office Minister, Timothy Renton, in which he encouraged officials to issue passports quickly, and generally facilitate easy entry and exit for 'businessmen', in the interests of promoting enterprise culture (JCWI 1988, p 2). There can be no justification for these kinds of provisions and practices unless racism is regarded as a 'fair' basis for policy.

The supposed threat that immigration poses to Britain's national identity and culture, and to the material and spiritual well-being of the British people, is linked to an assumption of illegal status, which is attached not only to black immigrants, but also to black people born and settled in this country. This assumption is carried over, in varying degrees, to all branches of the public sector, but its links with social security are particularly strong. DSS policy and its administration is largely premised on the beliefs that: black claimants have only themselves to blame for their circumstances; that they have no right to public funds and are expected to contribute to the economy not to live off its proceeds; and, finally, that they are amongst those most likely to abuse the system and hence must be expected to provide additional proof of their eligibility to claim. (For a fuller discussion of the implications of recent legislation, see Committee for Non-Racist Benefits 1987.)

Thatcherism as a political project, however, extends beyond the strands of nationalism and the new racism. A key element in this project has been an appeal to a set of related principles, adopted from classical liberalism. The most important of these include the sanctity of the market, the primacy of the consumer and a minimalist role for the state. These principles, in conjunction with the more overt forms of racism discussed above, have, albeit in more indirect ways, helped to structure racial inequalities.

For instance, the principle of 'consumer freedom', which can be witnessed in the liberalisation of markets in housing and education, has a number of important consequences. The prioritising of commercial over social objectives and the decline in public accountability and regulation both serve to inhibit the promotion of racial equality under the terms of the 1989 Housing Act. In the first place, black community and anti-racist pressure groups, including those within the Labour Party, will find it even harder to press for positive changes within a growing private sector. Section 71 of the 1976 Race Relations Act did at least provide an instrument, admittedly a pretty blunt one, for exerting pressure on local authorities to promote equality of opportunity. Second, housing opportunities for the homeless and the low paid, where black people are disproportionately found, will diminish with the reduction of subsidies and the emphasis on 'market' rents. Finally, small housing associations, which is what most black associations are, will find it increasingly difficult to compete with the larger profit-motivated associations. (For a fuller discussion, see Birmingham CRC 1988.)

In education, the recent case of Headfield School, Dewsbury, illustrates a form of parental freedom which has been sanctioned in a number of ways under the 1988 Education Reform Act. In the Dewsbury case, 'freedom' meant giving white parents the choice to opt out of a multi-racial school which was attempting to develop anti-racist policies and practices. Under the 'open enrol- ment' and 'opting out' provisions of the 1988 Act, parental rights become, in effect, rights to discriminate, individual freedoms exercised at the expense of group freedoms and rights. (See Ousley 1988, for a discussion of the implications of the 1988 Education Reform Act.)

The attack on state interference in people's private lives, when it is set alongside the argument about human nature and the threat to (white) cultural identity referred to above, provides a strong basis for opposing anti-racist initiatives. It becomes a powerful rationale for the status quo. Any attempt to review existing practices with a view to challenging racism is resisted, either because it interferes with the freedom of the market and with consumer choice, or because it threatens to discriminate against whites, or because attempts to regulate discriminatory behaviour are doomed to fail anyway. Multicultural, anti-racist initiatives in education have been particularly vulnerable to these counter-attacks. (See for example Palmer 1986.)

The poll tax illustrates these tendencies in two important ways. As with indirect taxation (for example, VAT), everyone will pay the poll tax, regardless of means. The argument for this kind of regressive taxation rests ultimately on the assumption that social inequalities are needed in order to encourage those with the highest 'skills' and 'abilities' to create a larger cake for us all to share, even if this means some people getting enormous slices and others virtually going without. Leaving aside the extremely dubious assumptions underpinning this argument, what is clear is that black people, who are amongst the lowest paid in society, are disproportionately hit by such taxation. Furthermore, since the tax is a charge on individual adults rather than on property, those living in multi-occupation dwellings with poor amenities, which are known to house disproportionate numbers of black families, will thereby be doubly penalised.

Of course, Thatcherism is not without its contradictions. The view held by Powell and others that black people are unassimilable is one which has come under pressure from those Conservatives who offer the prospect of assimilation in exchange for black identity and the denial of racism. The general election poster of 1983 offered black voters such a choice: either you are black or you are British: the choice between Labour or Conservative. The Conservatives want it both ways; they want the white nationalist vote but also, for the sake of expedience and maybe due to a fear of black revolt, they need to buy the black vote too. Such contradictions provide openings for the Labour Party to exploit, and can also provide the basis for developing coherent alternatives.

Before I move on to assess the Labour Party's response and its future role, there are two important points which serve to supplement, if not to qualify, the above analysis. Thatcherism does not exhaust racism. The new racism in the context of liberalism and authoritarianism has helped to provide new forms of legitimacy whilst at the same time delegitimising anti-racism. However, in acknowledging the popular appeal of these new forms, some older racisms should not be forgotten. There is a lot of life left in these too.

In the area of social services and welfare provision, for

instance, the long-standing principle of universalism, when applied alongside a failure to take account of cultural differences, effectively means that provision is made on a selective basis. Employment recruitment practices, including informal advertising and internal trawls, have long since helped to reproduce an all-white workforce. In education, selection on the basis of merit without a rigorous review of the assumptions, criteria and bias underpinning meritocratic principles, has also worked, over a long period, to the disadvantage of black pupils and students. In the youth service the principle of integrated provision for black and white, male and female, in the context of resources and activities all aimed at white boys, means, in many cases, a *de facto* segregated service. In some instances these policies and practices will have been supported by older cruder forms of racism, but more often racism has woven its way into the fabric of institutions in more subtle and indirect ways.

Racism is what makes these systems discriminatory. It is more a tangled web of institutional policies and practices than the attitudes and actions of a deviant individual. It can be a policy decision, or a rule, or a set of criteria, which provides a framework for day-to-day practice which leaves black people disproportionately worse off. More often, however, it is the failure to acknowledge the discriminatory effects of policies and their rationale, rather than any explicit or conscious intent to discriminate, which makes the system discriminatory. This failure to respond, however, cannot be disentangled from those dominant cultural assumptions regarding black people referred to above. These permeate policy frameworks and their implementation and help to sanction discrimination whether this takes the form of a conscious action or unconscious inaction.

Old and new racisms have helped to define, in a political sense, frameworks of policy and provision which discriminate both directly and indirectly and leave black people with fewer rights, curtailed access and at greater risk. The dominant view of black people as a threat to 'our' (ie, British) cultural and material wealth gives licence to those administering those policies to do so in a discriminatory way, and moreover, to expect to be rewarded for so doing. The effective pressure brought to bear on government by the immigration officers' union in the build up to the imposition of visas, and the additional resources diverted to inner city policing, are institutional examples of how it pays to be racist. (Note that the state is being rolled back in some respects, and forwards in others. Social authoritarianism is the other side of the neo-liberal coin.) At an individual level, when career prospects, including promotion and other incentives, are linked to working a system which effectively discriminates against black people, then instrumentally at least, it would appear to make greater sense to collude with racism than to challenge it.

The Labour Party's Response

The analysis of racism in terms of policies and their implementation, and the cultural context within which those exist, is an important but by no means sufficient basis for developing anti-racist strategies. Racism is not a static component of an institution or an inevitable effect of a policy, or a coherent, undynamic ideology. At any given moment the treatment and experience of black people cannot just be read off from policy documents, speeches, bills or Acts of Parliament. It is much more a *process*, subject at any moment to the influence of an array of political forces.

This is not to deny a role for policy documents and the like in this analysis. They help to mark out the terrain on which racist/anti-racist politics is waged. Such documents, however, cannot be examined in isolation from a much wider political context. The degrees and types of racial inequality are not just a result of institutional racism as articulated in the speeches of leading politicians or their policies. They are also the result of institutional racism 'on the ground' – in schools, hospitals, housing departments, police stations. But these inequalities result from other forces too: in particular, from the success of attempts to contain racism, and negotiate and campaign for anti-racism, as well as from the failure to mount any significant challenge to it. In other words, in addition to knowing about racist culture, racist institutions, policies and practices, 'on high' as well as 'on the ground', we need to know more about the forces of anti-racism, and the absence of those forces in contexts where they might exist.

It is against this background, including a personal one of working with others inside and outside the Labour Party in anti-racist politics, that I will examine the party's response to racism. The Labour Party can be examined at a number of levels: as a party in political control of a number of major towns (including Wolverhampton) and cities; as the major party of opposition nationally; as a party made up of individuals with strong links with the trade union movement, with professionals strategically placed in institutions; and, finally, as a party with potential and, in many cases, actual links with anti-racist and black organizations, both formal and informal. The nature and extent of Labour's response to the racisms discussed in the first part of this paper will provide the basis for a realistic assessment of Labour's role in the future.

Labour's manifesto of 1987 contained four paragraphs on race: the first was a commitment to equal citizenship rights for all; the second stated that Labour's policies on employment, education, housing, health care, local government, would benefit ethnic minorities because they are part of the community who are all going to benefit; the third was a commitment to promote racial equality via contract compliance and other positive measures and to make prosecution against racial attacks easier; finally, the party commited itself to non-discriminatory, firm but fair, immigration control (Labour Party 1987).

It is not easy or always helpful to analyse the Labour Party as if it speaks with one voice, especially when there are such clear differences between and within both the parliamentary and local Labour parties. However, if we take policy outcomes and public statements by the party leadership as a starting point here, the last decade can be broken down into three main periods. Initially, that is from 1979-83, the party spoke out strongly against racial discrimination in immigration and nationality legislation. At the same time, a working party of the National Executive Committee began to develop a detailed programme on positive action which was to have formed the basis of Labour's manifesto on race (Layton Henry *et al* 1986, pp 103ff). In fact, just prior to its election defeat in 1979, Labour had introduced an Ethnic Needs Bill which sought to overcome the anomalies and racist assumptions of the original Section 11 of the Local Government Act, 1966. At least in the immediate post-1979 period, the Labour Party was more optimistic about developing and presenting a programme of positive reforms on race to the electorate, and saw the first spell in opposition as an opportunity to work out the details.

In the second phase, however, following the general election defeat of 1983, the debate shifted from external policy to a major internal debate on the setting up of black sections in the party. The principle of black sections, which dominated conference debates on race in the mid 1980s, was consistently and successfully opposed by the leadership, backed by the block votes of some of the larger trade unions. The detailed programme of positive action never materialized. In fact, in the most recent period, that is, the run-up to the 1987 election and since, the Labour Party leadership has sought, in the main, to remain as silent as possible on race, save for openly distancing itself from local anti-racist initiatives.

These political trends are largely borne out in the first stage of the party's policy review, *Social Justice and Economic Efficiency*, published in 1988, and intended to provide a framework for detailed policy development in 1988-9. Of the seven groups reporting, only one, Democracy for The Individual and the Community, deals with racial discrimination and equal opportunities (*not* racism) in any detail. The presence on this group of the only black person (male) out of a total review membership of over sixty is indicative of Labour's failure to acknowledge the permeability of racism across every area of its policy review.

This is not to say that the principles relevant to racial discrimination and equal opportunities are not important in themselves. The strengthening of the race relations law; the repeal of the immigration and nationality laws; the principle of tighter control over government departments to review and provide evidence of progress on equal opportunities; and the use of contract compliance to influence positive change in the private sector (p 36) are all significant, assuming that they are developed in the next stage of the review and thereafter.

There are, however, a number of problems arising from the reliance on, and status of, the terms 'equal opportunity', and 'racial discrimination'. The problematic use of 'equal opportunities' is well illustrated in the report of the People at Work Review Group which, almost self-consciously, avoids mention of race by confining its discussion of equal opportunity to gender (p 10). Here 'equal opportunities' is used to eschew the problem of racism altogether. In this respect, 'racial discrimination', by definition, has to deal with 'race'. However, it is a term which lends itself more to a discussion of individual actions rather than the workings of institutions, and this is well illustrated in the Economic Equality Review (Labour Party 1988, p 18).

The absence of any reference to racism in the whole review document and even the sparse and scattered reference to racial discrimination and equal opportunities is particularly significant because it means that the problems identified in the first part of this chapter, that is, the racist policy frameworks and their implications for black people, are left untouched. A stronger race relations law and an empowered and hence more effective department with a co-ordinating role on race within government (p 36) cannot hope to compete with the racisms which proliferate in society's institutions. Such legal and administrative reforms by themselves are far too marginal to be able to influence specialist areas of mainstream policies and their delivery.

Nowhere in the document is any attempt made to examine racism in any of the major areas of policy. Education, housing and policing, for instance, actually fall outside the remit of any of the review groups in the first stage, despite the party's acknowledgement of the need to carry out a review of existing institutional practices as a necessary precondition for detailed policy development. Even in the policy areas which were discussed, and where there were opportunities to discuss racism, for instance in planning and in employment and the economy, such opportunities were not taken. The principle of rewarding socially productive investment, for example (p 23), could have been tied to anti-racism, but this would have required a detailed review of business practices in terms of their race dimension: in marketing, research and product development, investment and recruitment, promotion and training. The role/potential role of government in relationship to each of these together could have formed the basis for developing an anti-racist strategy applicable to the institution in question.

Overall, then, the weaknesses of the review to date lie in the lack of black representation on the review groups, the selective use of equal opportunity terminology, the absence of any review of existing institutional racism and the marginal character of its most significant proposals. The latter may have been appropriate in the 1970s when, strategically, it was necessary to fight to secure a place for anti-racism on the political agenda. They can hardly be described as visionary, or claim to serve as a basis for party policy into the 1990s. In this sense *Social Justice and Economic Efficiency* confirms a retreatist tendency within the party on anti-racism: a tendency, it would appear, that exists in other areas of Party policy and practice.

One of the most important clues to the views of the Labour leadership on race is contained in the 1987 election manifesto. It states,

> Our policies for employment, education, health care, local government and much else will clearly be of benefit to people of the ethnic minorities *as they will be to the whole community*.
>
> (Labour Party 1987, p 13, emphasis added)

There is a widespread assumption that policies aimed at redistribution between social classes will help black people because the latter are over-represented in the lower classes. It is also linked to the most common explanation put forward by the Labour Party in the aftermath of the street conflicts of 1981 and 1985, that the conflicts were not about race but the deprivation and disadvantage experienced by *all* inner city residents.

There has always been a strong resistance to acknowledging that racism is not just about class inequalities or deprivation but is something peculiar to black people (Ben-Tovim *et al* 1986). This resistance surfaces from time to time, for instance, in Labour's rejection of the principle of black sections. The argument that the latter are divisive, and that struggle for racial equality is one for the whole labour movement, has always ignored the reality of the party's record on race and its failure to promote black participation inside the party and anti-racist policies outside. The reality of black sections is that they were never, and are never, likely to divide the party or to marginalise anti-racism; (could it be more so than at present?) nor were they likely to take the party by storm in the way that their opponents have claimed or feared. In other words, the opposition to black sections, even in its own terms, was quite out of proportion to the 'threat' posed by their creation.

As a result, the voice of the Labour Party Black Section is detached from mainstream decision making. Its contributions to debates on education and their criticisms of current government policy articulated at the Second Socialist Conference at Chesterfield are removed to the 'extremes' of Labour Party opinion (Labour Party Black Section 1988). The effect of such manoeuvres is to help to reinforce, rather than to challenge, 'popular' opinions on race which have been so ably constructed and reconstructed by the Conservatives. Another effect is to alienate black activists and would-be activists from the Labour Party, and to lead them to consider alternative political options (Howe and Upshal 1988, p 12-13).

What the black sections debate did do was to distract the party from developing a detailed programme on racial equality to put to the electorate. At best, underpinning opposition to black sections from within the party was, and is, a genuine but flawed view that racial inequalities can be redressed by mainstream social reform. At worst, opposition to black sections can be linked to racist undercurrents not dissimilar to those discussed in the first part of this chapter. In those instances where Labour has acknowledged racism, it has tended to do so in terms of individual acts. Hence the manifesto, like the policy review, was particularly concerned with strengthening public order and making prosecutions against racial attacks easier. But in concentrating on the actions of individuals, the Party has effectively de-institutionalised its opposition to racism, a stance I shall now illustrate more fully.

The McCurbin Case

In this section, I shall briefly examine Labour's response to the death of Clinton McCurbin, a young black man, who was killed by police officers in February 1987, in Wolverhampton, whilst allegedly resisting arrest. The case will allow me to extend the above analysis of the Labour Party to include a more detailed assessment of those political processes which help to shape racial inequalities. There are other reasons for examining this case in more detail. Not only was the incident widely believed to have lost the Labour Party control of the council in the local elections of 1987, as well as a seat in the general election later that year; the ramifications of this and other cases have been cited to explain the national Labour Party's retreat on anti-racism.

At the time of the incident, local politics in Wolverhampton was dominated by what David Edgar has called the advocates of 'traditional, Tammany Hall, right wing Labourism' (*Guardian* 18 January 88). The deputy leader's response to the incident (the leader was fighting a seat in the European Parliament at the time) reflected those labourist traditions, and was typical of Labour's previous handling of such 'crises'. What was important was to be seen to be doing something in the eyes of the black community:

> I saw it very much as a humanitarian gesture which you would expect any caring local authority to make and as a clear commitment towards wanting to continue good community relations in the town.
> (Peter Bilson, Deputy Leader, Wolverhampton Council, reported in *Express and Star*, 10 March 1987)

In this respect the response was never meant to be anything but a gesture of goodwill, but a gesture it was nonetheless. The Labour Group pledged to pay for Clinton McCurbin's mother to return to England from the United States where she had been living, and also to pay the McCurbins' legal costs arising from the coroner's enquiry. As it turned out, the decision unleashed a backlash of response from which the Labour Party could not recover, at least not in time for the local elections in May. In a matter of days, a petition of over 6000 names was handed over to a Conservative councillor. The vast majority of *Express and Star* readers whose correspondence was published in the weeks following the incident were clearly extremely angry at Labour's response.

Their letters expressed opposition to the decision on two

grounds. First they claimed that the Labour Party was giving preferential treatment to black people, and thus was itself acting in a racist manner. Second, and not unrelatedly, the cash aid for the McCurbin family came to be seen as another example of Labour's financial extravagance, which, overall, could be witnessed in its proposal to increase the rates by 13.3 per cent. The familiar 'cash handouts for blacks' theme had been used before by the *Express and Star* and provoked a similar response from readers. It both pandered to local popular prejudice and appealed to a widespread local concern to minimise rates bills whatever the likely public cost. It enabled the local press to lump the Labour Party together with other 'loony left' councils and hence helped to undermine Labour's traditional working class vote in the subsequent elections.

The response can be partly explained by the relative isolation of anti-racists within the party. The gestural nature of the response was a fudge. On the one hand it was based on a commitment to do something, both in the interests of 'good community relations' and because of pressure from the black community. On the other hand resistance to institutionalised anti-racist strategies within the party ensured that the response had to be reactive and piecemeal. Both the black community *and* the right of the party were thus seemingly appeased.

These kinds of responses and initiatives are not just necessary compromises, but a consistent feature of Labour's response to racism. In practice they are little more than tokenism entwined in rhetoric. Anti-racist interventions become, as they did in Wolverhampton, *ad hoc* and reactive. Under such circumstances, policies on anti-racism are often little more than statements of principle and good intent, rather than being adequately resourced within a framework of implementation and evaluation. The limited impact of anti-racism is not confined to right-wing Labour politics. In the case of some 'left' local authorities, in Liverpool under Militant Tendency, and in some of the London boroughs according to Edgar, local Labour politics rely on tactics of intimidation and bullying, and on purges and plots. In these latter cases, anti-racism never gets a chance to percolate down, let alone filter up from the experiences of black people. In both cases, in 'right' and 'left' Labour councils, the appropriation of anti-racism by a ruling caucus of the local party coincides with minimal forms of participation and accountability to its own grass roots, let alone the wider black community.

The tokenistic nature of Wolverhampton Labour Group's response to McCurbin's death has to be understood in the context of Labour's already established relationship with the police in Wolverhampton. A feature of this relationship (notwithstanding the local party's opposition to the introduction of surveillance cameras in the town centre) was the party's consistent failure to attempt to exercise influence over policing methods and practices in the town. The deployment of police units in riot gear, the saturation policing of the town centre at the expense of policing other 'crimes' committed in greater number and away from the town centre, the pattern (not the exception) of picking up black young people and subjecting them to abuse and harassment, were all potential issues on a Labour Group/police agenda. Instead the Labour leadership, in common with the police and local business, regarded the town centre as *the* local policing 'problem', and the young people (young black people more precisely) who congregated there daily to be the cause of it.

The failure of the local authority to develop a critical dialogue with the police, and to take up and support concerns expressed by local black and anti-racist groups was seen by those groups as tantamount to offering tacit support to the police. The argument often stated by Labour's leaders that the local Labour Party had no control over the police may have been true in statutory terms. Nevertheless, there were a number of ways in which the police had been, and still are, dependent on the goodwill of the controlling Labour Group. For instance, police 'access' to the community, that is to schools, youth clubs and local authority departments, is often a matter of discretion on the part of the local authority. In Wolverhampton a number of forums which involved both the Labour Group and the police could have provided a basis for Labour to develop its own policy with regard to policing the town centre. Had it sought to trade its goodwill against a series of specific proposals with regard to local policing methods and practices, there might have existed a context in which a more serious and less gestural response to the McCurbin incident may have been possible.

Such proposals could have included the development of procedures for dealing with cases of alleged police harassment which had the confidence of local black people. They could have entailed the creation of more open participatory structures for considering the allocation of police resources in response to crime patterns in the town. They could have included a training programme which went beyond human awareness and dealt with racism in all its facets in the institutionalised policies and practices of policing. Had these been the areas for negotiation and campaign activity by the Labour Group, it is quite conceivable that the incident itself might not have occurred.

In terms of outcomes, Labour's response to the incident only marginally served the interests of the McCurbin family and arguably when it was too late. Beyond this, it lent weight to police demands for greater resources and widespread support for their handling of this and subsequent events. The Conservative Party, as it turned out, fell on its feet. In common with the local media and police, it used the issue to further its own ends, and in so doing, helped to secure the party's election victories.

The McCurbin incident not only serves to illustrate the failure of the local Labour Party to use its links at grass roots level with black and anti-racist community organisations and to use the collective experience of black people as a basis for informing political responses; it also illustrates the propensity to individualise racism, in this case police racism. This becomes a substitute for an on-going strategy to de-institutionalise racism which, in Wolverhampton's case, could have been pursued through the controlling Labour Group's relationship with the police. The background and events subsequent to the incident in Wolverhampton can also be used to illustrate the idea that racism is not just a deviant act perpetrated by one individual, nor can it just be read off from policies or the texts of political speeches. It is a process which must be analysed in terms of relationships around which power is contested, reinforced and created. The framework of provision and practice which results, at any given moment, from these relationships is ultimately what black people have to live with, and, in this case, die with. What underlies the failure to acknowledge racism and to make anti-racism a serious and integral part of Labour politics is complex and difficult to disentangle. Certainly there is a view which has surfaced periodically in Wolverhampton linking the experience of black to white working class youth, and resisting anti-racist politics in favour of a class-based response to the police. It is not just black young people, the argument goes, but working class youth as a whole, who suffer at the hands of the police. What is significant about this position is that it has been used to weaken anti-racism, rather than to develop an alternative, or even complementary, set of class-based demands or strategies. A reasonable inference to draw from this stance is that it is not about putting forward alternative class-based forms of response, but of resisting those which take racism as their focus. In Wolverhampton's case, and no doubt elsewhere, there exists a strong labourist parochialism, a predominant focus on the local white working class labour movement, which sits comfortably alongside a wider national 'parochialism' referred to in the first part of this paper. To this extent Labour is drawing, albeit less consciously, on those cultural reserves which are currently finding expression in Conservative government policy.

And Beyond Wolverhampton ...

Labour's failure to respond to the experience and treatment of black people on the one hand, and its attempt to impose anti-racism rather than work to construct an anti-racist consensus on the other, are well illustrated in a more recent incident, involving the death of Ahmed Ullah, a pupil at Burnage High School, Manchester. The tactic pursued by the headteacher at Burnage effectively sought to enforce anti-racist policies and practices on the school without consulting and involving white parents and pupils. The tactic was based on the assumption that anti-racism could only be secured by coercion, rather than developed from within the white and black communities. Under these circumstances the death, when it happened, provoked an angry response from white parents (and even the parents of Ahmed Ullah). They argued that the headteacher and the school's anti-racist policy had provoked rather than prevented racism, and even caused the incident itself.

There are important lessons here for a local Labour Party. These suggest the need to develop a policy framework (in this case through the LEA) which secures the participation of those groups of parents and pupils who must, in the end, support anti-racist education for it to work. Instead, as in the McCurbin case, the strategy pursued by the school, ironically, enabled the media, along with Conservative politicians, to use the deth of Ahmed to attack the principle of anti-racism.

The retreat on anti-racism, from the abolition of the Race Relations Committee in Birmingham, to the 'silences' on anti-racism in the major national review of party policy, cannot be justified on either political or moral grounds. The party leadership's reaction to members of the party's Black Section such as Sharon Atkin have served to feed rather than diffuse the media's hysterical outbursts on anti-racism. The leadership's strategy is partly based on the assumption that 'anti-racism' loses votes. Whilst certain versions of anti-racism may have that effect, as the McCurbin, Burnage and McGoldrick incidents testify (the last of these involved a headteacher from Brent who was suspended by the LEA for making an allegedly racist remark to an officer of the authority), these tend to be the ones associated with the *imposition* of anti-racism via slogans and rhetoric and tokenistic policies, from the top down. In consistently miscalculating or ignoring the response of the media and the mainstream readership of the media, they have indeed proved politically counterproductive. Gestures of goodwill, as in the case of McCurbin, are certainly no match for the dominant forms of cultural racism discussed above. In many respects, insofar as they are compatible with dominant media themes (for instance, 'cash handouts for blacks'), they are all too readily exploitable both by the media and political opposition. As a result, electoral support for Labour has been undermined.

Part of the problem with slogan-based politics is that responses, when they are made, are not linked to, or rationalised in terms of, a coherent and well-developed socialist alternative. Moreover the tendency to give maximum public profile to the response (the Burnage Report' was an exception, which still, nevertheless, got picked up and turned against anti-racism) may not only exacerbate local racist sentiments but also alienate the local black community. Rather than being seen to be doing something of a gestural nature in the eyes of the black community, a longer-term strategy seeking to challenge the framework of (for example, policing) policy and practice may win greater support and fewer sceptics.

For all its faults (see Gilroy 1987), the GLC did at least seek to popularise anti-racism through its publicity campaign, in addition to attempts to promote black employment and services that were more responsive to the demands of black communities. Particularly notable here were: training programmes for black staff; recruitment and promotion drives (black workers increased from under 7 per cent to over 11 per cent of the 23,000 workforce, Burney 1988, p 19); initiatives in the area of contract compliance; funding of black organisations; work on police monitoring; support for anti-racist campaigns; promotion of black arts; and, finally, funding of black businesses. Labour's attempts to popularise these initiatives were part of a wider attempt to make socialism popular. To this extent, the GLC stands apart from those local Labour parties which have shown more contempt for their electorates, including local black communities, and where anti-racism has been imposed, rather than created out of, and negotiated around, an anti-racist consensus.

In fact, looking back over the decade as a whole, the GLC's stance on anti-racism, for all its flaws, looks increasingly anomalous. Evidence cited in this chapter suggests that the argument for a coherent and detailed anti-racist programme for the next election has still to be won within the party. Throughout this chapter I have deliberately used the term anti-racism, not for the sake of being negative or provocative, but because rival terms such as positive action or equal opportunity can only be a part of an overall anti-racist strategy. Taken on their own, there is a danger that alternative terms can be limited to a discrete set of principles and activities, for example equal opportunity statements or positive action training programmes. Whilst these may provide important starting points, as well as forming part of an overall strategy, anti-racism requires a more fundamental and thorough review of institutions. The term makes clear that to talk of 'preferential treatment' or 'queue jumping', as opponents of positive action and discrimination suggest, is a nonsense; it points out that people have been lined up unfairly in the first place and that, anyway, having got to the front, black people are less likely to receive equal treatment. Labour has a role to challenge these common sense reactions to positive action and positive discrimination. Instead, its own ambivalence has served to undermine, rather than legitimate, such principles. I would add that 'liberal' critiques of positive discrimination, of the kind developed by John Edwards (1987), do not help the party to develop a coherent and defensible stance on anti-racism. On the contrary, by refusing to acknowledge the collective experience and effects of racism, their contributions only serve to endorse it.

Conclusions

The arguments developed in this chapter have been built around the need to develop an analysis of institutionalised racism out of the experience of working in anti-racist politics. It has involved an assessment of legislation, policy, speeches, manifestos and other documents, but not to the exclusion of the contexts in which they are interpreted, fought over and reworked, as well as left unchallenged. This means bringing together racism and anti-racism within the same analytical framework and it means conceptualising racism as a process not a product. It also means acknowledging that concrete material outcomes, as they structure elements of black peoples' conditions and experiences, are the result of the (unequal) interplay of racist and anti-racist forces.

The Labour Party, as a major political force which has traditionally stood for more equitable forms of distribution and social justice, offers some foothold for anti-racist politics. As this chapter suggests, however, the struggle for anti-racism is as relevant inside the party as it is outside. A number of implications for strategy within the party follow from this assessment and the paper will conclude by summarising these.

In the first instance, Labour's anti-racist strategy should start with black people's experiences of racism, which means establishing formal links with black and anti-racist organisations and campaigns outside the party as well as promoting black membership inside. Black people are unlikely to take the party seriously, so long as they are effectively excluded from its decision-making structures, as well as prevented from organising independently within it.

A second important principle of such a programme, which follows both from the earlier discussion of government policy and from the Wolverhampton evidence, is the need to develop anti-racism on the basis of an understanding and critique of white-dominated institutions. This calls for a detailed analysis of how institutions like schools and the police actually operate in places like Wolverhampton. This would enable the Labour Party, through the scope provided by its political status, through its links with trade unions and professionals promoting anti-racism in their own places of work, to contribute, in different ways, to the de-institution-alisation of racism. This means understanding the power relationships within those institutions, as well as identifying and collaborating with progressive forces inside and outside the party.

The tendency of the party to shy away from anti-racism may be partly about votes and elections. But the failure to develop an alternative, more credible and substantial programme suggests the problem is as much to do with the party's more deep-seated resistances to acknowledging and challenging racism in its institutional forms. To this extent, the party itself is helping to undermine anti-racism. The aim of an alternative programme would be to depoliticise anti-racism and make it part and parcel of everyday practice including professional practice, in the same way that racism appears natural, neutral and apolitical now. The party's present silence will not prevent a recurrence of deaths like those of McCurbin or Ullah, nor will it begin to deconstruct any of the other legacies of the 1980s. Moreover, the party cannot go on hiding behind a racist consensus without compromising its socialist commitment.

I would like to thank the following people for their comments on earlier drafts of this paper: Mel Jones, Maureen McNeil, Brenda Parkes, Mohan Singh and Kathy Stredder.

References

M. Barker, *The New Racism*, Pluto 1981.

G. Ben-Tovim, J. Gabriel, I. Law and K. Stredder, *The Local Politics of Race*, Macmillan, 1986.

C. Brown, *Black and White in Britain: The Third PSI Survey*, Policy Studies Institute, 1984.

E. Burney, *Steps to Racial Equality: Action in a Negative Climate*, Runnymede Trust, 1988.

Committee for Non-Racist Benefits, *Black Claimants: Targets for Cuts*, No 3, November 1987.

General Election Manifesto, Conservative Party, 1987.

Department of Environment, *Housing: The Government Proposals*, HMSO Cmnd 214, 1987.

D. Edgar, 'Let the People Sing', *Guardian* 18 January 1988.

J. Edwards, *Positive Discrimination: Social Justice, and Social Policy: Moral Scrutiny of a Policy Practice*, Tavistock, 1987.

P. Gilroy, *There Ain't No Black in the Union Jack*, Hutchinson, 1987.

S. Howes and D. Upsal, 'New Black Power Lines', *New Statesman/Society*, 15 July 1988.

Joint Council for the Welfare of Immigrants, *Bulletin*, Vol 6, No 3, 1988.

Britain Will Win, Labour Party, 1987.

Social Justice and Economic Efficiency, Labour Party, 1988.

Labour Party Black Section, *The Black Agenda*, 1988.

Z. Layton-Henry, *Race, Government and Politics in Britain*, Macmillan, 1986.

H. Ousley, 'Reforming Education: Opportunities Lost', *Local Government Studies*, January/February 1988.

F. Palmer (ed), *Anti-Racism – An Assault on Education and Value*, Sherwood, 1986.

David Purdy
Incomes Policy, Citizenship and Basic Income

It could be argued that incomes policy is a good idea whose time has gone. As the New Right's bid for hegemony consolidates its hold over British society, traditional socialist ideas seem ever less relevant to the contemporary scene. In general, this judgement is correct. It follows that if socialism is to avoid extinction, the Left needs to remodel its vision of the future, its strategic direction and its detailed policies. Neither sterile, fundamentalist posturing nor unprincipled, opinion poll politics will help us to make the necessary re-adjustments. It would also be a mistake to look no further than the next election. The crisis of the Left is too serious for such myopia.

In this essay, I outline a new approach to incomes policy, which draws on the painful experience of the past, meets the challenge of the New Right, and marks out a route to social transformation. Incomes policy should not be seen as a top-down instrument of economic control. Its constitutive principles, formative procedures, detailed design and practical implementation should all be parts of the transformatory process itself. Beyond the immediate exigencies of economic management, the larger purpose of incomes policy is to help promote a pluralistic, democratic and egalitarian reconstruction of the state and the economic system over which it presides.

The first part of this article proposes a definition of incomes policy which explains why the New Right's policies for incomes do not amount to an incomes policy. The second part reviews the attitudes of the British Left and trade unions towards incomes policies in the 1960s and 1970s. I argue that the Social Contract in the mid 1970s presented a golden opportunity for socialist advance which was tragically wasted because the principal historical actors possessed neither the vision, capacity or will to seize it. The third part establishes the connection between incomes policy and the ideal of citizenship which both motivated and grew out of the struggle to build a welfare state. Parts four and five show how this ideal should now be reformulated. What is needed is nothing less than a redesign of the institutions governing employment, work and income-entitlement. This involves a transition from welfare state capitalism to a new, though still capitalist, social dispensation under which every man, woman and child receives an unconditionally guaranteed minimum basic income. Incomes policy falls into place both as part of the political and ideological struggle needed to bring about this transition, and as an integral component of the new regime once it has been won.

What Do We Mean by an 'Incomes Policy'?

In one sense it is impossible for a modern government not to have some sort of policy for incomes. Through the systems of personal taxation and social security, the state, for good or ill, permanently modifies the primary distributive outcomes thrown up by the market. Similarly, the state's fiscal and monetary stance exerts some influence on wage and price formation. A recent example is the Conservative Government's Medium Term Financial Strategy. In the period 1980-83, the MTFS formed the very backbone of macro-economic policy, though it was later much softened and remoulded under Chancellor Lawson. One of its objectives was to bring about disinflation by forcing wage and price decisions up against the hard edge of market discipline. This was, to paraphrase Clausewitz on war, nothing more than a continuation of incomes policy by other means.

The same belligerent logic applies to the more detailed sallies which the government has launched under the banner of 'deregulation' – from the abolition of the House of Commons Fair Wages Resolution and the enforcement of competitive tendering for public services, to the drastic weakening of the Wages Councils and the imposition of the Restart scheme. The stated intention of this battery of initiatives has been to make the labour market, and therefore wages, more flexible. Profit-related pay, 'final offer' arbitration and individual employee share ownership schemes are designed to serve a similar purpose at the more prosperous end of the market.

The whole neo-liberal exercise in social engineering, celebrated under the watchword 'popular capitalism', has been accompanied by sedulous efforts to persuade us all to embrace the values of competition, selectivity, self-reliance, self-betterment, acquisitiveness and personal property ownership. Not the least important objective of this campaign is the commodification of the labour market. The neo-liberal ideal is an economy in which the determination of pay and other terms of employment is, as far as possible, released from the allegedly baneful rigidities imposed by legislative regulation, collective agreements, custom and practice or simply the capacity of workers to take organised, concerted action.

This all adds up to a policy with very decided repercussions for both aggregate shares of national income and the disposable incomes accruing to households and individuals. Yet at the same time, the Conservative governments have steadfastly repudiated the principle of an incomes policy as one of the more discredited relics of the nightmare era of collectivism. Admittedly, some commentators have professed to discern a partial, shadowy incomes policy in the government's selective efforts to restrain pay settlements in the public sector. But it is surely more correct to see the government's calculated adoption of a tough or generous bargaining posture in its capacity as direct employer or ultimate paymaster, as a simple consequence of budgetary restraint and the restructuring of the state, not as an embarrassing remnant of the *ancien régime*.

It would seem that a policy which is unavoidable has for nearly a decade been rigorously shunned. Evidently if we are to avoid falling into confusion, a definition of terms is required. By 'incomes policy' is meant an arrangement which is:

(1) intended to act directly on both the average rate of growth and possibly also the spread of money incomes

(2) concerned with the movement of primary or pre-tax money incomes
(3) devised under the auspices of the state, normally in collaboration with representatives of the interest groups in civil society whose behaviour the policy is designed to affect
(4) administered by means of a system of explicit rules governing the pay and pricing decisions of enterprises and industrial organisations
(5) normally extended to prices and non-wage incomes as well as wages and salaries.

Each component of this definition is important. First, only those policies which aim to produce a *direct* effect on wage and price setting qualify as incomes policies in the strict sense. Fiscal and monetary deflation, tax and benefit adjustments and labour market deregulation all impinge on wage and price outcomes *indirectly* by altering the environment and institutions in which they are determined. Neo-liberal policies with implications for incomes might conceivably be described as incomes policies at one remove. In reality, they are not even distant cousins, but issue from wholly alien sources.

Second, the chief aim of any incomes policy is to shift the time-path of pre-tax money incomes. In a decentralised and unco-ordinated system of wage bargaining and price setting, the interplay of individual, self-interested rationality produces results which are socially pathological. Some economy-wide agency is needed to impress on micro-economic behaviour the general social interest. Otherwise, no one incurs any responsibility or incentive to take account of the cumulative consequences of the decisions taken in each bargaining unit and enterprise. Incomes policy is a remedy for market failure. Without it, serious costs are inflicted on society as a whole. Obviously, the distribution of incomes *after* taxes and benefits also matters, and is a legitimate and unavoidable concern of public policy. Moreover, as argued below, any arrangement for regulating pre-tax income growth should be thoroughly and permanently integrated with the procedure for setting the parameters of the tax and benefit system. But whatever the arrangements for secondary income redistribution, there are compelling reasons for devising a primary system of regulation to fill the vacuum left by the anarchic play of market and power forces.

Third, the state is the social agency best placed and most likely to initiate the arrangements in question. But both democratic principle and practical statecraft make it imperative that the terms of any incomes policy should be negotiated in advance with the organised social interests whose behaviour needs to be regulated. Outside the circumstances of a temporary emergency, no policy either should, or indeed can, be unilaterally imposed by the state. Any stable and durable policy must harness both the authority and the intelligence of the principal industrial organisations representing employers and workers.

Fourth, no policy exists merely by declaratory fiat. Some mechanism of administration based on clear, public rules is needed to convert intentions into results. Partly, this is because pious exhortations by government ministers enjoining negotiators to observe unspecified restraint are about as effective as King Canute's legendary attempt to turn the tide. But what is more important is the popular consent required to sustain an incomes policy for more than one or two bargaining rounds. Each sectional interest group must be convinced that every other is being obliged to play by the same rules as itself. Once the necessity for *some* mechanism to ensure rule compliance is accepted, the question arises as to what precisely this should consist of. The pros and cons of traditional versus tax-based methods of administration are briefly reviewed in a later part of this chapter.

The need for popular consent also explains the fifth and final element of the definition. Barring a windfall improvement in its terms of trade, or an appreciation of its effective exchange rate, no country can permanently reduce/contain the rate of price inflation unless by one means or another it manages to reduce/contain the rate of growth of labour costs per unit of output. Since the trend rate of growth of output per worker depends on technical, institutional and cultural factors which change, if at all, only at a slow, secular pace, the key target variable of any anti-inflation policy is the rate of growth of money wages per

worker. Nevertheless, it does not follow that an incomes
policy need or should concern itself only with the movement
of pay. Workers and unions will not accept pay restraint
without some parallel regulation of non-wage incomes,
including corporate profits, personal property income,
self-employment earnings and the self-determined remune-
ration of groups such as company directors. It is notoriously
difficult to extend the coverage of an incomes policy to these
categories, but not impossible. The scope for fortifying
incomes policy by eliminating blatant inequities in income
tax assessment is indicated by the Australian government's
recent drive against high income group tax avoidance. There
is also a need for redoubled vigilance in the ongoing guerrilla
war against tax dodging in the informal economy. Non-wage
income restraint is essential to securing compliance with pay
restraint. Nothing is more apt to undermine the morale of an
army in the field than the sight of generals, officers and
mercenaries slinking stealthily out of the line of fire.

The Left's Attitude to Incomes Policies: The 1960s and 1970s

Since the mid-1960s, the British Left and trade unions have
regarded incomes policy at best with suspicion and usually
with venom. There are both structural and historically and
culturally specific reasons for this hostile attitude. Leaving
aside the implicit social contract of the Second World War
and the brief, though effective, voluntary pay restraint
practised from 1948 to 1950, the first really full-blooded
incomes policy was undertaken by the Wilson government
elected in 1964 in the name of 'planned income growth'. This
attempt to take Britain's ailing economy and system of
government through a process of post-imperial modernisation became stalled. It coincided with the emergence
from the industrial twilight of a self-confident shop stewards'
movement which was just beginning to flex its muscles in
bargaining with workplace management over pay and job
control. By 1966, against a background of labour unrest, a
chronic balance of trade and payments deficit and a classic
run on the pound, the much vaunted Tripartite Declaration
of Intent on Prices, Productivity and Incomes, had given
way to an emergency wage freeze. This was followed in short

order by a 'nil norm' and twelve months of 'severe restraint'. In the eyes of many trade unionists, the very term 'incomes policy' then acquired a negative, repressive image which it has never since lived down.

After this unpromising start, the institutional basis for an effective incomes policy was further weakened by the radical decentralisation of pay bargaining in the 1970s. The shift to single-employer, company- or plant-based negotiation in the private sector, now being copied in what remains of the public sector, reinforced trade union opposition to 'government interference'. It also laid the basis for a parochial, enterprise trade unionism which was consolidated by the Conservatives' successive reforms of employment and industrial relations law in the 1980s. Attitudes to incomes policy are also shaped by the way in which wage bargaining tends to be perceived in a capitalist market economy. Most pragmatically minded employers long ago gave up the fiction of unilateral control over wage fixing, and conceded that wages are a negotiable issue to be settled through collective bargaining at whatever organisational level suited them best. But, equally, most strategic enterprise decisions – on investment, location, technical change, product development, organisational structure and forward planning generally – remain non-negotiable issues exclusively reserved for managerial prerogative. It follows that workers at levels of the employment hierarchy below the most senior enjoy highly unequal access to different potential objectives of collective action. They are naturally inclined to cling jealously to their limited room for manoeuvre and self-assertion, and to resist any external encroachment on 'free collective bargaining'.

This subaltern perception is reinforced by the widespread, though oversimplified, belief that wage bargaining is a zero sum game in which wages and profits are strictly inversely related. The notion that capitalist profits are fair game forges an important psychological connection with the heroic age of trade unionism. Free collective bargaining is felt to symbolise continuity with the earlier historic struggle to win trade union legitimacy and recognition in the teeth of vicious resistance from employers, the judiciary and the police.

The Left's macho ideology and rhetoric have also played a part in the denigration of incomes policies. Notwithstanding the accumulation of evidence to the contrary, there are still plenty of hidebound revolutionaries around insisting that the wages struggle remains the royal road to 'class mobilisation' and 'socialist consciousness'. A more sophisticated version of this latter view relates incomes policies to the process of corporatist intermediation between the state and the working class in advanced capitalist democracies (See Panitch 1976 and 1981). Periodic attempts are made to restabilise crisis-torn economies by incorporating workers' organisations as auxiliary arms of the 'capitalist' state. On this view, the rise and fall of incomes policies mark the ebb and flow of the class war. It is worth devoting some space to a rebuttal of this assessment of corporatist tendencies, the better to appreciate the potential role of incomes policy in the contemporary socialist project.

In Britain throughout the whole period from the First World War to the late 1970s, the system of government was inflected by what Middlemas (1979) calls 'corporate bias'. By this he means that, despite occasional deviations, the long term trend of government policy was to encourage the peak organisations of capital and labour to step across the threshold separating state and civil society and to assume the role of 'governing institutions'. The 'social partners' came not only to share the state's central aim of avoiding crisis by maintaining social cohesion and political stability; they also began, inconspicuously and *sotto voce*, to negotiate over the terms of economic and social policy; and even acquired a recognised role in those areas of policy most closely tied to their own executive competence and sectional interests.

This system of corporate bias reached maturity in the 1940s. The unions' role as a governing institution receded in the 1950s. But the advent of incomes policies in the 1960s and 1970s gave a sharp new focus to the process of policy exchange. In the battle against inflation, the unions were called upon to underutilise the power to bid up money wages which they inevitably held as long as the state remained committed to a regime of full employment. Implicit in this appeal was an invitation to assume responsibility for the management of the national economy. But the unions could hardly be expected to help steer the ship unless they acquired some say in its destination, speed and the conditions on board. Incomes policy thus brought them closer to precisely those strategic zones of policy formation from which they are excluded under normal collective bargaining. The stage was set for what Colin Crouch (1981) calls 'bargained corporatism' – the regularised exchange of claim and offer in settling the terms on which workers would consent to pay restraint.

The logic of the principle 'no responsibility without power' extended well beyond the participation of the TUC General Council in economy-wide policy making at central government level. It drove a democratic wedge into decision making at every level of the economy – regional, local, industrial/sectoral and enterprise. The space created by this insertion from above was ready to be occupied by those movements at the base which were beginning to articulate demands for workers' control of production and popular participation in planning. For there was no inherent reason why the agenda of a negotiated incomes policy should be confined to budgetary and (infelicitously named) 'social wage' issues. Armed with a democratic vision, a transformatory strategy and a commitment to the politics of popular alliances, government, unions and people could become active partners in a social contract based on a wider and deeper agenda.

Incomes policy opened up a historic opportunity to establish a focus and purchase on public policy for all the diverse energies and movements which marked out the 1970s as a decade of disobedience and organic crisis – feminism, workers' control, ecological politics, the reorganisation of the labour process and the democratisation of the public service economy. The core institutions of the British state remained fundamentally authoritarian and paternalistic. But the surrounding system of corporate bias, which from 1971-72 onwards enjoyed its Indian Summer, contained deep tensions and ambiguities. Whether these resolved themselves into a traditional, oligarchic and bureaucratic cast, or, on the contrary, furnished growing points for a popular democratic revolution, was not pre-ordained. Everything depended on the imagination, intelligence and pressure which could be brought to bear to exploit their progressive potential.

The first stage in this battle 'in and against the state' was to win legitimacy for the principle that representatives of all major stake-holders in economic decisions should be involved in the appropriate decision-making process. As this principle gained ground, the question would inevitably arise as to how to co-ordinate the activities of pluralistic, participative institutions. In working out a socialist incomes policy, a new model state, in partnership with popular organs in civil society, would be obliged to address what is arguably socialism's toughest intellectual and practical problem: how to construct a mechanism of economic co-ordination which avoids both the open coercion of centrally planned, command economies, and the alienated, structural coercion of the market. (For a serious, detailed and inspiring model of democratic planning, which the author calls 'negotiated co-ordination', see Devine 1988.)

Thus lodged within the principle of a social contract were the seeds of momentous social transformation. What was lacking was a hegemonic agency capable of nurturing their growth. The effective moment of germination was brief: lasting from March 1974 to mid 1975. At this juncture, British capitalism was economically devastated; its natural party of government electorally defeated and for the time being politically disoriented; and its moral and intellectual predominance fractured. This was the crisis so long awaited by the Left – the peacetime equivalent of Britain's desperate plight in May 1940. The labour movement had the chance to emulate its wartime achievements by rallying a new historic bloc around the twin themes of national economic regeneration and democratic reform.

The chance was squandered. With a handful of exceptions, neither government, party nor unions grasped the strategic potential of the crisis; and each remained fatally disconnected from the social movements which could have inspired and sustained a bold, responsible and constructive social contract. In a re-run of the 1960s, incomes policy degenerated into a tense and protracted holding operation which ended in fiasco. Simultaneously, the political and ideological initiative passed into the hands of forces bent on destroying what remained of the post-war settlement, debilitating the labour movement and reconstructing a free economy guarded by an authoritarian state.

The notion that incomes policy is an incorporationist device by which the 'capitalist' state drains off working class militancy is an ahistorical abstraction. It presupposes that there is never any problem in deciding just what strategy and programme will best promote the long term interests of capitalism. Mrs Thatcher is the living refutation of this myth: her consistent charge against her 'One Nation' predecessors is that they vacillated, compromised and sold the pass to 'socialism'. It is also pertinent to ask whether and why the state in a capitalist social formation is irredeemably 'capitalist'. Certainly, industrial and financial capital are structurally privileged, and this circumstance imparts a strong bias to public policy. Short of a radical expropriatory programme, which is unlikely to be politically feasible, even if it were desirable, governments are obliged to pay attention to the state of business confidence in framing their policies. But this need not entail supine submission to self-defined capitalist interests. Nor does it follow that the state cannot be made responsive to non-capitalist interests.

The incorporationist thesis also presumes without argument that the outcome of policy bargaining is bound to be unfavourable to labour's interests; trade unions should, therefore, refuse even to enter the negotiating chamber. But even if we leave aside the lessons of Britain's own experience in the 1970s, this defeatist and purist argument for splendid isolation ignores the relevant international evidence. There are some capitalist countries where organised labour is weak – notably Japan and Switzerland – which have managed to maintain historically low levels of unemployment during the upheavals of the 1970s and 1980s, or, in the case of the USA, to regain them. But consider the countries where organised labour carries some political weight and has practised something resembling a process of policy exchange with the state. It is significant that the greatest success in keeping unemployment down has been recorded by those countries in which this process has become entrenched and enduring – Sweden, Norway, Austria and, to a lesser degree and more recently, Australia. The Swedish case in particular is instructive. Here, the labour movement's struggle for economic democracy based on the proposal for employees investment funds, shows that bargained corporatism by no means excludes radical class politics.

Viewed from inside Thatcher's Britain, the Swedish combination of full employment, advanced welfare rights and the preservation of a solidaristic, disciplined and combative labour movement, presents an enviable overall package. The British combination of monetary discipline, fiscal retrenchment, high unemployment and atomistic pay bargaining, has intensified the divisions between privileged employees in the core of the labour market and the underclass in the periphery. It has also fragmented and marginalised the labour movement which historically has provided the principal democratic and egalitarian resistance to capitalist power.

This is precisely why Britain's version of bargained corporatism was vilified by the neo-liberal Right. From their standpoint, the concessions which were, or might one day have to be, yielded up to appease the claims of organised labour, threatened the slow strangulation of free enterprise capitalism. What was required was an end to the insidious practice of crisis avoidance. The neo-liberal alternative economic strategy did not depend on labour's endorsement, and would not be vulnerable to the withdrawal of consent. It aroused no subversive aspirations for democratic reform, but insulated the state from consensual politics. At the same time, workers were encouraged to abandon old, collective values and loyalties and to assume a new identity as free, competing individuals exchanging their productive powers for a portion of capitalism's bounty.

Incomes Policy and the Logic of Citizenship

The British Left's ingrained hostility to incomes policy was a serious, possibly fatal, mistake. But the chastening experience of the neo-liberal counter-revolution should not be taken to imply that it is only attitudes which need to change, not the basic design and presentation of the policy itself. History moves on, and we need to keep up with it if we are to influence the future.

It would be anachronistic to advocate incomes policy simply as a technical adjunct of fiscal expansionism, enabling a higher level of output and employment to be attained at a lesser cost in terms of inflation. One reason is that this stale cost-effectiveness argument is double-edged. It carries the dismal corollary that if incomes policy failed to hold the line on inflation, a responsible government would be obliged to compensate by tightening its fiscal and monetary stance. This admission is logically impeccable, but ideologically enervating. It presents incomes policy as a useful, but, in the last analysis, dispensable tool of macro-economic regulation. Few hearts will beat faster at the recital of this defensive, 'new realist' pragmatism. Furthermore, the fiscal expansionist case for incomes policy presupposes that the goal of higher output and employment is indubitably desirable and must always take precedence over other policy objectives. As it stands, this is an unacceptable proposition. That it has for so long been uncritically upheld as the touchstone of progressive politics perhaps reflects the quite unwarranted belief that capitalism is incorrigibly prone to stagnation and incapable of developing society's productive forces.

Of course, budgetary stimulation is rationally defensible as a means of averting or escaping from a slump when there is little prospect of any spontaneous recovery in the private components of aggregate demand. But if, as in Britain since 1983, an output recovery is under way and looks unlikely to falter, it could be destabilising to widen the budget deficit and step up the pace of domestic credit expansion. There is room for informed debate about whether the government could and should have done *more* to stimulate expansion between 1983 and 1986. It is arguable that the fall in (true) unemployment might have occurred earlier and proceeded further without taking undue risks with inflation, the trade deficit and the exchange rate. But the regional bottlenecks, inflationary overheating and upsurge in imports which accompanied the consumer-led boom of 1986-8, suggest that any such claim is rather thin. This kind of argument for incomes policy rests on finely balanced judgements about the timing and magnitude of marginal fiscal adjustments, not a challenging case for a distinctly different strategy.

It might be retorted that a more expansionary short term policy would deliver long term benefits. Some such belief presumably explains Chancellor Lawson's refusal to use other instruments besides interest rates in order to curb consumer spending and protect the exchange rate in the face of a most imposing balance of payments deficit. Provided capitalists are confident that faster expansion can be sustained, a fuller rate of capacity utilisation will stimulate higher investment in equipment and skills, even if the *current* interest rate is historically high. If higher investment in turn boosts the economy's underlying trend rate of growth, an eventual return to 'full employment' becomes a less uncertain and remote prospect than it currently appears.

But this rehabilitation of the old (and previously failed) 'gallop for growth' formula is not intrinsically left-wing or progressive. The New Right no less than the Centre-Left fervently desires to create a prosperous and dynamic capitalism. Both the neo-liberal and the reconstructed Keynesian programmes propose different roads to the same destination. Neither pauses to consider the logically prior and more probing question whether the ecological and social damage caused by 'growthism' might not make a deliberately *restrained* growth path a saner, safer and more user-friendly option.

Even if we suppress doubts about the desirability of faster growth, there remains a problem of feasibility. Once it is conceded that there might have to be a trade-off between compliance with incomes policy rules and the stance of fiscal and monetary policy, the proclaimed socialist alternative to neo-liberalism is in danger of becoming indistinguishable from it. There is no guarantee that rough going might not cause the economic gallop to be reined back to a canter or even a trot. Indeed, this fate is highly probable. Suppose, against all current expectations, that the Conservatives suffered electoral defeat and incomes policy returned to the political stage. Even allowing for a gentle prologue, the policy would eventually have to confront the legacy of the neo-liberal years. Pressure would mount from trade unions and other interest groups, now even more attached to a sectional and economistic outlook and even less restrained by the ethic of solidarity and political loyalty than their forerunners. In the absence of any countervailing moral and intellectual conception of the world, the policy would be doomed to play only a walk-on part in the ensuing drama. And since this scenario could be anticipated by the electorate as well as by unfriendly critics, the chances are that the actors would never be given the opportunity to perform it in the first place.

This latter judgement might not hold good in the event of another really serious international recession. It is conceivable, though by no means inevitable, that the resultant shock wave might be enough to unseat the incumbent government. If the trade unions rose to the occasion, a durable incomes policy might then be put together as part of an emergency rescue package, the success of which would depend critically on co-ordinated international expansionary action. But it seems unwise to base a strategy on such desperate imponderables. What is missing from the conventional instrumentalist case for incomes policy is any *ethical ideal, ideological challenge* and *political strategy*. The themes which ought to form the basis for a renovated, progressive and hegemonic incomes policy are *citizenship, redistribution* and *democracy*.

The original idea of a welfare state was that every citizen should be guaranteed certain rights: first, to a standardised range of public services; and second, to a variety of contingency cash benefits designed to cover all the risks liable to cause financial destitution in a capitalist market economy. The costs of these provisions were to be defrayed from two sources: a progressive income tax system and, less satisfactorily, an employment-based national insurance system. This conception eventually materialised in the Keynes-Beveridge régime. Although it was deeply flawed by state paternalist and patriarchal distortions, this working model of a welfare state did exemplify what T H Marshall (1950) called 'the logic of citizenship'. By this, he meant that the (imperfectly realised) principle of universality proclaimed the fundamental equality of all citizens. It asserted that all were entitled to enjoy in common certain minimum social and economic rights. The countervailing force of this principle abated somewhat the unprincipled inequalities and insecurities thrown up by the market. It also paralleled and complemented, within the economic sphere of society, the earlier achievement of universal suffrage and political democracy.

The post-war collectivist state superimposed the logic of citizenship on to the logic of the market. By the 1970s, this state had become dyamically unstable. The contradictions between citizenship and market were acute. Claims inspired by the citizenship principle escalated. Claimant groups pressed for extensions in the range of depth of conventional forms of income support. Workers moved on from the old cry of 'work or full maintenance' to more ambitious demands for guaranteed job security and the right to socially useful work. Popular movements aspired to democratic control over the affairs of region, community, workplace and enterprise.

From a neo-liberal perspective, this revolution of expectations represented a breakdown of social discipline fostered by permissive indulgence towards every social variable from the money supply to methods of schooling and sexual mores. The surge of claims on finite resources overloaded the system of government and set off accelerating inflation. But the same phenomena can also be interpreted as signs that the prevailing institutional framework of economy and government was outmoded and ripe for transformation. At all events, the contradictions could be resolved only by a reformation of the state into a new pattern in which one logic or the other predominated. Given the labour movement's strategically inept pursuit of *its* state principle, it was the enemies of citizenship who prevailed and re-asserted the primacy of the market.

The critical question for socialists is how we are to renew the struggle not so much to recover the ground lost during the years of the neo-liberal ascendancy, as to establish forward momentum along a new line of advance. What is urgently needed is a refurbished state principle which is capable of re-empowering the claims of citizenship, and which cuts with, rather than against, the grain of contemporary social and economic trends.

Basic Income, Redistribution and Democracy*

The only way of meeting these exacting requirements lies in a radical redesign of the institutions governing employment, work and income-entitlement. The central motif of the new design must be an unconditionally guaranteed basic income for all. Basic Income (BI) is a new name for an old, and hitherto utopian, idea whose time has now come.

What is envisaged is a transition from welfare state capitalism to a new social dispensation. A BI society would still be capitalist, but the principle of citizenship would be replanted securely and without discrimination in its very constitution. BI would cultivate a potent counterforce against the tendencies of our present social order to reproduce poverty, unemployment, gender division, occupational hierarchy, commodification, growthism and consumerism. As explained below, a BI system creates a natural institutional focus for the conduct of macro-economic policy exchange and the regulation of wage and price setting. The transition to the new system would call for, but could also call forth, a broad popular alliance comparable to those which accomplished earlier advances in citizenship. This progressive historic bloc would bring together a rejuvenated labour movement, feminists, Greens, Democrats, claimants' organisations and other popular forces. Once BI was in place, the bloc would be in a position to mobilise argument and pressure to push beyond basic income capitalism to a freer, more egalitarian and more solidaristic society.

During the transition phase, the existing systems of social security, national insurance and personal tax allowances and grants are phased out and replaced by a *new universal right*. Every individual member of the entire population per-manently resident within the state's jurisdiction becomes entitled to receive *a guaranteed weekly income*. This individualised BI allocation is payable independently of any of the conditions hitherto used to determine benefit eligibility – current employment status, availability for work, past employment record, income from other sources, sex,

* This section is a highly condensed summary of arguments presented at greater length in Purdy (1988).

marital/parental status, household size and type, and so on.
A birth certificate activates entitlement for each new human
infant; a death certificate extinguishes each person's claim.
Between cradle and grave the only conditions of eligibility
are permanent residence within the national territory and
the regular filing of a tax return, just as enrolment on the
electoral register is a condition of maintaining the right to
vote in elections.

BI allocations are graduated by age. Thus, until they
reach whatever is agreed to be the appropriate age of
financial majority, children receive a lower grant than
adults. Legal title to children's BI resides with the child, but,
as with current child benefit, is transferred to his or her
primary carer. Similarly, whilst the official 'retirement age'
is abolished, senior citizens become entitled to an age
supplement in addition to the universal, adult rate of BI.
Supplementary transfers are also payable to the sick,
registered disabled and expectant/nursing mothers.

BI allocations are financed out of a progressive tax levied
at a rising scale on everyone's other – earned or unearned –
income, and assigned exclusively to this purpose. Personal
taxes and transfers are thus integrated into a self-contained
system, functionally independent of other elements of public
expenditure and finance. The scales of BI and BI
supplements are set and periodically re-set at some
consensually determined 'subsistence' level. In practice,
political feasibility and financial viability dictate that initially
these scales would have to correspond to the level of income
support available to single persons under the old social
security system. Similarly, to avoid straining taxpayers'
goodwill and political credibility, the calculation of
subsistence would at first have to exclude housing costs. For
a transitional period, housing benefit would be retained as
the last means-tested vestige of the old regime.

But there is no reason why 'subsistence' should forever
remain at this initial, parsimonious standard. Once BI was
installed, it would be natural and imperative to keep the
system under continuous review through an updated,
expanded and democratic version of policy exchange.
Working to the annual schedule of budgetary control,
government, industrial organisations and other interest

associations would negotiate over incremental regearings of the mutual relationships between wages, tax rates and BI transfers. This is why it is essential that taxes and benefits should ' be fully integrated. A closed system has the overriding virtues of social transparency and fiscal discipline. In contrast to all means-tested or categorical benefit systems, BI minimises the disconnection and social distance between taxpayers and beneficiaries. Everyone is a stakeholder and all taxpayers receive a weekly reminder of the level of income available to those with no other source of financial support. At the same time, debate, negotiation and power politics become focused in a clear, informed way on the consequences of adjustments in the wage-tax-BI nexus for the rest of the economy.

Amongst the many issues likely to figure on the policy exchange agenda is the most appropriate package of supply- and demand-side remedies for any actual or anticipated labour surplus or shortage in the monetised sector of the economy. In this sector, apart from commercialised self-employment and producers' co-operatives, most work will continue to be organised on the basis of formal contracts of employment. However, under a BI system, unemployment in the old 'claimant' sense disappears. There could, of course, still be a labour surplus: taking existing wage and non-wage terms of employment as given, the total supply of hours of labour offered to the labour market could exceed the total hours demanded by employers. If so, a wider range of remedies than are feasible in contemporary society becomes eligible for consideration. In particular, an opening is created to press for 'non-growthist' solutions to the (redefined) problem of long term unemployment. These would involve a steady reduction in standard weekly, annual or lifetime hours of employment, an egalitarian redistribution of job opportunities, and the promotion of measures to reduce the toilsomeness of labour and improve the quality of working life.

Under our present social arrangements, any such programme is blocked by an intractable clutch of interlocking barriers. Capitalism contains an in-built bias towards output-expanding, rather than toil-reducing, uses of the productivity growth which its own competitive imperatives continually engender. This bias is reinforced by the compulsive pressure of the dominant culture towards an unlimited growth of private material consumption. At the same time, low paid, full time employees are obliged to work long hours to earn a living wage. And the new underclass of long term unemployed, irregularly employed or 'economically inactive' social outcasts are excluded from the privileged lifestyle enjoyed by the affluent majority.

The redistribution of hours and jobs is also inhibited by gender and occupational privilege. Men's continued gender dominance as primary, if no longer exclusive, family breadwinners, skews the sex distribution of participation in and rewards from the still pre-eminent waged sphere of social reproduction. Women, juggling with the competing demands of homes and jobs, are still for the most part compelled to choose between poverty and financial dependence as unpaid family carers. Any serious cut in the standard working week would disturb men's structural privilege under the prevailing sexual division of labour.

Similarly, within each enterprise, any across-the-board reduction in standard hours of job time threatens the positional privilege of top job-holders in the social division of labour. Suppose that busy, and often workaholic, executives, administrators, technical experts and skilled personnel were required to lower their hours of work. Their previous workload would have to be accommodated by some combination of external recruitment to senior posts, internal promotion and retraining, and downwards delegation of the more highly prized, intrinsically rewarding, responsible, self-motivating and creative types of work. But each of these adjustments would tend to dilute local monopolies of expertise and control within each internal market, and to compress the structure of occupational pay differentials.

Since BI partially decouples personal income from employment, it begins to ease each of these obstacles. Shorter working hours no longer pose a threat to subsistence earnings. The disappearance of means testing eliminates the old unemployment and poverty traps. Women's increased financial independence strikes a powerful blow against patriarchy. No one is forced to undertake menial or oppressive jobs. Relative pay levels at the lower end of the job market tend to rise and employers receive a strong incentive either to automate toilsome tasks or to reorganise the labour process so as to reduce the burden of toil. And BI encourages everyone to reconsider the balance of their time-activity profiles from a standpoint which is not so much anti-work as pro-life.

No doubt the elevation of such sensitive redistributive issues on to the agenda of policy exchange would give rise to tension and conflict. BI is no more a panacea for social ills than was the introduction of universal suffrage. What is clear, however, is that the context of an incomes policy in a BI society is quite different from the past. Since wage bargaining has to be co-ordinated with the setting of BI scales and tax rates, wage norms cease to be a temporary expedient and become a permanent fixture. And the remit of negotiators extends in principle across the entire process of social reproduction. For example, the annual round of negotiation over the terms for compliance with any proposed incomes policy pay norm might centre on RETURNS (Redistributing Employment Time and Toil for Unemployment Reduction and National Solidarity). RETURNS could take a variety of forms – reductions in systematic overtime and the standard working week, longer annual holidays, rights to sabbatical and childcare leave, job splitting, retraining schemes, lifelong access to education and the promotion of more democratic methods of work organisation and management. A centrally negotiated framework agreement on these items would provide a benchmark for bargaining agendas and priorities within each enterprise.

The choice of mechanism for securing compliance with any negotiated wage norm is a secondary matter. Tax-based incomes policies seem more consonant on general grounds with the spirit of socially regulated, basic income capitalism. Traditional enforcement procedures have been based on centralised review bodies to vet claims and settlements with the threat of legal or commercial sanctions against breaches of policy norms. Experience suggests that this kind of arrangement is replete with risks of damaging collisions between policy makers and sectional groups. The resultant confrontations generate cumulative aggravation, and constantly threaten to discredit both the policy, the government presiding over it and the general principle of macroeconomic wage regulation. Tax-based policies leave negotiators at the micro level free to reach their own decisions without direct, third party intervention. However, firms whose employees' average gross hourly earnings grow at a rate in excess of the agreed basic pay norm incur a tax penalty levied according to pre-determined rising scale on either their payroll or their profits. Employers thus receive an incentive to resist settlements above the norm, and most unions can be expected to take this into account in framing their wage claims and bargaining strategies.

A disciplined and cohesive labour movement will primarily be concerned with the total package consisting of the wage norm and the associated non-wage terms which have emerged from the process of policy exchange. Provided this package is acceptable, the deterrent effects of tax penalties should be sufficient to minimise the degree of norm violation and satisfy the conditions for preserving public confidence in the policy.

Lest this judgement be thought unduly complacent, it is important to emphasise two points. First, in a BI system, income distribution depends more on the political processes of society and less on the mobilisation of sectional economic strength. Second, BI is both a response and a further stimulus to a broader cultural shift in the pattern of human development. BI marks a decisive break with the absurd and outmoded equation of 'work' with 'employment'. Society's total reproductive work also includes home-based childcare and housework, other unpaid voluntary labour, commercial self-employment and the alternative economy of personal and communal 'ownwork' undertaken mainly for its intrinsic gratifications with little personal monetary gain. BI rebalances the attractions of waged work against these other activities and uses of time. It thereby initiates an era in which personal decisions about whether to participate in the labour market and for what proportion of the week, year and lifetime, become genuine options for everyone, and not just, as hitherto in the history of capitalism, for those with ample, private means.

A solidaristic incomes policy also encourages people to regard employment as a source of privilege. Under our present social arrangements access to the job market and to its most favoured positions of authority, status and reward, is grossly unequal. As long as the growth of output and private consumption was the overriding purpose of social reproduction, these inequalities may have been morally defensible and practically unavoidable. If so, it follows that in a society seeking to restrain its assaults on the biosphere, a realignment of social priorities is indicated: material growth should yield precedence to social justice.

Under a BI regime employment policy unfolds within a setting which renders the power relations permeating the labour market visible, and therefore transformable. Space opens up for the long haul towards a truly classless society free from *all* forms of exploitation and domination. It is not only the ownership of capital, whether as personal wealth or as means of production, which biases the distribution of advantages and burdens in society. Jobholding itself is a major source of privilege. So too are marketable skills and educational credentials. And intersecting the social cleavages based on each of these advantage-conferring assets, are divisions formed by gender, race and physical or mental disability.

The egalitarian logic of a BI regime can best be appreciated by way of a schematic contrast with unadulterated liberalism. The pure liberal ideal is a society organised so as to promote the maximum degree of freedom for each individual compatible with the preservation of a tolerable degree of social peace. This principle allows all the cross-cutting class divisions, which run like fault lines through the social formation, to flourish unchecked. The installation of BI upholds personal freedoms, but mitigates systemic inequalities by consolidating *minimum* rights for all. Thereafter, the institutional framework and cultural ethos of the BI system would facilitate (though could not guarantee), a long term transition to a social order which provides the maximum freedom for each compatible with an *equal* degree of freedom for all.

Basic Income and the Labour Movement

It is hardly necessary to point out that the project outlined in the last section runs counter to the historically evolved culture and political orientation of the organised labour movement. Specifically, to espouse BI means abandoning four commitments:

(1) to the perspective of unlimited output growth
(2) to the goal of maximum ('full') employment as this was understood in the era of the long post-war boom
(3) to the principle of social insurance with its presumption that except for certain categories of deserving persons deemed to be incapable of participating in monetised work activities, income-entitlements should, on average and over the course of a lifetime, be *earned*
(4) to the pre-eminence of waged labour, whether as a source of income, power and social distinction, or as a source of personal identity and purpose.

It is also probable that many trade unionists and labour movement activists will be receptive to the kinds of objections to Basic Income which will be vigorously peddled by the New Right. It will be suggested:

(5) that an unconditional minimum income guarantee will encourage parasitism, deplete the supply of labour to the monetised economy, and undermine the work ethic.
(6) that it is unfair and socially divisive to pay BI allocations to both the idle and the industrious alike.
(7) that it is 'wasteful' to pay universal transfer incomes indiscriminately to both rich and poor regardless of *individual* needs and circumstances.

The first two of these points have been dealt with earlier. Neither unrestrained and unreconstructed economic growth nor the provision of sufficient 'full-time' paid jobs for all who might conceivably wish to take them, can any longer be regarded as desirable, or even feasible, objectives. As regards the third point, there are several reasons for jettisoning the once radical, but now defunct, principle of social insurance. An employment-based insurance system necessarily discriminates against those who do not participate in waged labour, or who participate only intermittently or on a 'part-time' basis. It also fails to provide for the financial needs of 'full-time', low paid family breadwinners, including nowadays large numbers of single parents responsible for primary childcare – most of them women. More generally, contributory insurance benefits are too inflexible to cope with new forms of social deprivation, or with changes in public perceptions of deprivation. In a dynamic society the safety net of secondary income support, which has to underly the national insurance system, tends to be supplemented by the growth of new, non-contributory benefits designed to alleviate new types of poverty.

Since universal, non-contributory benefits are expensive, the supplementary system of income support is inherently vulnerable to the incursion of means-testing. But means-testing complicates the social security system, inflates its administrative and policing costs, tarnishes its public reputation, and, by helping to diminish benefit take-up rates, reduces its effectiveness. Furthermore, once means-testing is seen to be an endemic feature of social security, opponents of universality can lay claim to both realism and compassion in demanding that the entire system be reconstructed in the (spuriously precise) name of 'targeting' benefits towards those whose needs are greatest.

Finally, in practice, though not, it seems, in either official or popular belief, the national insurance contributions of 'regular' employees do not 'pay for' their *future* benefit entitlements such as state retirement pensions. They are simply an alternative, and *regressive*, form of personal income taxation, levied at whatever rate is necessary to ensure that the National Insurance Fund's *current* revenues equal its *current* outgoings.

Just as National Insurance has now outlived its useful social purpose, so too, though over a longer timespan, we need to look forward to the gradual supersession of the traditional system of employment (point 4). Of course, society will continue to need a labour market in order to harness and allocate the time, effort and skills of human beings to the public, monetised aspects of social reproduction. But it will become increasingly anachronistic and intolerable to maintain a rigid gearing between society's arrangements for getting its work done on the one hand, and the distribution of income, power and esteem on the other.

Point (5) expresses the fear that the introduction of BI at a minimum subsistence level will induce labour and/or other factors of production to withdraw from the monetised economy on such a scale as to bring about either total economic collapse, or, less drastically, an unacceptable, though finite, fall in measured GDP. A full examination of this issue is beyond the scope of this essay, but two general observations are pertinent. First, if we consider *individuals* as distinct from *households*, those whose *sole* source of income is their BI allocation, will still have a lower income than anyone who performs any amount of paid work, whatever the tax rate on earnings. Both the traditional principle of 'lesser eligibility' and the incentive to financial self-betterment will remain intact.

Second, depending on personal preferences, BI will prompt most 'regular' employees to opt for shorter weekly, annual and lifetime hours of paid work. Other things being equal, this marginal contraction in the supply of hours offered to the labour market, will reduce the prevailing labour surplus. In these circumstances, one of the tasks of a democratically negotiated employment policy will be to set the gearing between BI scales, personal tax rates and wage levels in such a way that the monetised economy is not subjected to a persistent labour *shortage*. Doubtless, like most other tasks of macroeconomic policy, this will be a difficult balancing act, but surely not an impossible one.

This leaves the last two ethical objections to BI (points (6) and (7)). We should certainly be concerned if some people elect to live in impoverished idleness. It is important to insist not only that all who *wish* to do so should enjoy the *right* to contribute to society's reproductive work; but also that all who *can* work, *ought* to. Apart from the fact that paid work is bound up with the distribution of social advantages, any kind of work is an integral part of a rounded human experience. That is why the prevailing inequality in the social division of labour is so repugnant. Equally, in so far as work is toilsome, the burden should be fairly shared out. The critical question is how to ensure compliance with this general precept. Generalised, legally enforcible work obligations, backed ultimately by the coercive power of the state, would be alien to the libertarian spirit of BI. They would also be anachronistic in an age when the protestant work ethic is in retreat. Moreover, if we reject the authoritarian and punitive impulse behind 'workfare', and if we take an appropriately catholic view of what activities can legitimately be counted as contributing to society's reproductive work, it is hard to see how any system of labour compulsion could be effectively administered and invigilated.

We are, therefore, left with economic incentives and internalised moral norms as the best ways of discouraging parasitism. If, nevertheless, some people remain impervious to all incentives and moral pressure, then that, in the last analysis, is their right in a society which values personal freedom. Under a BI system this right is theoretically available to everyone without distinction. Moreover, as we have just seen, there is no reason to suppose that the number of people who actually exercise the right to be idle at any one time will seriously impair social reproduction. In these conditions, as often happens in human affairs, the cost to society of carrying a minority of passengers is lower than the cost of attempting some draconian method of getting everyone to pull their weight.

That BI is paid to rich and poor alike is the logical corollary of establishing a truly universal, non-means-tested transfer system. It will always be possible for the opponents of BI to devise some hypothetical, selective and means-tested system, which offers greater immediate gains for the very poorest income groups at a lesser total cost in taxes levied, provided one is prepared to swallow the assumption that benefit take-up rates approach 100 per cent. However, what really matters in comparing different transfer regimes is not their immediate distributive impact, but their long term transformatory potential. A BI regime establishes a clear focus and channel for all society's classes, disadvantaged and privileged alike, to press their claims and counter-claims on the distribution of resources, roles and power. Political argument and negotiation revolve around the proportions between BI, taxes, wages and property incomes, and the associated configuration of the social division of labour. Strong economic and political constraints will continue to inhibit egalitarian and emancipatory achievements. But at least a BI regime creates an environment congenial to their pursuit.

Not the least of the virtues of the BI project is that it brings together two levels of discourse which rarely connect, and are often at odds. At one level it addresses individual human beings in all their singularity. At the other, it deals with the totality of relationships which, *pace* Mrs Thatcher, some of us persist in calling society as a whole. The individual person has been conspicuously absent from the socialist and labour movement tradition, almost anathematised as a category of thought. BI enables the movement to repair this deficiency and to contest the neo-liberal attempt to monopolise the ground of individual freedom and rights, but without abandoning a proper concern for the inescapably collective aspects of social existence.

By embracing the BI project, the movement also reconnects with its own historic traditions. The advance of citizenship began with the centuries-long struggle to establish the supremacy of Parliament over Crown and to shift the basis of political representation from property to persons. It is now time to learn the lessons of the struggles in our own century to build a welfare state; and to reformulate the claims of citizenship in preparation for a new wave of social transformation.

References

C. Crouch, *The Politics of Industrial Relations*, 2nd edition, Fontana 1981.

P. Devine, *Democracy and Economic Planning*, Polity Press 1988.

T.H. Marshall, *Citizenship and Social Class*, Cambridge University Press 1950.

K. Middlemas, *Politics in Industrial Society*, Deutsch 1979,

L. Panitch, *Social Democracy and Industrial Militancy*, Cambridge University Press 1976.

L. Panitch, 'Trade Unions and the Capitalist State', *New Left Review* 125, Jan-Feb 1981.

D.L. Purdy, *Social Power and the Labour Market*, Macmillan 1988.

Ruth.Lister

Social Benefits – Priorities for Redistribution

Seven out of ten people live in households receiving some form of social benefit; social security accounts for about 30 per cent of public expenditure. Inside the Conservative Party, it has been an important terrain over which the battle between traditional One Nation Tories and the newer Thatcherite breed has been fought. In the post-war reconstruction, social security was seen as a central plank in the building of a fairer society. Yet it is many years since it can be said to have been a vital issue for the Left. The sheer complexity of much of the social security system, combined with a perception that it is an issue only for 'the poor', has relegated social security to the second division of left politics. Indeed, social policy as a whole has been down-graded politically. But, as Malcolm Wicks (1987b) has argued, 'social policies are not just about service provision and benefit regulations, but rather, decisively shaping the structure of society, its values and therefore its future'.

Alan Walker (1983, p 61) has argued that the view that the welfare state:

> now requires only minor adjustments (the fine-tuning of heaven) has contributed to the removal of the issues of poverty and social security from the radical political agenda. In fact the battle for socialist welfare has yet to be won.

If the battle is to be won (or even waged), the welfare state must be reclaimed as central to the socialist project of the creation of a just society based on egalitarian and democratic principles. This is an issue to which I will return at the end of this chapter, after considering what a realistic socialist benefits policy might look like. But first such a policy needs to be set in the context of current government policies; Labour's alternative as presented to the electorate in 1987; and the inability of either to tackle the central failings of the social security system.

Towards a Residual Welfare State

If asked to sum up Conservative social security policy in one word, many people would probably answer 'cuts'. Cuts there have certainly been: according to the House of Commons Library, prior to the implementation of the Social Security Act 1986, a cumulative total of over £11 billion had already been sliced off the social security budget since 1979. This has been masked by an overall *increase* in spending, largely as a result of the growth in the number of, especially unemployed, claimants. The Social Security Act 1986, which was implemented in April 1988, involves further cuts both in the short and longer term; child benefit has now been frozen and further cuts, particularly in child benefit and housing benefit, can be expected.

This litany of cuts, at a time when massive sums have been redistributed to the better-off through reductions in taxation, is bad enough and has contributed to a deterioration in the living standards of the poor relative to those of the rest of society. But linked to this policy of cuts, and of more fundamental significance, has been the way in which social security policy has become less and less a force for social integration and more and more a force for social division. This has manifested itself in a number of ways. (For a more detailed account see Walker and Walker 1987, and Lister 1989.)

First, and perhaps foremost, has been the continual and growing emphasis on 'targeting help on those in greatest need' – a euphemism for means-testing and confining benefits to the poorest who can then all too easily be branded as failures, while the rest of us have less of a stake in defending the social security system.

A second central theme, which has come increasingly to the fore since the 1987 election, is that of a reduction in the role of the central state as 'the next step in the long evolutionary march of the welfare state ... away from dependence towards independence' (Moore 1987). Private provision, particularly in the field of pensions (which is in fact subsidised by public tax reliefs), is being encouraged so that public/private welfare will become an increasingly important source of social division. The contraction of benefits provided for young people and the replacement of supplementary benefit single payment grants by discretionary loans under the cash-limited social fund have both been justified as means of reducing 'dependence on the benefit culture'. In fact, what we are seeing is a shift from public to private forms of dependence as claimants are forced to turn to family, charities and money-lenders. More people are also likely to turn to local authorities for assistance. And another element in the reduction of the role of the central state has been the transfer of responsibility for the administration of certain benefits to local authorities (housing benefit) and to employers (sickness and maternity benefits).

Behind the rhetoric of self-reliance and personal independence, the social security system's control functions are being strengthened. The rules governing the entitlement of the unemployed to benefit have been tightened significantly and commentators such as Joe Rogaly of the *Financial Times* and Melanie Phillips of the *Guardian* have predicted further moves down the road to some form of workfare system. Tackling the so-called 'why work? syndrome' has been a dominant goal from the beginning, as has been the crackdown on 'fraud and abuse' – in both cases with a profound impact on social security policy and administration. 'Blaming the victim' is a well worn method for driving a wedge between benefit claimants and those in work. At the same time, the black community has been the subject of increasing control as links between immigration and benefit status have been strengthened.

Conservative social policy has been summed up well by Malcolm Wicks (1987a, p 9) as a

> move towards a residual welfare state, characterised by increasing inequality, deepening poverty, greater reliance on the means test, a growing role for the private market and consequently social division and conflict.

A central part of the task facing a future Labour government will be to reverse these damaging and dangerous trends.

Labour's Limited Anti-Poverty Package

Alan Walker (1983, p 51) argued after the 1983 election that:

> Labour's social policies do *not* start from the position that a
> fundamental change is required in the structure of the welfare
> state, in particular a change in the relationship between clients
> and claimants and those who administer benefits and services.

A similar point was made more recently by Robin Cook,
Shadow Social Security Secretary:

> A key element in our failure to resist the Fowler offensive
> against social security was the impossibility of mobilising the
> vast army of claimants to defend a DHSS by which they felt
> oppressed rather than supported. Labour urgently needs new
> models of welfare provision which are accessible and
> responsive.
>
> (Cook 1987)

The 1987 Manifesto did not provide such models. Instead, it
offered, in the words of Roy Hattersley (1987a), 'a very
limited anti-poverty package'. The limitations of this
package would have been understandable had it been part of
a longer term strategy with clear objectives. But it was not.
Even the earlier policy statement to the 1986 Conference
had been depressingly vague about longer term social
security policy. However it did, at least, set out some longer
term objectives, namely 'to end completely the present
means-tested system of benefits' and to provide 'benefits for
women in their own right'. What was lacking was any sense
of what the path from short term reforms to longer term
aims would look like and of how exactly the aims would be
achieved. Nor were any clear targets set for future benefit
levels. Moreover, there was a strong implication that future
progress would be dependent on economic growth. Insofar
as there was a policy for redistribution, the party shrank
from spelling out its full implications to the electorate,
thereby damaging the credibility of both its social security
and taxation policies.

It is ironic that election post-mortems on both the Right
and the Left of the party appear to have led to the
conclusion that Labour must reassert the priority of

economic over social policy, as if the latter had somehow
seriously challenged the former. As will be argued below,
the development of social security policy has been
consistantly undermined by its subordination to economic
priorities and Labour's pre-1987 Election statement of
policy was no exception. While *Social Justice and Economic
Efficiency*, the first report of Labour's Policy Review, does
not show any signs of an explicit reversal of these priorities,
it does at least recognise that

> economic strength requires the firm foundation of a fair social
> policy to ensure every member of society contributes their full
> potential.
>
> (Labour Party 1988, p 17)

The chapter on economic equality begins to provide a
framework for reform but there is still a considerable
amount of work to be done to develop the 'clear,
comprehensive and practical strategy of achieving our social
objectives' (p 21) that it promises.

The Indefensible Status Quo

It is perhaps inevitable that during a period when it has been
essential to defend a benefits system under attack, there has
been little time or energy for developing proposals for
radical reform of that system. But there has always been a
danger that defence against attack might be interpreted as
defence of the status quo as a good thing in itself. It is time
that the labour movement went on the offensive, exposing
the flaws in the social security system which have been
aggravated by the Fowler reforms, and campaigning for
policies that will tackle those flaws rather than simply paper-
ing over them.

Criticisms of the operation of the social security system
can be grouped under four broad headings:

Increased reliance on means-testing

In 1948, 1 in 33 of the population was dependent on
means-tested national assistance. Instead of this safety net
withering away, as envisaged by Beveridge, it has enmeshed
more and more people, as the national insurance scheme has
failed to provide adequate security. By 1987, more than 1 in

7 of the population was living on supplementary benefit, that is over 8 million people. Dependence on supplementary benefit (renamed income support in April 1988) has accelerated in recent years, partly as a result of cuts in the already inadequate national insurance benefits and partly because of the inability of the unemployment benefit scheme to cope with mass long term and recurrent unemployment. Thus, while in the early 1960s fewer than a fifth of the unemployed relied entirely on supplementary benefit, the proportion is now about two thirds.

When account is also taken of the working poor, it has been officially estimated that, by 1983, about 14 million people were living in households receiving one of the main means-tested benefits (Hansard 1986). This reflects the fact that, whichever party has been in power, means-tested benefits have all too often been the 'cheap but ineffective response to poverty' (Berhoud, 1987). The result is a social security system which is complex, stigmatising and divisive and which fails in its objective of targeting help on those in need because large numbers of those in need fail to claim the benefits to which they are entitled. Take-up is especially low among ethnic minority communities; and the definition of public funds as the key means-tested benefits effectively excludes from entitlement those immigrants subject to the 'recourse to public funds' rule, and creates uncertainty and anxiety for others.

At the same time, means-tested benefits serve to trap people into poverty as increases in other income mean reductions in benefit. Under the post-April 1988 system, it is estimated on the basis of 1987/88 tax rates that over half a million low paid workers face an effective marginal tax rate of over 70p in the pound (Hansard 1987). Means-tested benefits are also against the interests of women living with men, as entitlement is based on the couple's income and ignores the possibility that the income might not be shared fairly.

Second class treatment
It is the income support scheme that has come under most criticism for the poor service that it provides for claimants. Indeed, the DSS's own *Handbook for Good*

Practice speaks of the 'two nations' of supplementary and contributory benefit offices. The strains on the system, as too few staff try to cope with too many claimants, have further reduced the quality of service provided. Many claimants experience the DSS as an alien, hostile bureaucracy. As one quoted in the GLC Claimants Commission Report observed 'the system could do with a little humanity in its working' (GLC, 1985). In the words of the former Union Coalition for Social Security, of which the DSS trade unions were members:

> the squalor, the sense of dereliction and fortification of many offices simply confirms a social view of 'claimants' as a marginal and undeserving group of people and by association this perception rubs off on the staff who provide the service.
>
> (UCSS 1987)

Inadequate benefit levels

Benefit levels are too low to meet claimants' basic needs, particularly in the case of families with children. For example, the income support rate for an under 11 year old child amounts to just over £1.67 a day, on top of which 93p a day is paid as a family premium regardless of the number of children. Even a retired senior DHSS official concluded of the supplementary benefit scheme that

> it is hard for many, and impossible for some – particularly families with dependent children on the basic rates – to maintain reasonably decent living standards for any appreciable length of time without help from other sources. For them life on SB is a bleak struggle to make ends meet.
>
> (Beltram 1984, p 189)

In the past single payments went some way to helping families eke out their meagre benefit. Now many will be living semi-permanently below the inadequate minimum set by parliament as they repay their social fund loans out of their weekly benefit. Already, cuts in single payments have meant that many claimants can no longer look to the DSS for help with essentials such as beds, bedding, cookers and household equipment; these, it appears, are no longer recognised as essentials (Cohen and Tarpey, 1988).

Sexism and racism
Despite the eradication of direct sex discrimination, thanks to an EEC Directive, too many benefits still reflect assumptions about, and perpetuate the dependence on men of, married and cohabiting women. Response to women's changing economic and social position has been slow and grudging and there is still scant recognition of many women's aspirations for autonomy and financial independence.

Similarly, little effort has been made to meet the needs of claimants for whom English is not their first language or to take account of cultural differences in the rules governing entitlement. Moreover, as noted above, the right of immigrants to social security is dependent on their immigration status which has given rise to passport checking on a wide scale. And, as Hilary Arnott has observed:

> the prevalence of passport-checking is linked to the racist attitude displayed by some DHSS officers, as evidenced in the Policy Studies Institute's tempered observations: 'Since racial prejudice is so widespread in society, it is not surprising that it should be found among local office staff'. All this cannot inspire black people with the confidence that they will be treated correctly and given their rightful entitlement.
>
> (Arnott 1987, p 66)

The Economy Rules OK
These long-standing flaws in the social security scheme reflect two fundamental and related constraints upon it: the primacy of economic over social policy, and social security's control functions, particularly with regard to the labour market. These co-exist with its welfare functions.

Alan Walker (1983, p 45) has criticised the division between economic and social policy and the consequent public burden model of welfare that has characterised the thinking of both Conservative and Labour governments:

> Economic hegemony creates a false division between economic and social policy which, in turn, reinforces the ascendancy of the one over the other. In fact, economic policies are based on

implicit or explicit assumptions about the sort of society and
social relations that a government is trying to create or
reproduce. Economic policies imply a set of social values and
distributional goals ... and are therefore also social policies.

It is all too often forgotten that economic growth is but a
means to an end. It is important that socialists are clear as to
what that end is and that it then informs economic policy
rather than vice versa. To quote Alan Walker (1982, p 29)
again,

> socialist social policy would reintegrate the social and economic
> spheres and replace economic hegemony with social need as the
> main determinant of both social and economic priorities.

For too many years the poor have been asked to put their
faith in the crock of gold at the end of economic growth.
But, as Roy Hattersley (1987b) has argued,

> all the evidence confirms that the idea that the poor are dragged
> to prosperity by the rich – the 'trickle down' theory – is
> sophistry invented in an attempt to justify vast disparities of
> wealth and income.

The social security system has helped to soften the impact
of the market economy and the inequalities of the wages
system, but it has never been permitted seriously to
challenge them nor the ideology which underpins them.
Thus, from the start, the contributory principle has been
central, and private and occupational welfare have been
encouraged and subsidised for those who can afford them,
and earnings-related benefits, which mirror the inequalities
of the market, are now well entrenched.

While greater emphasis has been placed on the control
functions of social security by the present government, as
Pete Alcock (1985) has noted, 'under capitalism, social
security has always been a weapon for labour discipline'.
Control has been exercised not only through the eligibility
conditions attached to benefits for the unemployed but also
through the level at which those benefits have been set. The
social security system discriminates systematically against
the longer-term unemployed and the old Poor Law 'less

eligibility' principle (often translated into the language of 'why work?', and (primarily male) work incentives) is a more important influence on benefit levels for the unemployed than is need. Similarly, as noted above, the social security system perpetuates the economic dependence of women upon men, echoing the old principle of the family wage, and acts as an arm of internal immigration control.

The contradictions between the welfare and control functions of the social security system are experienced by claimants in various ways – from the whole ethos of the delivery of benefit, with its greater emphasis on the control of fraud and abuse than on ensuring full entitlement, through to the administration of particular rules such as those governing 'voluntary' unemployment, cohabitation and the rights of immigrant claimants. It would be unrealistic to expect such contradictions to be resolved overnight, but if progress is to be made to a socialist benefits system, they must be explicitly recognised.

A Broader Strategy for Redistribution

The extent to which social security is tied into the wages system is one reason why social security policy cannot be developed in splendid isolation. Socialism cannot be built in one sector; without a fairer wages structure and some form of minimum wage, progress on radical reform of social security is likely to be limited. Similarly, as David Piachaud (1987, p 60) has argued,

> It is futile to think about, let alone plan, social security and income redistribution without thinking about the distribution of work. 'Picking up the pieces' is no substitute for tackling the causes of inequality – as Humpty Dumpty learned to his cost.

Nor can a social security system ignore changes in the patterns of work.

The burden of tackling poverty and inequality cannot fall on the social security system alone, as the first report from Labour's Policy Review recognised. To take a concrete example: although means-tested support for the working poor through FIS and now family credit has been deliberately developed as a cheap alternative to an adequate child benefit scheme, it would be extremely expensive to replace such support solely by means of an increase in child benefit. Instead, it will also require tackling the low pay which is subsidised by these means-tested benefits, and improving access to good jobs for mothers. This in turn means improving childcare services and parental employment rights. Such an approach is also essential in tackling gender inequalities and the sexual division of labour which underpins them, and in facilitating the integration of domestic and employment responsibilities.

A socialist benefits policy must also take account of the social division of welfare identified by Richard Titmuss 25 years ago. Thus it is the interaction of the social security and other public welfare systems with the parallel occupational and fiscal systems of welfare that determines the overall distribution of income, opportunities and life chances. The rest of this chapter is therefore predicated on the assumption that reform of social security is an integral part of a broader strategy for redistribution that embraces:

a fairer wages structure including, in particular, a statutory minimum wage and more effective equal pay laws;
a fairer distribution of paid and unpaid domestic work between women and men;
an expansion of employment opportunities and improved access to employment for those groups currently disadvantaged in the labour market;
improved services, including those designed to facilitate the combining of paid employment with the care of children or other dependents;
investment in housing and insulation programmes which, as well as improving living conditions and tackling fuel poverty, is to be commended on grounds of conservation and job creation;
genuinely progressive taxation of income and wealth, including independent taxation of women and men.

Having set out the broader context for a socialist benefits policy, the next priority is to establish the principles upon which it should be based.

Values and Strategic Principles

Debate about social security policy needs to be rescued from the clutches of the technocrats (for whom there still remains an important role) and re-established as central to the building of Labour's new Jerusalem. This means going back to first principles so as to establish the purposes of a socialist social security system and the values that inform it. As David Blunkett and Bernard Crick (1988) have argued:

> everything we aim for: short term repairs, middle-term new building and long term redistribution of income and work, must be guided and informed by our values as well as our ultimate aims.

Richard Titmuss (1968, p 116) pointed the way two decades ago: 'socialist social policies,' he maintained, are 'totally different in their purposes, philosophy and attitudes to people from Conservative social policies. They are (or should be) pre-eminently about *equality, freedom and social integration*' (my emphasis). Linked to the concept of social integration is that of *social citizenship*: the acceptance of the right of all members of society not just to basic economic welfare and security but also 'to live the life of a civilised human being according to the standards prevailing in the society' (Marshall, 1950, p 11). Important to the notion of social citizenship is the way in which people are treated. Echoing Tawney, Nicholas Deakin has argued that a social policy based on the value of *democracy* 'would have something important to contribute about institutions and their responsiveness to the needs of their customers' (Deakin, 1987, p 188). It would also begin to address the powerlessness experienced by social security claimants.

A bridge between these abstract values and a set of strategic principles to guide social security policy is provided by what the *Faith in the City* report called 'the spirit of collective obligation' (ACCUPA, 1985, para 9.45). At a time when the virtues of self-reliance and independence are constantly being extolled by government ministers, it is important to reassert the notion of social or collective responsibility based on an understanding of our mutual *inter*dependence. This understanding lies at the heart of a socialist social security policy. It points to a social security system that performs a number of functions:

> the provision of genuine security against risks such as unemployment or disability and against contingencies such as old age;

the sharing of responsibility for the costs of raising the next generation and of caring for dependents so that these do not fall solely on the shoulders of individual families and in particular individual women;

the redistribution of income (in conjunction with the tax system) along a number of dimensions including: from better-off to worse-off; waged to unwaged; healthy to sick; those without to those with children; men to women and over the life-cycle of the individual.

In the words of the Director-General of the ILO:

in the long term social security has much more far-reaching objectives than the mere fight against poverty. Social security must aim at the maintenance of the level and quality of life and at the strengthening of the individual feeling of security. Increased prosperity would not justify the progressive dismantling of social security: quite the contrary. Besides, new fears emerge as technology evolves. Changes in individual and family behaviour create new requirements for social solidarity ... it will not be enough merely to respond to needs as they arise; it will be necessary to prevent the risks from arising: hence the importance of preventive measures in the future development of social security systems.

(ILO 1984, p viii)

The fight against poverty remains a priority, but as Neil Kinnock (1984) has noted, we 'need to revise our attitudes to the welfare state and gear it much more to the permanent eradication of poverty instead of the relief of poverty'. By placing the fight against poverty in the context of social security's broader aims, the dangers of the political marginalisation of claimants are reduced. This is an important strategic reason for setting as a central goal of socialist social security policy a progressive reduction in means-testing. Means-tested benefits, confined to the poor, isolate them so that the rest of society no longer has a real stake in defending and improving what is becoming an increasingly stigmatised system associated with failure.

More controversially, a socialist benefits policy that treats all claimants as equals will have to abandon the contributory principle. By the same token that contribution tests establish the right of certain groups and individuals to benefit, so they exclude other, often particularly vulnerable, groups and individuals. The upholding of the contributory principle requires that the alternative benefits provided for those excluded are in some way inferior. Supporters of the contributory principle used to argue that it protected benefits against cuts, an argument that has clearly been disproved by the present government. Now it is claimed that the principle legitimates the benefits in the public mind. But it is not clear that it is the presence of contribution tests, rather than the absence of means tests, that is the key element in terms of public acceptability. And again the legitimation of one type of benefit implies the inferior status of other kinds.

While it would be unrealistic to call for the immediate abolition of contribution tests, the Labour Party must reconsider its longer-term commitment to the contributory principle. There are signs that this is, at last, beginning to happen. The social security section in *Social Justice and Economic Efficiency*, having endorsed the insurance principle, goes on to argue that

> social insurance must allow for those denied the opportunity to earn an income high enough or for long enough to build up an adequate contribution record ... Where necessary, payment of basic benefit should not turn on contributions but on qualification for the conditions it covers – old age, unemployment, maternity or disability.
>
> (Labour Party 1988, p 19)

In praising the insurance principle the document could, effectively, start the process of burying it.

The principles of equality and social citizenship also mean no discrimination in either the rules governing benefit or in its administration. Everyone must have equal access to and treatment from the system regardless of race, gender, marital status and sexual orientation. Nor must one claimant group receive inferior treatment to another, which means that the systematic discrimination against the long term unemployed, which condemns them to a lower standard of living, must be ended. Elimination of racial discrimination will require an examination of how the connection between benefit entitlement and immigration status can be severed;

and a 'rigorous' examination of possible ethnocentrism in all aspects of the social security system is required, together with the 'clearest and most unequivocal statement of intent to root out racism, conscious or not, from the social security system' (Gordon and Newnham, 1985, p 74). Similarly, if a socialist social security policy is also to be feminist, it is not enough simply to outlaw direct discrimination against women. The system must respect and enhance the autonomy of individual women and men. This means that another goal should be that the individual and not the couple should be the basic unit of entitlement. This goal, contained in the 1986 policy statement, is absent from the first report of the Policy Review; nor is any mention made of the need to tackle racism in the social security system, although it is expected that thought will be given to these issues during the next stage of the review.

The treatment received by claimants in practice depends not just on the rules but on the quality of the administration of benefit. At the most basic level this means enough well trained and well paid staff to provide a good quality service in a decent environment. A system which provides clear rights with the minimum complexity is another important element – although the vision of the totally simple system is probably something of a chimera. More fundamentally, it requires a shift in emphasis in the culture of benefits administration away from the preoccupation with the control of fraud and abuse to a greater concern for ensuring everyone receives the benefit to which they are entitled. In fact, a well staffed service is the best form of prevention against abuse as the report of a NACRO working party has pointed out (NACRO, 1986).

At the same time, a more democratic system would need to be more responsive to the views of those it serves, and to devise forums that enable those views to be expressed. There are inevitably limitations on the degree of 'user control' possible in a centralised system like social security. But there should be scope for some element of consumer say in how the service is delivered at local level. While the social security section of *Social Justice and Economic Efficiency* calls for a more 'user-friendly' DHSS, it does not take on board the difficult question of how to apply the principle of democratic participation, identified in the 'Consumers and the Community' chapter. It is essential that work be done on this question during the next stage of the review.

Last but by no means least is the question of the level of benefit. Whilst the determination of that level is, in part, a technical matter, it first involves the more fundamental conceptualisation of human need. Marshall's notion of social citizenship, referred to earlier, implies a responsibility to ensure not only that basic physical needs are met but also those social and cultural needs determined by the wider society. Broad support has been expressed for the principle that 'to keep out of poverty people must have an income which enables them to participate in the life of the community' (SBC, 1978). This principle is endorsed in *Social Justice and Economic Efficiency*, which states that the party 'will seek help in researching an adequate income' (Labour Party, 1988, p 20). Drawing on the work of Peter Townsend and the London Weekend Television *Poor Britain* survey, Meghnad Desai has suggested that 'an increase in supplementary benefit level of between a third and a half is obviously needed – needed in the way need is defined by the citizens of Britain, by the community' (Desai 1986, p 18).

In practice, a more sophisticated analysis is required that takes account of, for instance, the needs of children relative to adults which, the evidence suggests, the current system underestimates. The establishment of a participation standard as a goal also raises a number of political questions concerning the relationship of social security to the wages system (as discussed above) that will need to be addressed. These include first the role of earnings-relation. It is arguable that there should be no role for earnings-related benefits, which mirror market inequalities, in a socialist system. But, as noted above, earnings-relation is now well entrenched and it is probably unrealistic to argue for its immediate removal. But it should be possible to argue for a diminution of its role, with greater emphasis placed on adequate flat rate benefits. And in the context of a fairer wages structure some degree of earnings-relation would be less problematic. It is thus dispiriting to see that the Policy Review is asking 'to what extent should earnings-related supplements be restored to unemployment or other insurance benefits?' (Labour Party 1988, p 20).

An even more fundamental issue is that of the relationship between incomes in and out of work, especially for the unemployed. The belief that those in work should be better off than those out of work runs deep in our society and is not confined to those on the Right. Might an attempt to counter these beliefs head on, in the name of meeting need, lead to a backlash against the unemployed? Again, the answer lies outside the benefits system in measures to eradicate low pay as well as improve child benefit. With a statutory minimum wage it would be easier to set benefit levels at a similar level. In the meantime there is scope for doing more to meet the needs of the unemployed by, at the very least, providing them with the same benefits as other claimants, without challenging the 'less eligibility' principle head on.

Models for Reform

Before outlining a model for reform of social security based on the above principles, it is necessary to explain briefly why other models, which would scrap the existing system and start again from scratch, have been rejected. Broadly speaking, two alternative approaches can be identified: negative income tax (NIT) and basic income.

NIT combines tax and benefits in one system, paying benefit to those below the tax threshold and taking tax from those above it. It has a superficial attraction in its relative simplicity; it is often believed that, by integrating the tax and benefit systems, it resolves the problems created by their current lack of co-ordination. In fact, it aggravates the worst of these problems – the poverty trap – by taking means-testing to its logical conclusion and making it more efficient. By the same token, it provides a more blatant subsidy of low pay and would therefore depress wages at the bottom. While it would be simpler than the current system, the price would be less flexibility in responding to the fluctuating circumstances of those on low incomes. It would also be difficult to base NIT on the individual rather than the couple as the unit. In short, it is incompatible with the principles outlined above and has nothing to offer socialists or feminists. Technocratic magic wands provide only illusory gains.

Whilst NIT schemes have been favoured by the Right, basic income draws support from across the political spectrum. In its pure form, it would provide an unconditional tax-free cash payment to each individual in place of existing benefits. In practice, most basic income supporters have conceded that modifications would be necessary to reduce the cost, at the expense of some of the simplicity and freedom from conditions which are the scheme's main attractions.

Basic income would be compatible with the principles outlined here, but the way in which principles are implemented has to take some account of political realities. It is debatable whether a social security system which deliberately 'challenges the link between income and wages' (Sheffield City Council, 1987) would command the necessary political support once it was clear that that was what it was doing. An attempt to use the social security system to challenge directly the primacy of the wages system could well misfire, if public opinion was not ready for it. The result would probably be either a basic income in a much diluted form, or one set so low that it left those totally dependent on it worse off than now. There is, nevertheless, a case for leaving basic income on the table as a possible longer-term option (see Chapter 2).

The model proposed here would be compatible with any future move towards a basic income scheme. Its goal is a comprehensive system of non-means-tested, non-contributory benefits, paying the same level of benefit to different claimant groups. Each individual would receive benefit in his or her own right. Extra would be paid to help meet certain costs such as children, housing and those created by disability. Unlike basic income, benefit would not be paid indiscriminately but would be 'targeted' on the basis of those contingencies associated with inability to support oneself through paid employment.

It would build on the present system of contributory and non-contributory benefits by extending the contingencies covered and gradually harmonising them into one system of non-contributory benefits as contribution tests were phased out. (If, as seems likely, contribution tests were replaced by some form of presence or residence test, as exist under the non-contributory scheme at present, these must not make it more difficult for immigrants to claim than under the contributory system, nor must they be applied in a racist manner.) Once benefit levels were harmonised at the contributory benefit level (leaving open the question of whether a short and long-term rate were retained), they would be raised gradually to a level that made dependence on income support unnecessary and enabled recipients to play a full part in society. Assuming a fairer tax system, the benefits that provided income maintenance (as opposed to meeting costs) should then be taxable.

This is not the place for a detailed blueprint, and indeed a number of questions still need to be resolved, but some of the main elements of the proposed reform are sketched in briefly. The first step is to ensure that those contingencies already covered are done so on an equitable basis. Thus, the present patchwork of benefits for those with disabilities would be replaced by a comprehensive disability income scheme that did not discriminate according to the cause of disability (Disability Alliance, 1987). This should also lead to a widening of eligibility for invalid care allowance.

Unemployment benefit would be extended to cover those out of work for more than twelve months and would be paid at the same rate as other benefits. Some socialists argue that the unemployed should not be subject to an availability for work test. This is understandable in the current context when the rule is often used to push the unemployed into low paid work with poor conditions. But, as Esam and his colleagues have argued:

> implicit in the idea of unemployment is some kind of test of willingness to participate in the labour market. It would have to be a condition of receiving benefit that the individual was willing to work should a suitable job be available.
>
> (Esam, Good and Middleton 1985, p 55)

In the context of a positive employment policy and a statutory minimum wage, the availability for work rule would simply reflect the reciprocal rights and obligations integral to a socialist benefits model.

The main contingency not covered by the present system is parenthood. The inability of one parent or the sole parent to earn because of the care of children is an important cause of poverty, particularly among women. Any benefit introduced to cover this contingency would have to be combined with an extension of and improvement in child-care facilities at home. And to facilitate shared responsibility for parenting in two parent families and the combining of paid employment and child care, there should be provision for paid parental leave (in addition to improved maternity benefits and leave), and to cover parents who have to take time off to care for a sick child (see Hurstfield 1987, for a description of the Swedish system). Consideration would need to be given to whether special provision would be necessary for lone parents, even if only as an interim measure. More generally, the benefits system has to be modified to accommodate part-time work. One approach gaining support is the provision of benefit on a pro-rata basis according to the number of hours worked, although this might cause problems in the case of unemployment benefit which would need to be resolved.

The final group for whom there is no adequate provision at present is young people. There needs to be a proper statutory allowance covering young people in education or training after school-leaving age.

Turning to costs: disability costs would be covered by the disability income scheme. As regards children, European experience suggests that

> as a first step towards developing a coherent policy on child support, it is essential to establish the costs associated with children. Equally necessary is debate, followed by explicit decisions, as to how the costs of children should be apportioned between individuals and the state, parents and non-parents.
>
> (Walker, Lawson and Townsend 1984, p 321)

The goal should be an adequate child benefit scheme paid at the same level irrespective of the parents' employment status, so that other benefits would not need to include additions for children. In the context of a fairer tax system (see chapter 4), the case for taxation of a generous child benefit would have to be considered. At the same time, the cuts in the school meals scheme should be reversed and, ideally, free meals should be extended to all children as originally intended after the war.

Provision for housing costs has been a constant Achilles'

heel in attempts to reform social security, largely because of their size and variability. There is broad support for some kind of unified housing benefit system that treats owner-occupiers on the same basis as tenants. Equally, there is reluctant acceptance of the difficulty of avoiding some element of means-testing in such a system. One model that deserves further study is that put forward by the Association of Metropolitan Authorities (1987), incorporating both a universal flat rate and a means-tested element.

Getting to There from Here

The obstacles to the implementation of the kind of programme outlined above should not be underestimated, not least because it has to be viewed as part of a broader strategy for redistribution. It is therefore important that it can be introduced gradually. This should not be confused with *ad hoc* incrementalism lacking both clear goals and a long term strategy.

The obstacles are of two types: institutional and political. A rigid departmental approach to policy making is inimical to the kind of strategy now required. It is encouraging that the Policy Review is attempting to cross some of these departmental boundaries. As Malcolm Wicks (1987a, p 182) has argued

> a radical government must consider the machinery of government in the light of its social policy objectives ... We need a genuine joint approach to social policy that actually works and this requires a strong prime ministerial interest in the alternative social strategy and a revamped Cabinet Office to oversee and implement government social policy decisions.

This could then be backed up by the use of social impact statements to monitor the implementation of policy. A further crucial requirement is the muzzling of 'the wolves in the Treasury' (Donnison 1982, p 209) who have been the curse of social policy making whichever party has been in power.

To argue that implementation of a radical social strategy depends upon political will, is perhaps, to state the obvious. But that political will cannot be assumed and it will require pressure from below. First, there is a major educative task to be undertaken within the labour movement, in order to re-establish social security as a central political issue. (The Labour Social Security Campaign has been attempting this but it cannot be left to a small unresourced group.) Second, public support must be built up. At one level, it will mean convincing those in work that we all have a stake in the future of the social security system, and those not in work that Labour is committed to recasting the system in a less oppressive, more 'user friendly' mould.

At another, more fundamental, level it requires Labour to take the ideological initiative and reassert the case for social responsibility and social justice more generally. This has to start now. The battle for hearts and minds cannot be won in the occasional electoral skirmish. As Stuart Hall (1987) has observed, 'Thatcherism has been intervening ideologically with consummate skill *ever since 1979*'.

It is a cause for hope that, despite Thatcherism's success in changing the climate of ideas, opinion polls consistently reveal a bedrock of support for collectivist values and for a fairer distribution of resources. It is true that such beliefs may well often co-exist with more punitive attitudes towards certain groups of those in poverty. But the challenge for Labour is to appeal to and build on the socially responsible side of people's attitudes, in the same way that the present government has appealed to their individualism. As the 1950 Labour Manifesto put it, 'we appeal to what is good in people, not to what is bad. We rely on fellowship and friendliness, not on fear and greed' (Blunkett and Crick 1988). Labour must be able to inspire people with a vision of an alternative, fairer, society. A decent social security system must be central to that vision.

References

P. Alcock, 'Socialist security: where should we be going and why?' *Critical Social Policy*, Issue 13, 1985.

AMA, *A New Deal for Home Owners and Tenants*, 1987.

Archbishop of Canterbury's Commission on Urban Priority Areas (ACCUPA), *Faith in the City*, Church House 1985.

H. Arnott, 'Second class citizens' in A. Walker and C. Walker, 1987 (see below).

G. Beltram, *Testing the Safety Net*, Bedford Square Press 1984

R. Berthoud, *The Independent*, 29 May 1987.

D. Blunkett and B. Crick, 'The Labour Party's Aims and Values' The *Guardian*, 1 February 1988.

R. Cohen and M. Tarpey, *Single Payments: The Disappearing Safety Net*, CPAG 1988.

R. Cook, 'The Hole in Labour's Heart', *Marxism Today*, August 1987.

N. Deakin, *The Politics of Welfare*, Methuen 1987.

M. Desai, 'Drawing the line: on defining the poverty threshold', in P. Golding (ed), *Excluding the Poor*, CPAG 1986.

Poverty and Disability: Breaking the Link, Disability Alliance 1987.

D. Donnison, *The Politics of Poverty*, Martin Robertson 1982.

P. Esam *et al*, *Who's to Benefit?* Verso 1985.

GLC, *Report of the GLC Claimants Commission*, 1985.

P. Gordon and A. Newnham, *Passport to Benefit*, CPAG, Runneymeade Trust 1985.

S. Hall, 'Blue Election, Election Blues', *Marxism Today*, July 1987.

Hansard, 14 April 1986 c271-2 HMSO.

Hansard, 30 November 1987 c464 HMSO.

R. Hattersley, *Financial Times*, 6 May 1987a.

R. Hattersley, The *Guardian*, 18 September 1987b.

J. Hurstfield, 'Parenthood and part-time work: the Swedish approach' *Poverty*, No 68, CPAG 1987.

ILO, *Into the 21st Century: The Development of Social Security*, Geneva 1984.

N. Kinnock, *Marxism Today*, June 1983.

R. Lister in M. McCarthy (ed), *The New Politics of Welfare*, Macmillan 1989.

T.H. Marshall, *Citizenship and Social Class*, Cambridge University Press 1950.

J. Moore, *Speech on future of the welfare state*, 26 September 1987.

NACRO, *Enforcement of the Law Relating to Social Security*, 1986.

D. Piachaud, *The Distribution of Income and Work*, Oxford Review of Economic Policy, Vol 3, No 3 1987.

Sheffield City Council, *To each according ...*, 1987.

Supplementary Benefits Commission (SBC), *Annual Report*, HMSO 1978.

R. Titmuss, *Commitment to Welfare*, Allen and Unwin 1968.

UCSS, *Draft Claimants' Charter, 1987*.

A. Walker 'Why we need a social strategy', *Marxism Today*, September 1982.

A. Walker, 'Labour's social plans: the limits of welfare statism', *Critical Social Policy*, Issue 8, 1983.

A. Walker and C. Walker, *The Growing Divide*, CPAG 1987.

R. Walker *et al*, *Responses to Poverty: Lessons from Europe*, Heinemann 1984.

M. Wicks, *A Future for All*, Pelican 1987a.

M. Wicks, 'Shaping the State', *Social Services Insight*, 20 February 1987b.

Jim Tomlinson
Employment Policy and Economic Management

It cannot be said too often that the Labour Party's central economic policy concern should be unemployment. But perhaps it is worth emphasising why that centrality remains appropriate. Above all, the reason is that unemployment radically increases inequality. On average unemployment probably reduces household incomes by 40-60 per cent. This reduction in the standard of life is, of course, visited unequally on the population; liability is highly concentrated amongst those who in any case have poor life chances. Two points emerge from these consequences of unemployment. First, the concern for unemployment cannot be 'absolute'. It must be tempered with a concern to create well paid jobs: or the inequality created by unemployment will remain if the alternative is low paid employment. Second, the key concern must be with those who are unemployed for a substantial period of time, for it is they who suffer the main costs of unemployment.

The number of long term (over 1 year) unemployed has grown enormously since the early 1970s. Good data is only available for men, and this shows a rise from around 300,000 in 1979 to half a million by 1981, one million in July 1982 and 1.3 million by mid-1986. It has since fallen to just under 1 million. This is not just a bulge arising from the 1980/81 economic collapse; as many entered long term unemployment in 1985 as in 1981. In excess of 80 per cent of 'days lost' through unemployment are attributable to long term unemployment (Haskel and Jackman 1987).

In addition to the fundamental economic cost of unemployment, on its present scale it worsens the whole texture of social relations. As Beveridge remarked over 40

years ago, mass unemployment alters the whole relation
between 'masters and men'. This can currently be seen in
everything from employment law to popular discourse on
'scroungers'.

Whilst unemployment has been falling since mid-1986,
insofar as this reflects underlying expansion of employment
rather than statistical sleight of hand, it is on an unsustainable
basis: we have had a good old-fashioned Tory consumer
boom, fuelled by a fall in private savings and accumulation of
debt. Already by late summer 1988 the balance of payments
consequences of this had led to a sharp tightening of interest
rate policy, and the prospects are for a slowdown in the
economy which will end or reverse the fall in unemployment.

How can this position be improved? It is orthodox but still
helpful to discuss this issue initially under two main heads –
macro-economic and supply-side.

Macro-economic Policy

The key issue here is how far governments can use the
weapon of demand expansion to reduce unemployment. Two
separable sets of discussions bear on this issue. On one hand
we have the whole debate within academic economics, the
Keynesian versus monetarist/new classical dispute, bearing
on the response of the economy to demand expansion. On the
other hand we have those who would see the key issue as the
'practical' *constraints* on such demand expansion. Those who
would emphasise such constraints can in turn be divided into
two. First, there are those who effectively argue that
advanced capitalist countries like Britain are now so inter-
woven with the world economy, especially via capital markets, that no individual country can do much to determine its
own economic destiny (Holland 1983, Stewart 1983, Morrell
1987). Second, there are the arguments which emphasise the
balance of payments constraint on British growth (Smith
1984, 87; Cutler et al 1987).

This focus on 'practical' *constraints* on a policy of demand
expansion seems the most helpful starting point for
discussing the scope for unemployment reduction via
macro-economic policy.

The argument that, under conditions of internationalisation of economic activity, 'national economic management is obsolete' gains credence from the British experience in the mid-1970s and the French in the early 1980s. In both cases governments of the Left had to reverse expansionary policies because of 'loss of financial confidence', flight of capital, fall in the exchange rate and resultant inflationary pressures. The important question is not whether these events took place, but what significance is to be attached to their occurrence? Do they show that national economic management is now a chimera, an unhelpful illusion to be jettisoned?; or only that the constraints on national economic management have tightened, and that such management requires more difficult economic and political conditions to be undertaken with any degree of success?

I have argued elsewhere (1988) that the latter is the appropriate conclusion. The point is illustrated with reference to the success of Swedish economic management in the 1980s, especially the devaluation policy followed in 1982. The success of this policy has been conditional on a number of features of the Swedish political economy. It has reflected the well-known 'corporatist' character of Swedish economic management and bargaining between the 'social partners'. In particular, this meant that wages did not rise rapidly to offset the competitive advantage brought about by the devaluation. Consent to this was partly secured by the creation of wage-earner funds, a partial socialisation of investment (Hashi and Hussain 1986). Sweden also has a substantial insulation of domestic capital markets from international finance. And it also, of course, has a highly efficient (private) manufacturing sector, renowned for producing high quality goods. The point of this brief outline of the Swedish 'model' is not to argue that it can be replicated elsewhere, but to indicate that under certain political/institutional conditions national economic management is still possible – even in highly internationally integrated economies, as the Swedish economy is. In addition, the Swedish case points us towards the major areas of importance when the constraints on economic management are under discussion.

Demand expansion, if not fated to fail because of international economic integration, may prove a very limited provider of employment if the economy faces a severe balance of payments constraint. That this is the position in Britain seems well illustrated by the events of the 1980s. From a current account surplus of over £6 billion in 1981, the growth of the economy since then, which has barely scratched the surface of unemployment, has led to a current account deficit of nearly £3 billion in 1987, and probably £10-15 billion in 1988. The latest monthly figures available (July 1988) show a deficit of £2 billion – the largest in relation to GDP since post-war reconstruction. Moreover, this decline took place despite a substantial decline in the effective exchange rate (from an index of around 95 to the low 70s). Britain thus appears to face its traditional problem of a balance of payments constraint on economic expansion, coupled with low price elasticities for its traded manufactured goods (eg, Hotson and Gardiner 1983) which suggests that the pound will have to depreciate persistently and substantially just to keep the current account from deteriorating further as output expands. At best, then, a left or centre-left government would find itself wanting to see the exchange rate fall to maintain competitiveness, whilst wanting to restrict that fall because of its inflationary consequences. At worst, the exchange rate fall might not even yield a proportionate improvement in the trade balance, given the growing importance of *non-price* factors in international trade (Stout 1976, Cutler *et al* 1987).

Manufacturing competitiveness then remains vital to Britain's capacity to reduce unemployment. Manufactures provide half of Britain's exports, and as North Sea Oil runs down this proportion is likely to increase. By July 1988 the economy was ceasing to be a net exporter of oil – the balance for that month being only £64 million. Traded services in general are too volatile to provide sufficient offset to a deteriorating balance in manufacturers. The much vaunted financial services make up under 4 per cent of exports, and market share has been lost faster in this area than in manufactures in recent years (Key 1985). It is a myth that Britain has an obvious comparative advantage in such services.

As is well-known, employment in manufacturing as a proportion of total employment is on a downward trend in all advanced capitalist countries. This trend has been stronger in Britain, and the absolute number of jobs lost has been higher than elsewhere in the OECD world (Rowthorn and Wells 1987, p 211). Nevertheless the scope for 'bucking the trend' and seeing substantial job increases in manufacturing is slight. The importance of a successful manufacturing sector lies not in direct provision of employment, but in the capacity to satisfy the full employment level of domestic demand for manufactures, and to finance by export any associated deficit in the non-manufacturing trade balance (Rowthorn and Wells 1987, Introduction).

Employment creation in any sector is therefore constrained by the British appetite for manufactured imports, and the relative lack of appetite of the world for British exports. It is calculated that every 1 per cent rise in British income raises demand for such imports by 2 per cent, but a rise in world incomes of 1 per cent raises demand for British exports by only 1 per cent. In the long run it is clear that the only solution to this problem is a 'supply-side' one, ie, it needs to be based on improving the efficiency of manufacturing industry. This will be discussed below. But what about the short run? One of the obvious proposals here is for selective import controls to secure the domestic market. This argument is persuasively made by Cutler et al (1987, Ch 4).

The economic arguments seem compelling. The traditional free trade arguments based on relative efficiency (comparative advantage) seem less compelling when trade is mainly swapping manufactures for manufactures, rather than swapping goods produced from very different resource bases (as in Ricardo's original wine and cotton example). The impact of protection on domestic production efficiency seems an open question on the basis of historical experience, and is not a sufficient reason to oppose protection if that protection is coupled with appropriate supply-side policies. Domestic content regulation (ie, specifying a minimum British share in the costs of a good) could be quite easily administered in the car sector, where company car tax subsidies are an obvious instrument; similar devices for consumer durables could cover the two largest areas of import surplus in manufactures.

The problems with protection are essentially political, in the widest sense. Protectionism runs against the grain of the rhetoric of post-war policy in the advanced capitalist world. Though this rhetoric has not prevented various 'Voluntary Export Restrictions', or protectionism via the Multi-Fibre Agreement on Textiles, it cannot be lightly disregarded. Whilst Ricardo's theory of comparative advantage may not have entered the public consciousness, the appeal of high quality imports, and the correlate argument of not 'feather-bedding' domestic manufactures both have substantial weight. Also, of course, there is the danger of retaliatory measures given both the ideology of free trade and its embodiment in various international agreements to which Britain is a party. Above all, protectionism would clearly be a blow against West Germany and its hegemony in the EEC.

Overall, protectionism involves a very complex political calculation – are the potential economic benefits worth the possible political costs? It seems impossible to make a summary judgement. But what needs to be explored are ways of reducing the possible political costs. For example, the encouragement of foreign multinationals to locate plants in Britain behind protective barriers might to some extent undercut the argument that this was a form of feather-bedding British industry. (The issue of multinationals is returned to below.)

The final macro-economic argument concerns capital flows. Arguments that say that the current scale and volatility of international capital flows render national economic management more difficult are clearly correct. Can anything be done to ease this constraint? First it should be noted that much of this growth of capital flows is not based on long-run trends towards greater internationalisation of production, but on the instability of exchange and interest rates under the post-1972 floating exchange rate world. In other words a return to a more stable international monetary regime would help reduce the scale and volatility of capital flows – though it must be said that Britain's role in any such return is likely to be marginal – the key actor remains the USA (Strange 1986).

Second, there is the issue of exchange controls. The kind of comprehensive controls abolished in 1979 seem difficult to envisage as an option – they leaked substantially even before their abolition. When transactions are made on telephones they cannot be 'policed' in the way possible in the early post-war years. However this is not to say nothing could be done. It should be noted that whilst most capital flows take the form of movements in and out of bank deposits the *net* movement is dominated by portfolio investments. Here there is an existing proposal, made by Roy Hattersley before the last general election, which would seem to be bold, innovative and potentially successful. This proposal aimed at regulating the portfolios of insurance companies, pension funds, etc, by withdrawing tax subsidies if certain guidelines on the composition of assets were not adhered to. This proposal was originally put forward as a means of financing a National Investment Bank, but here the concern is with the balance of payments. Regulation of the capital account via such tax regulation would seem the best way of trying to deal with the short-run problems of demand expansion leading to a current account deterioration (Williams *et al* 1988).

Probably nothing could prevent a substantial fall in the exchange rate if a Labour government were elected. In part this is no problem – the exchange rate needs to fall substantially for reasons of competitiveness. The problem is to stop it getting out of hand – and also to stop its fall simply feeding back into the economy in the form of higher inflation – a point returned to below.

The Left has traditionally been sceptical of the priority accorded by the Right to the defeat of inflation. This was a sound instinctual response to the 'moral panic' about inflation of the mid 1970s, and the absence of good evidence of the economic damage done by inflation. However *politically* inflation is a big problem, rationally or otherwise: the electorate and financial markets dislike inflation and therefore it cannot be disregarded. Over the short run there may be a trade-off between inflation and unemployment (for example, via a falling exchange rate). But the danger is that in the longer run high inflation may compel a reversal of policy and therefore undermine employment objectives. Given this problem, Labour must explore the possibilities of using an exchange rate target (after an initial fall in the rate) to provide credibility to its anti-inflationary position. This does not mean fixing the exchange rate for all time; but it does mean a substantial degree of fixity to give credibility to the target. Such a policy would bring into focus the politically painful trade-off between reassuring financial markets and ambitious reductions in unemployment. But given the constraints, such political pain is unavoidable; to 'go for broke' on employment in the short run, and ignore inflation, may be politically fatal.

Supply-Side Policies

Britain in the 1980s has not seen a 'productivity miracle'. Manufacturing productivity growth 1981-84 was certainly notably above other major capitalist economies, but this followed a period of declining relative growth, and since 1984 the relative trend has been similar, and the *absolute* position still inferior (NEDO 1987). This picture of sharp cyclical changes within a still markedly inferior trend is borne out by a large scale survey of manufacturing companies, which found little in fundamentals had changed between 1975-85. In the broad area of production engineering the picture was still one where machines were used inefficiently, components hung around for long periods doing nothing, and new technologies were marginal to overall performance (New and Myers 1987).

Why is British industry so inefficient? If there is a one line answer it must be managerial inefficiency. British managers are ill-trained, where they are trained they usually have the wrong kinds of skills (Armstrong 1987), and they are obsessed with 'labour' problems (Williams *et al* 1987). This latter is particularly striking given the actual cost composition of manufacturing activity – where direct labour costs make up on average only 18 per cent of the total, compared with 52 per cent for brought-in components (30 per cent are overheads, New and Myers 1987). Hopefully one thing that might emerge from the last nine years of union-bashing is the *economic* irrelevance of such a posture. What is to be done in this area? Of course in broad terms the answer must be to create a better, more appropriately trained managerial body which is less prone to the prejudices of previous generations. This is, indeed, a labour of

Sisyphus. However it may be helped by the encouragement of foreign, particularly Japanese, companies and management to site in the UK. This is not because Japanese management has 'all the answers', but because their strength does seem to lie precisely in the area of British strategic weaknesses – broadly, production engineering.

Of course such arguments raise the legitimate question of how different such inward manufacturing investment will be from the expansions of US multinationals in Britain in the 1960s – and their subsequent contraction in the 1970s and 1980s? First of all it must be said that in large part this contraction was part of a general contraction of manufacturing, nothing to do with the ownership of the companies. But undoubtedly it also reflected the peripheral, branch plant status of some of this investment. Japanese investment is not necessarily of a similar character. It is partly growing because of the 'structural' surplus in Japan's balance of payments current account which reduces the scope for profitable domestic investment. Partly, also, it reflects a long term strategy for penetrating EC markets whilst circumventing hostility to Japanese imports. On both these counts it is likely to be less mobile than much American capital in the past. 'Japanisation' is no miracle cure, nor are all Japanese practices desirable, but Japanese managerial competence has helped, and can help, the revival of British manufacturing.

Other supply-side policies are also important but can only be very briefly mentioned here. Plainly British Research and Development has been a longstanding problem. It has been too low in total, and misdirected towards military and inappropriate areas like aircraft and nuclear power. It also seems to have been poorly integrated with other parts of company activity (Smith 1984, 1987). This problem should be more amenable to government policy than many other economic policy areas simply because so much of British Research and Development is publicly funded. A fairly rapid redeployment of scarce skilled labour resources in this area would seem a feasible option.

Traditionally, in talking about the supply side, the Left has focused on the low level of investment in the UK economy. It is true that over a long period Britain has devoted a smaller share of GNP to investment than major competitor countries, and this has left a legacy of much lower investment/head for workers in manufacturing (NEDO 1987). Net investment in manufacturing has been negative in most of the years of the 1980s as scrapping has exceeded new investment. However it is important to distinguish between a macro-economic aggregate called investment, and investment projects; the former is really only the summation and consequence of the latter. The problem is to increase the number of efficient and profitable investment projects, which will then be reflected in the aggregate of investment. The share of investment in GNP has macro-economic and therefore political implications (see conclusions below), but it is not itself something to be operated directly upon.

Of course the efficiency and profitability of investment projects depend upon the forms of calculation employed by enterprises to judge such issues. Hence overall investment levels may be inhibited if there are general forms of calculation in the economy which, for example, tend to be hostile to risk and/or long pay-back periods. There is plenty of evidence of this in the past in the UK, most notably because of the peculiar relations between finance and industry in the UK, the over-active stock market, and the conservative lending practices of the banks (Williams *et al* 1983). The growth of foreign banks in Britain has done something to reduce the latter problem. The former, with its capacity to produce an emphasis on short-term profits and financial conglomerates with no productive rationality, remains to be tackled. In the long-run this must involve reducing the role of the stockmarket, a role which is marginal to the provision of industrial finance (Mayer 1987), but which inhibits more strategic investment policies by firms.

It must be a central political objective of a Labour government to reduce both the economic and political clout of the City. This involves a whole series of reforms, embracing pension funds, the stockmarket, the role of the Bank of England and a whole host of other issues which cannot be discussed here. But the cutting edge of such a policy must be to stress the *anomalous* character of the stockmarket in the British system in comparison with major industrial competitors (with the exception of the USA, which also of course has a poor post-war productivity record).

Reducing Unemployment

So far it has been suggested that the capacity of macro-economic policy has not been reduced to nothing by the internationalisation of the world economy, but it is more constrained. And in the British case this is compounded by the chronic weakness of the balance of payments and the limits on depreciation of the exchange rate as a cure for this weakness. Fiscal policy is thus limited in its capacity, both because of the likely response of international finance to any uncongenial fiscal posture, and because of the British appetite for imports if output does expand. This does not mean nothing can be done. The British government's fiscal stance through much of the 1980s (though loosened after 1981) has tended to be tighter than other European countries, without them suffering losses of financial confidence. In addition to the constraining effects of any exchange controls which can be designed, financial confidence may be helped by a relatively modest reflation, which in any event would be necessary because of the balance of payments constraint.

An expansion of publicly financed training is the kind of fiscal expansion which fits all three of these desiderata. It thus bridges the gap between the need for short-run 'employment' and the need for long-run improvements in skills. As a number of studies by the NIER have shown, Britain remains substantially deficient in training, especially in 'craft' skills, a long-run position exacerbated by the collapse of privately financed training in the 1980s. Training also has political advantages: it is widely accepted as a 'legitimate' use of public money; it is based on adaptation to economic change, not resistance; it deals with the problem of mismatch between jobs available and workers unemployed; and it has widespread support across the political spectrum.

This is not to say training is an easy fix. For success it requires not just broad political support as a 'good thing', but detailed political support institutionalised via re-vamped tripartite industrial training boards, necessary to fight the inevitable union and employer resistances. It also doesn't come cheap, especially as it must offer decent incomes to participants (unlike the current Community Programme which has predominantly attracted only young people because of the low income it gives (Haskel and Jackman 1987). And at the end of the day it must be training for jobs, and hence other policies must be pursued at the same time to secure this outcome.

The widespread political support for more training is both a political possibility and a political danger. A possibility because it tends to undercut some political opposition to fiscal expansion; a danger because of the pressure to reduce the programme to a lowest common denominator of half-hearted skill training at low cost.

This is precisely the character of the new plans announced by the Government in February 1988 (HMSO 1988). These stand as a monument to rhetoric with little substance. The rhetoric speaks of a need for a 'revolution in attitudes to training and retraining'. The substance amounts to a training programme for 600,000 people per annum at a cost of £1.5 billion. Those involved are usually to be paid £10 per week above current benefit entitlement. Most training is envisaged to cost £17.50 per week per trainee. Clearly this is primarily a way of reducing the dole queue, not of retraining the population. But the opportunism and bad faith of the current government in this area should not obscure the potential of training as a political, as well as economic, priority.

Conclusions

Views about the rapidity with which unemployment can be reduced depend above all on the likely macro-economic circumstances when a non-Conservative government takes office. The signs, particularly from the deterioration of the current account, are that those circumstances will be serious. This means that growth of the economy will be slow, and therefore there will be no painless solutions whereby everyone gains as unemployment falls. Other things being equal, putting people back to work sharply worsens the balance of payments constraint, as raising low incomes sharply raises the appetite for imported manufactures. Hence for a number of years the import appetite of the populace in general will have to be reined back. Coupled with this, any sharp upward movement in investment (public and private) will reduce the *share* of national income going to consumption, and in the context of a slow-growing economy this is likely to mean absolute falls.

Another way of putting this point is to say that a radical reduction in unemployment is likely also to involve a policy of redistribution of income. This has a number of facets. It means *some part* of higher public expenditure being financed by increased taxes, given the constraints on fiscal deficits. It also means willy-nilly some kind of incomes policy. The purpose of this would be to manage the redistribution of resources from consumption to investment and to maximise the employment impact of the slow growth in demand. Of course this will be met by the charge that economic problems are being tackled at the 'expense of the working class'. The answer to this must be yes, in part they are. A radical redistribution of income *and* switch from consumption to investment cannot be secured solely at the expense of middle class consumption – there is no pot of gold to be robbed. The consumption of the employed working class must also be contained for the benefit of the unemployed. (This argument is developed on in Tomlinson 1988A.)

The traditional left recipe for reducing unemployment, 'Keynesian' style expansionary packages, was tried in the context of sharply rising unemployment for the first time in the mid-1970s. One limitation of such a policy quickly became apparent – the leverage of private finance via its role in gilt purchase and currency sales. Any attempt to reflate the British economy in the early 1990s would face the same difficulties. At the same time the underlying current account position has deteriorated further since the mid-1970s. The trade position in the late 1980s is only sustainable because mass unemployment cuts import demand via its effects on unemployed households' income. It has been calculated that a family with two children on Supplementary Benefit spends just £6.68 on import-intensive clothing, footwear and durable household goods, whereas the all-household average in the Family Expenditure Survey is £36.20 (Bradshaw and

Morgan 1987). This emphasises the balance of payments consequence of any return to full employment.

These constraints do not mean that the traditional Labour emphasis on expanding social welfare and infrastructure spending is absurd. Such programmes however have to be designed to take into account import content as well as overall financial implications. Thus, for example, Labour's 1987 programme rightly emphasised the low import content of construction projects in comparison with most forms of expenditure (Labour Party 1987, p 15). At the same time we need to be thinking of devices for aiding the balance of payments position in the short-run whilst some form of expansion of domestic industrial capacity is pursued. The advantage of using controls on portfolio investment is that it both helps the capital account of the balance of payments and may also help gilt-finance of public borrowing. But such 'devices' provide at best a breathing-space for policies to correct the underlying problem of manufacturing efficiency. Those who want to reduce unemployment must in the long-run provide policies on this front, or fail.

References

P. Armstrong, *The Abandonment of Productive Intervention in Management Teaching Syllabi: An Historical Analysis*, Warwick University: Industrial Relations Research Unit 1987.

J. Bradshaw and J. Morgan, *Budgeting on Benefit: The Consumption of Families on Social Security*, Family Policy Studies Centre, Occasional paper No. 5, 1987.

A. Cutler, K. Williams and J. Williams, *Keynes, Beveridge and Beyond*, RKP 1987.

HMSO, *Training for Employment*, CM 316, 1988.

I. Hashi and A. Hussain, 'The Employee Investment Funds in Sweden', *National Westminster Bank Review*, May 1986.

J. Haskel and R. Jackman, *Long Term Unemployment and Special Employment Measures in Britain*, LSE Centre for Labour Economics Discussion Paper No 297, 1987.

S. Holland, *Out of Crisis*, Spokesman 1983.

A. Hotson and K Gardiner, 'Trade in Manufactures', *Bank of Englad Discussion Papers*, Technical Series No 5, 1983.

J. Key, 'Services in the British Economy', *Bank of England Quarterly Bulletin*, 1985.

Labour Party, *New Jobs for Britain*, 1987.

C. Mayer, 'New Issues in Corporate Finance', *Centre for Economic Policy Research*, Discussion Papers, 1987.

F. Morrell, 'Our Future Lies in Europe', *New Statesman*, 6 March 1987.

NEDO, *Britain Industrial Performance*, 1987.

C. New, and A. Myers, *Managing Manufacturing Operations in the U.K. 1975-1985*, Cranfield 1987.

B. Rowthorn and J. Wells, *De-Industrialisation and Foreign Trade*, Cambridge University Press 1987.

K. Smith, *Britain's Economic Crisis*, Penguin 1984.

K. Smith, *The U.K. Economy in the Late 1980s: Trends and Prospects*, University of Keele Working Paper 87:6, 1987.

M. Stewart, *Controlling the Economic Future*, Wheatsheaf 1983.

D. Stout, *International Price Competitiveness, Non-Price Factors and International Trade*, NEDO 1976.

S. Strange, *Casino Capitalism*, Basil Blackwell 1986.

J. Tomlinson, *Can Governments Manage the Economy?*, Fabian Society Tract, No 524, 1988.

J. Tomlinson, 'Industrial Policy and Macroeconomic Policy' in P. Hirst and J. Zeitlin (eds), *Reversing Industrial Decline*, Berg 1988a.

K. Williams, J. Williams and D. Thomas, *Why Are the British Bad at Manufacturing?*, RKP 1983.

K. Williams, J. Williams, A. Cutler, and C. Haslam: 'The Economic Consequence of Mrs Thatcher: Labour's Economic Policy Options for 1991', unpublished paper, University College of Wales, Aberystwyth.

Ian Gough and Len Doyal,
with the Sheffield Group

Conclusion: Socialism, Democracy and Human Needs

Policy Schizophrenia

Socialist thinking about policy in Britain has suffered for too long from a three-way split between economic policy, social policy and constitutional reform. In this it has mimicked British culture and history – or rather British culture and history up to 1979. Since then the governments of Mrs Thatcher have set about reintegrating the three policy domains along the lines of 'the free economy and the strong state': welfare goals are subordinated to business profits and the British constitution is centralised to remove obstacles to 'UK Ltd' emanating from civil society. This belated bourgeois revolution is one reason why the Left's traditional schizophrenia can no longer be sustained, and why all the essays in this book begin to consider economic policy in relation to social policy, and question the constitutional framework and practices of the British state within which both must be negotiated.

The post-war Labour government bears a major responsibility for deepening the split between social and economic policy. On 5 July 1948 Beveridge's social security scheme and Bevan's National Health Service launched a remarkably developed and pioneering 'welfare state'. Yet, apart from a remote hands-off form of Keynesianism, the Attlee government failed to create a systematic form of industrial and economic intervention despite substantial nationalisation; indeed it paved the way for a reassertion of the international role of sterling and the City of London, and the laissez faire supply-side policies which accompanied this.

This combination is unique among Western nations, where economic and social interventions are more congruent. In the USA both are dominated by market principles; in Europe, statist or corporatist forms of economic intervention complement 'Beveridge' or 'Bismarck' welfare systems. In Britain, by contrast, the Jeckyll and Hyde struggle between 'nice' social policies and 'realistic' economic policies has come to haunt the Labour Party and the Left. True, the Alternative Economic Strategy in the 1970s began to appreciate the interdependence of the two, but the linkage was conceived in narrowly Keynesian terms – social spending would boost home demand – and resulted in an even more dangerous disparity between socialist ideals and capitalist reality.

Opinion poll and survey evidence continues to show support for major welfare services such as the NHS as well as for increased taxation to finance improvements (Taylor Gooby 1985). The First Report of the Labour Party Policy Review also points to approval for the welfare policies traditionally associated with Labour. However, it would be self-deluding to believe that this is evidence of an inexhaustible reservoir of public support for welfare, which is waiting to be tapped by a well orchestrated and presented electoral campaign. Thatcherite policies have been increasingly carefully directed at undermining collective investment in, and endorsement of, welfare, replacing these with individual, market based initiatives, and arguing (seemingly successfully) that, however apparently desirable state welfare may appear, it is not viable because of its contradictory impact on economic policy. Indeed the evidence is that, in spite of 'blips' and setbacks, the Conservative claim to be able to manage the economy more responsibly than Labour still commands support (Crewe 1987). Crudely put, voters prefer Labour's social policies but Tory economic policies; when choosing how to vote a majority regard the latter as more salient. Therefore without some fundamental rethinking of the interrelation of social and economic policies, it is unlikely that existing patterns of party support can be overturned.

If economic and social policy have developed in isolation, left thinking about the British constitution, political institutions and our system of governance has hardly developed at all. The labour movement is second to none in treating the British constitution with a reverence which would put Burke and Bagehot to shame. Not until the shock of Labour's third election defeat in 1987 did constitutional issues have much purchase within the Left, whilst the Labour leadership persists in ridiculing and outlawing such rethinking. Again this can be traced back to the post-war settlement: the fact that the welfare state and the nationalisation programme could be introduced without challenge to the British political system seemed to demonstrate the latter's neutrality and flexibility. Senior Shadow Cabinet members such as Roy Hattersley continue to argue that an election victory and a renewal of 'corporate bias' will see us through another round of social democratic reform. In fact however, as Marquand (1988, ch 7) shows, the period from the early 1960s to 1979 witnessed a plethora of institutional innovations, but with no underlying system of values or indeed common purpose; and, as Rustin points out here, since 1979 constitutional reform is proceeding apace, but in all the wrong directions.

These gaps and inconsistencies in thinking matter, since the three policy domains are increasingly interrelated and implicated in the deterioration of the British economy and the polarisation of British politics. In 1964 the incoming Labour government under Harold Wilson attempted what was arguably the most interventionist economic policy in British history, only to be deflected by the international exposure of sterling as a reserve currency, and his government's refusal or inability to devalue soon enough. In other words planning for growth and welfare was stultified by the unreconstructed nature of the British economy and economic policy making. In 1974-79 a similar pattern followed: interventionism was followed by quasi-corporatism and then by quasi-monetarism. Only since 1979 has the incompatibility of economic and social policy been overcome, via a ruthless subordination of the latter to the former – of collective goals to market individualism.

The linkages between economic failure and constitutional conservatism are still more important, and have been notably explored by writers as varied as Nairn (1988, part 3) and Marquand (1988, chs 6 and 7). In brief, Britain has failed to develop the forms of state intervention or political bargaining and consensus politics required by the nature of its political economy. On the one hand British welfare statism and piecemeal government intervention block US-style market adjustment mechanisms, while no Continental or Japanese style 'developmental state' has developed to take their place. On the other hand, a powerful labour movement (still more extensive than in any of the other big-7 economies), entrenched interest groups and a system of 'corporate bias' are not integrated into the policy-making process via explicit forms of corporatism or consociational democracy along Scandinavian, Austrian or even West German lines.

This is economically and politically harmful. Economically, because evidence is growing that advanced capitalist countries with intermediate levels of centralisation in the labour market perform less well than those at either 'extreme' – the decentralised market-led adjustments of the USA and the negotiated adjustment mechanisms of Sweden (Calmfors and Driffill 1988). The 'inbetween' countries do less well, because the individualism and blind compulsion of the market conflict with the politicisation of economic and social issues and the construction of a common purpose, which are intrinsic to societal bargaining. Politically, the absence of constitutional reform is harmful because the absence of clear rules and rights in the 'traditional' Westminster model places a great burden on trust and moral agreement, which is withering with economic decline and political polarisation.

Thatcherism represents a clear recognition and resolution of this impasse. Economic and social policy are re-fused by subordinating the latter to the former. Economic policy has involved tax cuts, de-regulation of capital, product and labour markets, and privatisation. Social policies have encouraged market 'exit' from state provision, notably in housing, old people's homes and pensions. They have enlarged occupational provision and tax expenditures. They have held benefit levels constant and thus reduced them as a share of average incomes. They have encouraged a dual labour market and further developed social security in the direction of a 'residual', targetted system. And finally they have redistributed income towards the *rich* in an unprecedented way. The emergence of mass unemployment as a result of the macro-economic policies of the early 1980s pressed heavily on an already inadequate welfare state; the only response was a plethora of half-baked training and make-work schemes, stealthily coalescing in the direction of American-style workfare. This all amounts to a drive towards an American-style resolution of economic and social policy: neo-liberal supply-side economics plus a residual welfare system. In the process it is widening the gulf between Britain and Europe.

At the same time the contradictions between economic and social policy and the political system have been tackled by the development of the 'strong state'. The trade union movement has been targetted on all fronts, and with the abolition in 1988 of the Manpower Services Commission the last vestige of Britain's quasi-corporatism has disappeared. Local government has been restructured and stripped of its financial independence in order to undermine local and regional centres of political opposition and strategic alternatives, as much as to control public finances. And the central state has acquired new powers to direct policy developments, as in education, and to remove obstacles in the way of de-regulation. The whole project amounts to a determined attempt to squeeze independent organisations in civil society which seek to replace market-led adjustment with political negotiation. This too is an attempt to create in Britain the freedom of manouevre capital enjoys in the United States – but without the restraining framework of its Constitution.

It will also have the effect of distancing us from the consociational democracies of northern Europe. This is a tendency which is rather belatedly receiving some recognition on the Left in the Labour Party and the Trades Union Congress, and new relationships are being developed with European leaders. However, it is not just the political appeal of socialist support in Europe which should direct us to closer assessment of Britain's role within it, but the stark contrast which European social and economic structures provide with the Thatcherite capitalism.

The need therefore is to devise an alternative package of economic and social policies and constitutional reforms in Britain which are compatible, yet which express genuinely socialist goals and strengthen all the social forces with a potential in their realisation. The solution, we shall argue, is:

> The prioritisation of human needs as the fundamental goal of both socialism and the welfare state
> The development of a social economy to meet needs
> Commitment to a 'dual strategy' combining top-down and bottom-up initiatives to democratise the British state and British society.

We will go on to apply these principles to some aspects of economic and social policy; and, to enable all this to happen, we will conclude with a call for reform of the antiquated British constitution.

Socialism and Human Needs

Socialism must embody specific beliefs about the good life, and one of the encouraging trends of recent years has been the reopening of just this question in an open, enquiring manner. Many, such as Roy Hattersley (1987), for example, now urge us to tackle the New Right head on and 'choose freedom' as the watchword of modern socialism. Yet we remain unconvinced. However absurd the Thatcherite's narrow negative view of freedom is (ie. freedom from state oppression), and however impressive the thinkers propounding an alternative, positive conception of liberty, it is too tricky and ultimately confusing to confine the essential ideas of socialism to that value alone (which is not of course to deny that freedom – both political and social – is absolutely central to socialism). Others, such as Beetham (1987), argue that radical democracy captures the heart of modern socialism. Undoubtedly this is an absolute pre-requisite, but again it seems insufficient and too protean – democracy to what ends? Both these reformulations concede too much to liberalism. They are not wrong, but insufficient to grasp the core ideas of socialism.

What we want to argue is that socialism is primarily about utilising the earth's resources to meet people's needs.

'Putting common human needs first' captures the heart and soul of socialism, incorporates the goals of freedom, equality and democracy, yet combines them with the 'collective endeavour' and what used to be called 'fraternity' of socialism. Moreover production to meet needs answers the pressing problems of today and the coming century. It confronts the immorality of hunger and want in the Third World alongside waste and greed in the First. It recognises the limits to growth and the ecological threats to the biosphere which have fuelled the recent expansion of 'green' consciousness. It reiterates the irrationality of global capitalism, the absurdity of an economic system based on short-sighted self-interest which ignores sustainable patterns of production, and creates glaring inequalities and mounting debt. It is vital to point out that socialism is not just about caring/sharing and the welfare state, but the only *rational* basis for managing the planet.

What are human needs? The essential common-sense of the idea of human needs has been wilting under a sustained philosophical attack in recent years by those arguing that needs are relative to particular cultures, so that no unifying, absolute needs exist or can be empirically identified. Elsewhere Doyal and Gough (1984) have rejected this cultural relativism as wrong and reactionary. Needs, for us, are the universal preconditions for creative and fulfilling human action. All people, whatever their gender, age, nation, class, religion, ethnicity, have basic needs which, if unsatisfied, will prevent them acting successfully within the societies where they live. Whatever their life-goals they will be unable effectively to identify and pursue them if their basic needs are unfulfilled.

Health and *autonomy* are the two fundamental human needs. By health we roughly mean the absence of physical illness, and by autonomy the consciousness and skills to participate fully in social life with self respect and the respect of one's peers. To achieve health and autonomy certain intermediate needs require at least minimal satisfaction. The list includes: adequate and nutritional food, warm and dry housing, a non-hazardous environment and work, appropriate health care, good parenting of children, a significant support network in the community, literacy and appropriate education, participation in employment or other significant activities, and physical and economic security. All of these intermediate needs are also universal, as can be confirmed by trying to imagine a society or culture where they would diminish rather than enhance individual capacities. Socialism then begins with the view that these basic needs of all should be satisfied before the desires of a few.

In addition, particular groups of people have specific needs which require satisfaction for their health and autonomy to be safeguarded. To take an obvious example, all women who wish to give birth require access to safe childbirth facilities. Other specific needs are due to social exploitation, oppression, inequality; for example those of black children suffering racist abuse, or the homeless oppressed by bailiffs and landlords. Our perspective must recognise the host of specific needs, but we also argue that forms of oppression that lead to these are to be condemned because they undermine the *universal* needs for health and autonomy. In other words there is the basis here for a reconciliation between the specific need groups behind the new social movements of the 1970s and 1980s, and the older interests of the labour movement. Instead of counterposing the interests of gays, blacks, the disabled, etc. to the interests of 'traditional Labour supporters', we can say, simply and without dissembling, that they share a common interest rooted in their common needs for health and autonomy. Specific group needs are recognised but not reified.

Immediately, however, a practical and moral problem arises, for if it is granted that basic needs are universal, it is certainly going to be far harder to reach agreement on what they are in detail, or on the 'satisfiers' or the best policies to meet those needs. Who is to decide? ask Hayek and the neo-liberals. Welfare professionals, bureaucrats, the state? For we white, Western, middle class males there is the further danger that policies to meet needs will merely reflect our interests – and our power. Nor is that all – the issue of priorities between groups of needs and between the needs of different groups will always lie at the heart of political controversy. Is there then any way out of the impasse which threatens to undermine the socialist project of meeting common human needs?

The democratic socialist solution is to agree on procedures which enable us collectively and rationally to settle disputes over what specific needs are and how they can best be met. There is space here only to make two general points.

First, knowledge about needs stems from two sources and assumes two forms: the codified, 'scientific' knowledge of experts, professionals, etc, and the 'experiential' knowledge of individuals and groups of people in their everyday lives. Much air has been wasted debating the respective merits of professional versus grass-roots definitions of needs. In our view both contribute something valid, and the aim should be a dialogue between the two, as rational and as democratic as we can achieve. When trying to maximise the health and autonomy of the elderly, for example, both the gerontologist and the elderly and their associations will have knowledge to contribute if mistakes are not to be made. Of course in practice a host of obstacles will be encountered – particularly in asserting the felt needs of the powerless against the expertise of professionals and officials, and of women, blacks and other disadvantaged groups against the power of white males and other privileged groups. These issues are returned to in the section on social policy below.

Second, this ideally requires that everybody has the constitutional right and the material wherewithal to participate in decision making. This means, of course, that traditions of representative and participatory democracy – in both the political and the economic spheres, in both the state and civil society – are central to the socialist project. So too is the specifically socialist goal of equality, and, more importantly in the medium term, Tawney's (1952) aim of ensuring that existing inequalities do not operate to exclude some members from participation in society. In other words the desire to satisfy human needs also embraces traditional democratic socialist concerns about the societal *means* for achieving this goal. Putting these two concerns together leads to a 'dual strategy' for reform, embracing top-down centralised rights *and* bottom-up decentralised initiatives. The strategy can perhaps be encapsulated in the concepts of *citizenship* and *democracy*. Both of these are concepts which have recently been placed on to the policy agenda by others too (Plant 1988). We will now go on to discuss some of their implications for planning and policy development.

Planning to Meet Needs

What does all this mean for economic and social policy? In brief, the fundamental goal of *both* should be the optimal satisfaction of people's needs. 'Production to meet needs' is by no means redundant as the guiding thread of socialist policy, but we must think through more carefully what exactly this entails. We need a new model of the economy. Let us begin by distinguishing three stages which must be gone through for resources to be transformed into the satisfaction of needs (Doyal and Gough, 1990). First an adequate quantity and quality of goods and services to meet needs (need 'satisfiers') must be produced. Second, they should be distributed according to the urgency of individuals', families' and households' needs. Third, these use-values have to be transformed into need-satisfactions through appropriate and equitable consumption within families and households; and the total work involved needs sharing equitably and adjusting so as not to harm individuals' health and autonomy. To these a fourth stage must be added (we could call it material reproduction) wherein people, capital goods and the natural environment are reconstituted for further rounds of production in the future.

It is transparently absurd to claim that an unregulated capitalist economy could effectively organise this process (which is perhaps why most careful neo-liberal thinkers are more cautious, and leave the field to Conservative politicians). It cannot ensure that production units prioritise health, education, housing and other services which satisfy needs; it cannot ensure that what is produced is distributed according to the urgency of people's needs; it fosters ignorance and helpnessness in the spheres of consumption and work; and it cannot adopt a collective, long-term perspective about future labour and capital requirements, let alone about the biosphere and natural resources.

All this is to restate the obvious for many of us, but on the other side of the coin are the worse failures of the state socialist economies of the Eastern bloc. For example the

Soviet Union has just endured an unprecedented health crisis of *rising* infant mortality and adult death rates, due to poor nutrition, alcoholism, pollution and inadequate health services, amongst other factors (Davis 1988). No advanced capitalist country has suffered such an overall absolute decline in basic health needs since the Second World War. Moreover political unfreedom inhibits individual autonomy and the procedural foundations for a democratic society to meet needs. Of course many of these defects now have a chance of being tackled if perestroika and glasnost run their course. But the universal recognition today that there are serious weaknesses in centrally planned economies means that we cannot simply counterpose public ownership and central planning to the nonsense of the New Right. Clause 4 does not provide us with an unambiguous guide as to how to achieve a democratic economy to meet human needs (Murray 1987).

We would do better to study the experience of Sweden and some of our other European neighbours (see, for example, Korpi 1983). Sweden combines the highest and most equal levels of need-satisfaction in the world with a successful economy. The secret appears to be high levels of state social *and* economic intervention guided by a highly mobilised labour movement. The integration of social and economic policy, together with a high level of participation in civil society, enables the Swedish labour and socialist movement to pursue a strategy of managing yet transforming capitalism. Though there are many constraints put on its actions by capitalist elements, it provides the best model yet of something approaching democratic market socialism, and has demonstrated its clear superiority over both the unregulated, 'me-now' capitalism of Reagan and Thatcher *and* the experience of unreformed state socialism.

The only feasible answer for Britain too in the foreseeable future is an economic framework which embraces plural forms of ownership without unaccountable concentrations of private power; a mixture of plan and market with the added encouragement of a third, co-operative, communal sector within civil society; and democratic forms of participation within the workplace and in the wider society – in other words what is probably best called democratic market socialism. The *goal* of production to meet human needs can embrace a variety of institutions and policy instruments.

The lessons of this for the Labour Party and other forces on the centre-left are clear. First, they must come to an agreed and coherent position on the role of markets and the private sector. We should pinpoint clearly those domains where unregulated market provision is harmful to the satisfaction of any individual's or group's needs, either directly as in health, or indirectly as in the freedom of capital to locate new investment where it pleases. The rationale for state intervention then is market failure – not only in the domain of distribution, but also in production, need-transformation and material reproduction. The best form of state intervention is a more pragmatic matter: it can embrace direct state provision, industrial direction, macro-economic management, supervision and regulation, taxation and subsidies, state transfers, consumer protection, environ-mental targets – and public ownership. But the ultimate rationale for state intervention is to improve the level of welfare via the satisfaction of basic needs – to bring about a 'welfare society'. The view that democratic market socialism is 'neither fish not fowl' is wrong: on the contrary, it amounts to a rational search for the best combination of public and private, of planning and markets, guided by a clearly moral and unselfish set of goals.

Within this framework we must recognise and endorse the role of regulated markets. It is simply wrong automatically to counterpose need and market. There are some intermediate need goods, for example clothing or foodstuffs, where market-guided production, if suitably regulated by the state, is obviously superior to centralised planning and state production. If this is accepted, it then follows that we must recognise and endorse the role of regulated profits. If one is operating a transitional economic strategy, whether local or national, then 'reasonable' profits have to be accepted as not only politically necessary but also as desirable, for without profitability the most desirable, prefigurative, democratic, use-value-producing enterprises simply cannot survive in the present capitalist environment (Rustin 1986). Hence a feasible socialist strategy means regulated markets and regulated profits, within a framework of planning to meet needs.

But democratic market socialism is more than 'plan plus market'. It is also about fostering alternative 'third' forms of production and distribution within the community, especially consumer, wholesale and production co-operatives. A politics of need requires a new politics of consumption: new ways of organising consumers and users, which begin to socialise what are at present individual decisions. Consumers should be able to take into account when deciding on a purchase such factors as: the way that a product has been made, its impact on the host community, the political complexion of overseas states which contribute to its manufacture and the environmental impact of each stage of the production process. Publicly funded consumer unions, as well as a revived co-operative movement, could help to fill this gap. Help to produce co-operatives through favourable taxation and subsidised loans would also encourage the emergence of a third domain of production and economic practices within Britain. In this way alternative patterns of production and more community-willed steering mechanisms can be encouraged to complement the dominant mechanisms of plan and market.

The Dual Strategy

Nevertheless, at the end of the day, socialism is about collective control over the main features of the economy, which involves a greater role for the state and the public sector. Hence we must pay special attention to the democratic control of the state. If we recognise the necessity for an enabling state to enhance individual's autonomy, we must ensure that in the process it does not disable that very autonomy. As suggested, therefore, we must develop the idea of a 'dual strategy' for the state (Doyal and Gough, 1986 and 1990). In a nutshell we must *both* centralise and decentralise the contemporary British state if it is to enhance collective welfare and empower the mass of the population.

Only the state can guarantee individuals *rights* to the satisfaction of their basic needs; and it is right and proper that the basic citizenship rights should be guaranteed by the central state. Neither the market nor communal solidarity could do this. Only the central state can redistribute income, undertake national economic and social planning, properly provide many basic services like health and education, enforce equal opportunities policies, co-ordinate innovation and research policies, regulate transport and communication, redirect economic investment between regions and so on. The emergence of 'post-Fordist' economic structures will undermine the desirability and feasibility of some past forms of state intervention – both economic and social – but it will not undermine the need for a public purpose or public policies to steer the economy to improve need satisfactions. For this a strengthened central steering mechanism is required, linked to social policies which recognise the enforceable rights of all citizens.

But the other 'leg' of the dual strategy must encourage 'bottom-up' initiatives and local forms of democratic control. Clearly the state guarantee of basic rights can only be a base upon which the shape and structure of different forms of welfare provision can be built. The assumption, characteristic of the post-war welfare state, that state control of the definition and delivery of all forms of welfare was the only guarantee of equality of access, was a recipe only for paternalism and the exclusion of those who did not fit into dominant models of need. We must ensure that future forms of social and economic planning take their shape from the democratic involvement of the diversity of consumers in developing initiatives and participating in local control.

The model of local authority democracy in the provision of local services is a very limited example of such wider democratic control. Indeed the periodic election of largely unaccountable local politicians can often mirror at local level the autocracy of central government. A wider diversity of regional and local government, with responsibilities for different levels of planning and control may be more appropriate. To this could be added consumer representation on local planning and administrative bodies, and the involvement of community groups and community representatives in local democratic forums. Within a framework of social rights, local and community experiments could take on a new lease of life, in the knowledge that they will not usurp the needs of weaker groups – as, for example, the recent education reforms are likely to. In this way many of the most invigorating innovations of the new left councils, the women's movement and so forth, can be harnessed to enrich the idea of an empowering state – without counterposing this to the idea of more central state planning and intervention. Again we can draw strength from both centralising and decentralising strands of thinking in the contemporary socialist/feminist movement.

Clear criteria can be specified so that the respective roles of the two 'legs' are understood. The old principle could be revived that all decisions should be devolved to the level of the smallest group affected by the outcome. Let us take education as an example. The management of many aspects of a school's daily life should be delegated to a democratic forum representing parents, teachers and, on some issues, pupils; but the recent dispute at Dewsbury has shown that policy making on admissions, which affects other children in the locality, must be retained at local authority level; and the content of the core curriculum, which underpins the right of all children to receive a certain level and quality of education, should only be settled at national level. This provides an attractive partnership of state-guaranteed rights and local initiatives. In the rest of this paper we spell out some of the implications of the dual strategy for economic policy, social policy and constitutional reform.

Economic Policy

To begin with it would be prudent to draw lessons from past experience in Britain and from other Western countries. The first teaches us that Morrisonian nationalisation has been a failure and is neither desirable nor feasible as a general model for state control in a welfare-oriented economy. It is undesirable because it is profoundly undemocratic. It is unfeasible because, as Charlie Leadbeater argues in this book, the development of new, post-Fordist structures and practices have undermined the control which a simple transfer of ownership to the state can yield. The second lesson is that other Western countries have devised more successful methods of economic regulation. Broadly speaking the non-English speaking countries can be divided into three forms of economic co-ordination: banker co-ordination as in West Germany, statism as in France and Japan, and social corporatism as in Sweden. The prime role is exerted by different actors – finance capital, the state and the labour movement – but in all of them there is some body which acts as the 'regulative intelligence' and 'steering mechanism' of the economy. This contrasts with the situation in Britain – even before 1979 – where no such societal actor seeks to guide the economy in the pursuit of coherent, longer-term goals. The result has been a deteriorating economy. An impressive weight of evidence now demonstrates that countries with systematic interventionist policies and consensual approaches to policy making can sustain innovation and growth without inflation. They are also more likely to favour forms of economic development which prioritise welfare – especially the socialist 'societal bargaining' procedures of Sweden. These lessons suggest the following priorities for economic policy.

First, a new relationship between finance and industry. At present UK financial markets are excessively oriented to market pressures, and have not developed the institutional links with industry which are found in Continental Europe. The alleged consequences include: 'short-termism' in fund management˝ and stock market preferences (a tendency which has worsened in recent years), a lack of commitment to firms' investment plans, an excessive number of takeovers and mergers which have yielded little in the way of company performance, and a dramatic outflow of capital abroad. All these tendencies have accelerated since the easing of controls in 1979, 1980 and 1984. On the other hand, the City has exerted great influence, via the Bank of England-Treasury nexus, on the making of macro-economic policy. This resulted in the pursuit of a strong pound and high interest rates until the mid-1970s, and continues to fuel opposition to any form of industrial strategy today. These problems must be overcome if resources are to be put to more rational use.

There can be no doubt that nationalisation of many of the central financial institutions is the only just and effective policy, but at present it is not feasible – indeed it is less feasible than the state ownership of lower priority manufacturing enterprises and utilities. Not only do these institutions have political clout, they can also precipitate a sterling and balance of payments crisis, and all political actors know this. Hence a reforming government must either act drastically and immediately within hours of gaining office, or it must adopt a gradualist strategy. Both have their problems, but the former is self-contradictory, for the likelihood of a party advocating such policies gaining power would precipitate countervailing measures before the actual election which could dramatically undermine its electoral chances and the post-election economic situation. There seems no alternative, then, to a strategy of step-by-step regulation and control of the financial markets, but this does not mean that early achievements need be limited. As Jim Tomlinson argues here, key changes could include the establishment of a National Investment Bank, the systematic use of pension funds as sources of long-term finance, selective exchange controls, and discriminatory taxation of pension fund assets held abroad.

An industrial strategy is a second necessary ingredient. The absence of an industrial strategy in Britain runs against current practice in most OECD countries except the United States – and even in the US the procurement programmes of the Pentagon act as a hidden form of industrial policy. Since 1979 the de-regulation of product and labour markets, cuts in state support expenditure and privatisation have made a coherent industrial policy more difficult to achieve. Moreover history has moved forward and undermined some of the starting assumptions of the earlier Alternative Economic Strategy. Its economic feasibility has been challenged by moves towards post-Fordist accumulation patterns noted earlier. Its political feasibility has been undermined by Thatcherism's successful strategy to divide the political constituency committed to traditional socialist solutions. Finally its desirability has been challenged by many of the currents forming the new social movements. In the 1980s the AES was criticised as too statist, too growth-oriented and insensitive to environmental costs of economic growth, too parochial and unaware of the necessity for international and European co-operation, sexist in its focus on white male sectional interests, and devoid of any vision of a society inspired by different moral values.

The papers by Jim Tomlinson and Charlie Leadbeater in this volume advocate alternative priorities and new policy instruments. These include limited protectionism to restrict manufactured imports, controls over the power of the city and greater government direction of investment projects, the expansion of state training and the introduction of incomes policy; these policies would go alongside new forms of social ownership, based on the use of the central state and civil society to influence markets, investment and employment policies, rather than direct nationalisation of production. Thus more but different forms of state intervention are a necessary ingredient of a feasible socialist economic programme today. There is no evidence that state intervention *per se* is unpopular or ineffective in advanced capitalist countries including Britain. On the contrary, it is outdated and ineffective state intervention which is both electorally and economically damaging – it must be replaced with a wider range of both top-down and bottom-up controls over economic activity.

This leads us to the third area of economic reform: the development of a new social contract: a system of 'societal bargaining' whereby more collective and democratic processes of decision making are gradually developed which involve organised groups in civil society as well as the state. Again the Swedish labour movement has shown how a disciplined, imaginative and solidaristic movement can obtain full employment, advanced welfare rights and partial economic democracy by offering to Swedish capital the *quid pro quo* of wage moderation, labour mobility and acceptance of new technology. It is true that the records of social contracts in Britain and Sweden are as different as chalk from cheese. As a result many British trade unionists and socialists are vehemently opposed to any form of 'incomes policy', or at best unaware of its potential. But a bargained social contract is the crucial contribution that the trade union movement can make towards establishing a renewed politics of need in contemporary Britain. It is contradictory for a country to have a powerful union movement claiming to represent the general interests of the working class (as Britain does) and for it to act simply as one sectional interest group among many.

So some kind of social contract is an essential policy component, as Dave Purdy argues here, and, as Charlie Leadbeater points out, this must have a local (micro) as well as a national structure. If successful this would yield a sustainable rate of economic growth. The *quid pro quo* in any social contract could obviously take a number of forms. Dave Purdy's aim of a state guaranteed income for all may be a long term goal in satisfying the basic needs of all citizens; but in the meantime, as Charlie Leadbeater suggests, there are all sorts of trade-offs that could be negotiated for workers and consumers in terms of conditions of employment, environmental standards, pricing policies, and so on.

Examples of bottom-up involvement in local economic planning already exist, to some extent, in the local economic strategies of the sort pioneered in Greater London, Sheffield and the West Midlands in the 1980s. In particular the GLC tried to develop a quite distinct mode of operating 'within but against the market' in order to pursue goals which were explicitly committed to human needs. As such it represented a fertile experiment in need-oriented economics and popular planning from below, involving many of the new social movements representing specific groups and fashioning new constituencies of support amongst ethnic minority groups, women, gays and lesbians. On the other hand the GLC initiatives operated in an environment of limited funds, chronic shortages of skilled planners and managers, opposition from bureaucrats and parts of the trade unions and Labour Party, and the unremitting hostility of the Thatcher government which eventually abolished the GLC. Yet the experience of the GLC lends support precisely to our case for a *dual* strategy, combining central economic planning and regulation with autonomy and initiative from the grass roots.

Social Policy

Future social policy must avoid the paternalism and the professionalism of the post-war welfare state. Central control of services, and the exclusion of consumers of welfare from any collective involvement in their definition and delivery, has led to an alienation from *statist* welfare which the Thatcher governments of the 1980s have been able readily to exploit. It has also led to services modelled largely upon the (presumed) needs of only those citizens whose voices were most powerfully represented within state structures – the employed, white, skilled, male working class. Other needs, and the majority of people, were largely excluded from state welfare. The dual strategy would permit us to avoid such paternalism and exclusion in the future. The top-down/bottom-up notions of citizenship and democracy provide a challenge to paternalism and professionalism; and yet they also offer an assault on the individual, private market-based consumerism of Thatcherite welfare policies. Let us begin with 'top-down' rights.

The notion of a right to state support is certainly a challenge to the marginalising and stigmatisating effects of discretion and targetting pursued by the current government, as Marshall and Beveridge recognised. Citizenship rights can have a unifying function, because all have equal rights to final states of need satisfaction. (However since we do not all start equal in the citizenship stakes, this does not exclude transitional policies of positive discrimination.) Rights can be enforceable through an impartial legal process, which can be seen to be open and fair, and they can empower those who possess them within the broader political sphere. Enforceable rights challenge and restrict professional control over welfare services and the paternalism inherent in discretion.

Beveridge's recognition of the need for a rights basis to social security benefits was at the heart of his proposals for social insurance. However, the insurance proposals were flawed, because they were based upon a notion of rights earned through employment – thus restricting real entitlement. Future social security benefits must be based upon rights determined by status (not contribution) – and upon rights which are understandable by all, and enforceable on behalf of all. Contrasting such demands for citizenship with current Thatcherite welfare policies is an important strategy for Labour. The new Social Fund, with its basis in discretion, priority and judgement, provides an excellent model against which to counterpose a new concept of rights to welfare. In the long run new rights might take the form of a state guaranteed income for all as argued by Dave Purdy; but in the shorter term, as Ruth Lister discusses, the notion of the right to a state income, without test of means, for those who are unable to provide for themselves through wages, is a readily understandable and potentially popular demand.

In other areas of social policy, too, the introduction of citizenship rights not only challenges the market individualism of Thatcherism, but also takes us beyond many of the central features of post-war welfare. Indeed it was the Conservative government's own 1980 Housing Act which first introduced statutory rights for council tenants, now recognised by all to be a positive step. Future housing policy must build on these by developing more far-reaching strategies to guarantee a right to buy or a right to rent for all, including those currently excluded from both state and private housing. The continued existence of widespread homelessness in Britain is not compatible with the collective obligation to meet basic needs. Enforceable rights must also be extended to cover rights to decent standards of housing and to support for repairs to maintain houses whether in the public or private sector.

In education, rights for the consumers of services have not been widely understood or accepted: the expectation that the professionals know best is more difficult to challenge. In higher education, however, consumer choice (at least of areas of study) has always been at the centre of planning. The introduction of credit accumulation and transfer within higher education is providing a more flexible and powerful means of determining service provision. The new National Council for Vocational Qualifications (NCVQ) is also extending consumer flexibility to further education and training. It can and should be extended into primary and secondary education, backed up by a core curriculum to ensure basic standards. Accompanied by developments in democratic involvement, discussed below, rights in education could challenge professional domination without undermining professional expertise.

If anything, health and social services have been still more dominated by professional judgement and control. However, citizenship rights can and should be introduced here too. To operationalise citizenship rights Plant talks of the need for 'cash, rights, entitlements and cash surrogates [vouchers]' in health service provision (1988, p 13). Recent debates over mental health services have also raised the issue of consumers' rights to demand service provision to meet health needs (e.g. a right to community based mental patient care). Private health provision champions consumer choice. Collective health care cannot, and should not, seek simply to mimic it: the advantage of collective planning for preventative medicine and the central co-ordination of expensive training and investment is overwhelming. However, as Roland Petchey argues, we must seriously consider empowering consumers of public health through the use of enforceable rights to prevention and treatment. Vouchers are almost certainly too crude a tool here, but more general rights to health care are an enhancement of, not a contradiction to, state provision of basic health needs.

In the personal social services, too, the promotion of an active rather than passive approach to the need for care must be fostered. It has always been a central aim, if not always realised, of social work practice to work to empower clients to ensure where practicable that they are the authors of the resolutions to their problems. Rights to services, such as aids for disability, assistance in the home, day care, nurseries, community services and so on, would considerably enhance this process; and ensure that social workers could act more as advisors and advocates for their clients.

Rights on paper, as all lawyers know, are no more than that. To make them real requires a greater democratisation of services, referred to below. But it also depends upon a renewed commitment to information, advice and advocacy in social policy. The growth of *welfare rights* services in the 1970s and 1980s has been a valuable challenge to the deterioration in welfare provision over this period – most notably through the successful campaigns to encourage claimants to take up rights to social security benefits, especially when these have been under threat. The extension of rights-based advice and advocacy work within all aspects of state welfare would help to change the role of all professionals from one of paternalism and judgement to one of information and support.

Such developments would also begin to open up the legal system itself. A legal system which has traditionally protected private wealth before all else has never been very responsive to the needs of the broader society for legal enforcement of rights. Development of welfare rights throughout social policy will challenge this limited role for law. This will create greater pressure for the extensions of tribunals to replace courts, and the reform of courts themselves along the Family court model; it will also increase the demand for para-legal workers and lay advisors to work within these bodies. Such developments may in turn lead to a challenge to the monopoly of the legal profession. If the campaign for social citizenship can open up even the most powerful and unresponsive of state services and professional bodies to an empowered citizenry, it would contribute to the other constitutional reforms discussed below.

Another more controversial component of a top-down strategy to extend citizenship rights would be a programme of positive or reverse discrimination. The simple fact that many disadvantaged groups suffer continuing and debilitating discrimination implies that the achievement of distributive justice in the future requires selective discriminatory practices in the present. The success of existing equal opportunities policies in Britain has been limited in removing the stains of secondary sexism and racism (Solomos 1986). These policies should be strengthened and reviewed in the light of the various demands which different examples of discrimination make. For example, successful positive discrimination in employment will be constrained by the requirements of the job at hand; this suggests limitations on the degree to which already existing skills and qualifications can be held constant in favouring one disadvantaged group of applicants. In housing policy, on the other hand, the same restrictions do not apply. Our reasoning is, in any case, consequentialist: reverse discrimination is concerned not to rectify past injustices but to achieve greater equality in the future. Once race, gender and other attributes cease to be grounds on which inappropriate judgements of difference are made, these programmes become redundant and can be wound up. But in the meantime they modify the operation, though not the rationale, of equal rights policies.

All these top-down state rights must however be accompanied by bottom-up, democratic control within civil society to ensure at local and community level that services are geared to the varied real needs of real people. This requires a revitalised conception of the role of democracy in the development of welfare. The post-war welfare state was largely based upon the assumption that the elections which had produced support for a Labour government represented democratic support for the state-based social policies which it introduced. The democratic road to socialism thus became subverted to ensuring the re-election of a government which would continue to provide statist welfare. In fact, of course, state-provided welfare has largely resulted in a separation of the state (and its services) from the people, and this version of the democratic road has therefore lost out to the Thatcherite appeal to individual freedom and the private market. New forms of democracy in the welfare state are now essential if popular support is to be weaned away from the apparent attractions of the market, and a new collective commitment to welfare is to be fashioned.

Most fundamentally, democracy means ensuring accountability, through bottom-up participation in the range of welfare services. It means involving consumers in the determination of the 'shape' of the services they receive. This is not an accountability based on the periodic election of governments or local councils, who then govern autocratically, but the continued involvement of people in the planning and implementation of social policies throughout the state and civil society. Given the range of services, and the different circumstances of groups and individuals, however, there can be no single, simple model of democratisation. Forms of participation must be tailored to the needs and processes of particular individuals and groups in particular areas, as in the example of education and school management discussed above.

Clearly there are some aspects of services where central

government must decide and where basic rights will dominate the form of provision, for instance social security benefit levels, minimum wage rates, or the core curriculum in schools. However, in many other areas of social policy the provision of general rights need not determine the form of provision of services for all consumers. Services controlled by local authorities already vary up and down the country depending upon the policies and priorities of different authorities. However they do not necessarily reflect real variations in local conditions or local needs. To achieve this, however, requires the participation in planning and policy implementation of those who know and understand these variations; in other words tapping the experiential knowledge of the locality. As Gabriel argues, this involves listening to and working with different ethnic minority and community groups. It is therefore a much broader concept of democratic participation than that currently represented by local government.

Governing bodies in schools are an example of a participatory approach to democracy. They are not a model to be followed blindly – especially not in the form provided for under the new Education Reform Act. But their involvement of users and providers of education in a local democratic forum at which important local decisions can be discussed and determined, is a good example of how a professionalised process could be opened up and users given more involvement in, and responsibility for, their services. Indeed democracy of this kind is providing a form of *ownership*, which could challenge the individualistic, market based ownership of Thatcherism, as well as the alienating public ownership of state based welfare. Similar kinds of democratic forums could be developed in housing, building on tenants' associations and residents' organisations. Some progressive local authorities have already shown the way here, with tenant representation on council committees. Tenant co-operatives in the rapidly growing housing association sector also demonstrate that collective control and ownership of services can be effective and representative at a small scale, local level.

In health and social services, consumer and community groups could be encouraged to articulate local needs and priorities, whilst representative involvement in higher level decision making could include a consumer voice in planning major resources and investments. Coupled with a rights-based approach to service delivery, this could move services away from professional domination without conceding to new right arguments for consumer sovereignty through the market. Even in social security democracy can, and must, be put on the agenda. There is a short reference to a 'user-friendly DHSS' (now DSS) in the Labour Party first Policy Review report, but little discussion of how the most oppressive and alienating of state services could be made more responsive to consumer needs. The only way it can be, and the only way people are likely to be convinced that this will be done, is once again through forms of democratic accountability. The idea of local plebiscites on benefit rates would be a recipe for division, not unity, at least in the short term. But, as Ruth Lister suggests, decisions about the delivery of benefits – about office location and design, staff training and development, and access to information and new technology – could all be open to accountable debate in local forums of workers and consumers.

An appeal for citizenship and democracy in social policy represents a commitment to the dual strategy in the planning and delivery of welfare services. It provides a fundamental challenge to the belief that a return to the post-war welfare state is the only alternative to the private market individualism of Thatcherism, and opens up the promise of a future welfare state which is not based upon the divisions, exclusions and stigmatisation, which is the (accurate) vision of welfare for too many people in Britain today. It also opens up, therefore, the possibility of forming new social alliances for welfare with dispossessed and excluded groups, such as women, black people, people with disabilities, and others; rather than basing state-provided welfare only on the needs (and political clout) of the white, employed, male working class. It suggests a new model of interdependence between state and civil society, constructed both by and for the people.

Constitutional Reform

As Mike Rustin shows, Britain now has probably the most powerful yet least representative central government in the Western world, coupled with the least accountable state machine. Rolling back recent moves towards the strong state is one sound reason why constitutional reform is a necessary ingredient in any strategy to enhance democracy in Britain. But, as we have argued throughout, a dual strategy for economic and social policy means that it is essential to any democratic socialist strategy for meeting human needs. If we are to move away from the anonymous coercion of market forces, towards consensual, politicised economic decision-taking, an open, accountable, democratic framework is essential. And if welfare needs are to be guaranteed as social rights this too requires a move away from the unwritten British constitution towards an explicit system of basic laws, and a reformed judiciary and administrative system. Economic, social and constitutional reform are inseparable.

Constitutional reform is at last making a welcome appearance in debates over socialism and social democracy emanating from the Left and Centre (see Marquand 1988, and Keane 1988). It has also received widespread support from the large number of signatories to the Charter 88 call for a Bill of Rights in Britain. As Mike Rustin discusses, there are a number of constitutional reforms which must be openly debated within the labour movement. These would include reform of Parliament to strengthen its control over the executive; Keane (1988) discusses such ideas as restricting prime ministerial patronage, more convenient sitting hours, extra research facilities, greater use of televised standing committees, and other changes. Reform must be extended to Whitehall too, for instance via provision of legislation for freedom of information and new forms of accountability and scrutiny for civil servants. Opening up the legal service to enhanced citizenship rights will also require reform of the legal profession and the courts. We must also recognise the immense power of the media in any society dominated, as Britain is, by mass communication – legal restrictions on ownership and control are required here as well as democratic extension of access to telecommunications and the press.

The problem with this sort of 'list' approach, however, is that no coherent rationale or guiding thread is adumbrated. The analyses put forward in this book point towards three unifying issues in the contemporary agenda. First, economic trends are undermining the concentration of power and policy making at the level of the nation state. On the one hand, internationalisation is making regional economic blocs more important; on the other hand post-Fordist trends render local and regional economic strategies more salient. This points towards a coherent new plan to democratise and improve decision making. On the one hand, the Left must continue its reappraisal of the EC, collaborate more with sister parties in Europe and work for a new 'social Europe'. On the other hand, power and economic and social policy-making should be decentralised to a new Scottish Assembly, to regional bodies in Wales and the English regions and to local authorities unencumbered by *ultra vires*.

Second, Charter 88 and its call for a new Bill of Rights should be wholeheartedly endorsed. The time for a codification of Britain's unwritten constitution is over-ripe, for at least three reasons. First, it would offer some protection to the individual against the depredation of the strong state. Second, it would help lay the basis for a more consensual approach to solving Britain's continuing economic problems. And third, if, as we argue, citizens' rights include enforceable social rights within the state to the satisfaction of basic needs, it would offer constitutional backing to economic planning for needs. On all these grounds it appears now as the indispensable element in a post-Thatcher renaissance.

Finally, electoral reform to introduce proportional representation is a *sine qua non* for all the above. This would simply bring Britain into line with the majority of the world's democracies, and all European democracies except France. And, as Mike Rustin argues, the case for it is becoming unanswerable. The present electoral system is likely to perpetuate minority Conservative rule. In effect, it disenfranchises many voters and it acts as a major obstacle to women and minorities entering Parliament, amongst other defects. On top of this the electoral arithmetic facing the

Labour Party remains unfavourable and with boundary and population changes afoot, it is unlikely to improve. Commitment to electoral reform must become central to a new commitment to constitutional reform.

Such a commitment would open the way to some kind of an electoral pact with other parties. This is probably the only secure method of ending Conservative government in the foreseeable future. It is not often that morality and expediency align in such convenient fashion; it would be still more remarkable if the Labour Party and other opposition elements turned their back on both. A coalition government committed to electoral and constitutional reform would provide a feasible and realistic launching pad for the integrated, welfare-orientated economic and social policies set out above. It will not provide socialism in Britain overnight; but it will mark a significant shift in direction towards a social economy and a democratic state.

References

D. Beetham, 'Choose democracy', *New Socialist*, 49, May 1987.

L. Calfors and J. Driffill, 'Centralisation of wage bargaining', *Economic Policy*, April 1988.

I. Crewe, The *Guardian*, 15 June 1987.

C.M. Davies, 'Developments in the health sector of the Soviet economy 1970-90', paper delivered at Socialism and Social Policy conference, Leeds Polytechnic, April 1988.

L. Doyal and I. Gough, 'A theory of human needs', *Critical Social Policy*, 10, 1984.

L. Doyal and I. Gough, 'Human needs and socialist welfare', *Praxis International*, 6,1, 1986.

L. Doyal and I. Gough, *A Theory and Politics of Human Need*, Macmillan forthcoming.

R. Hattersley, *Choose Freedom*, Penguin 1987.

J. Keane, *Democracy and Civil Society*, Verso 1988.

W. Korpi, *The Democratic Class Struggle*, Routledge 1983.

D. Marquand *The Unprincipled Society: New Demands and Old Politics*, Fontana 1988.

R. Murray, 'Ownership, control and the market', *New Left Review*, 164, 1987.

T. Nairn, *The Enchanted Glass: Britain and its Monarchy*, Radius 1988.

P. Plant, *Citizenship, Rights and Socialism*, Fabian Society No 531, 1988.

M. Rustin, 'The non-obsolescence of the right to work', *Critical Social Policy*, 18, 1986.

J. Solomos, 'The Politics of Anti-Discrimination Legislation', in R. Jenkins and J. Solomos (eds) *Racism and Equal Opportunities Policies in the 1980s*, Cambridge University Press 1986.

R.H. Tawney, *Equality*, Allen and Unwin 1952.

P. Taylor Gooby, *Public Opinion, Ideology and State Welfare*, RKP 1985.

Notes on Contributors

The Sheffield Group:
Pete Alcock is Senior Lecturer, Applied Social Studies Department, Sheffield City Polytechnic
Andrew Gamble is Professor of Politics, Sheffield University
Ian Gough is Senior Lecturer, Department of Social Policy and Social Work, University of Manchester
Phil Lee was until recently Senior Lecturer in Applied Social Studies, Sheffield City Polytechnic. He is now a Lecturer in Social Policy and Social Work, Leicester University
Alan Walker is Professor of Social Policy, Sheffield University

Contributors
Allan Cochrane is Sub-Dean (Research) and Lecturer in Geography, The Open University
Len Doyal is Principal Lecturer in Philosophy, Middlesex Polytechnic
John Gabriel is Lecturer in Cultural Studies, University of Birmingham
Charlie Leadbeater is a journalist on the *Financial Times*
Ruth Lister is Professor of Applied Social Studies, University of Bradford
Doreen Massey is Professor of Geography, The Open University
Chris Pond is Director of the Low Pay Unit
David Purdy is Lecturer in Economics, University of Manchester
Mike Rustin is Head of the Sociology Department, North East London Polytechnic
Jim Tomlinson is Lecturer in Economics, Brunel University

Index

New Times

The Changing Face of Politics in the 1990s

Stuart Hall and Martin Jacques (editors)
in association with Marxism Today

Marxism Today has established itself in the last five years as Britain's foremost political monthly. Its reputation was consolidated by its brilliant analysis of Thatcherism – a term pioneered by Stuart Hall and Martin Jacques.

The magazine has now moved on to an analysis of *New Times* – the fundamental political, economic and cultural restructuring that has taken place in the last decade throughout Western Europe and North America.

The profound changes which have occurred have redrawn the political map – and the new terrain has so far seemed more propitious for the Right than for the Left. The essays gathered in this collection are beginning to chart the new landscape and to make a start on an analysis of a new politics for the 1990s.

New Times is an agenda-setting collection which has important implications not just for Western socialism but for any serious consideration of the future of politics.

Contributors: Neal Ascherson, Sarah Benton, Rosalind Brunt, Beatrix Campbell, David Edgar, Stuart Hall, Dick Hebdige, David Held, Paul Hirst, Martin Jacques, Charlie Leadbeater, David Marquand, Frank Mort, Geoff Mulgan, Robin Murray, Tom Nairn, Mike Rustin, Gareth Stedman-Jones, Fred Steward, Goran Therborn, John Urry, Gwyn A. Williams.

paperback £8.95

Bending the Rules

The Baker 'Reform' of Education

Brian Simon

Kenneth Baker's 1988 Education Reform Act sets out, through a series of carefully calculated 'reforms', to undermine the foundations of Britain's educational system. In this lively, polemical and highly praised book, Britain's foremost educational historian makes clear the enormous dangers posed by this piece of legislation.

In *Bending the Rules* Brian Simon provides an invaluable brief guide to the 1988 Act as well as the arguments needed to counter this threat to our schools.

> 'Well written, well informed and well researched ... I commend it.'
> Anne Sofer, *Times Educational Supplement*
> 'A systematic demolition job on the Baker Bill. The book is useful in expounding just how big a change the Education Reform Bill is seeking. It also makes many sensible criticisms of the government's proposals.' David Thomas, *Financial Times*
> 'Wise and scholarly' Peter Wilby, *Independent*

paperback £5.95

Beyond the Rhetoric:
Politics, the Economy and Social Policy in Northern Ireland
Paul Teague (editor)

All too often writing on Northern Ireland focuses on the military and sectarian conflict taking place in the province, ignoring the economic and social background to that bloody and dramatic struggle. This highly praised book delves beyond the rhetoric into the harsh realities behind Northern Ireland's current plight – some of the worst poverty and unemployment in Europe, an economy heavily dependent on government spending and the service sector, multinational companies which come and go following the dictates of the world economy. In addition to looking at the politics of the Protestant and Catholic communities in the wake of the Anglo-Irish Agreement, the often ignored affairs of another participant in the drama – the Republic of Ireland – are also examined.

This book brings together a group of acknowledged experts writing in a measured tone rarely associated with the subject; also, for the first time, it offers a pluralist perspective on Northern Ireland, with authors occupying positions across the spectrum of the left.

Contributors: Paul Bew, David Canning, Frank Gafikin, Peter Mair, Barry Moore, Mike Morrisey, Liam O'Dowd, Brendan O'Leary, Henry Patterson, John Rhodes, Bill Rolston, Bob Rowthorn, Paul Teague

'The book has two particular attractions ... it represents the first considered analysis of politics in the wake of the Anglo-Irish Agreement ... the second strength is the unusual attention it gives to the dire state of the province's economy.' Robin Wilson, *Marxism Today*

'Fortunately dogma has given way to socialist pluralism.' Austen Morgan, *Fortnight*

paperback £6.95

Banking on Sickness

Commercial Medicine in Britain and the USA

Ben Griffith, Steve Iliffe and Geof Rayner

Privatisation poses a major threat to the National Health Service. What is not so well known is the variety of ways in which individuals and companies operate for profit within the NHS. From doctors and consultants taking on private medical work to the contracting out of hospital cleaning and other services, from the massive profits made by the drug companies to the ambiguous position occupied by opticians, dentists and others, there are numerous ways in whch commerce invades health care.

The Thatcher years have witnessed a major growth of private health insurance and US-owned private hospitals and clinics which subvert the egalitarian principle on which the NHS was founded. Meanwhile, 'private' but non-profit medicine in the area of pregnancy and abortion services continues to play an invaluable role.

The complexities of commercial medicine are explored in this clear and lucid book, the first to examine a crucial aspect of commercial medicine. *Banking on Sickness* is essential reading for health service workers and all those worried about the future of health care in Britain.

> 'Considerable food for thought ... an interesting and thoughtful discussion about the compatibility of private (or commercial) medicine with a tax free-funded health service ... Obviously this is a book which many colleagues will buy one to burn or to hurl through windows.' David Mant, *Lancet*

> 'This informative and timely book ... pulls together a wealth of valuable facts and arguments.' Jane Salvage, *City Limits*

> 'This book provides the most up-to-date critique of private medicine in Britain and will be particularly interesting to those concerned with contemporary health policy.' Anne Marie Rafferty, *Nursing Times*

paperback £6.95